THEODORET OF CYRUS
ON DIVINE PROVIDENCE

ANCIENT CHRISTIAN WRITERS

THE WORKS OF THE FATHERS IN TRANSLATION

EDITED BY

WALTER J. BURGHARDT
THOMAS COMERFORD LAWLER

No. 49

Theodoret of Cyrus
On Divine Providence

TRANSLATED AND ANNOTATED

BY

THOMAS HALTON

Gardiner Professor of Greek
The Catholic University of America

NEWMAN PRESS
New York, N.Y./Mahwah, N.J.

COPYRIGHT 1988
BY
WALTER J. BURGHARDT
AND
THOMAS COMERFORD LAWLER

Library of Congress Cataloging-in-Publication Data

Theodoret, Bishop of Cyrus.
    On divine providence.

    (Ancient Christian writers ; no. 49)
    Translation of: Peri pronoias.
    1. Providence and government of God—Early works to
1800.   I. Halton, Thomas P. (Thomas Patrick)   II. Title.
III. Series.
BR60.A35 no. 49   270 s   88–25459
[BR65.T753]   [231'.5]
ISBN 0-8091-0420-2

Published by Paulist Press
997 Macarthur Boulevard
Mahwah, New Jersey 07430

PRINTED AND BOUND IN THE UNITED STATES OF AMERICA

CONTENTS

NOTES

INDEXES

THEODORET OF CYRUS
ON DIVINE PROVIDENCE

INTRODUCTION

Theodoret of Cyrus was the last great theologian of Antioch. His literary output was extremely large, and much of it survives.[1]

Garnerius,[2] followed by Ceillier,[3] Bertram,[4] and others, gives the date of Theodoret's birth at around 386. Tillemont[5] favors 383 and in this is followed by Montalverne,[6] Altaner,[7] and the moderns generally. The early years were spent with the Syriac monks at Nicerte, near Apamea, where he led a life of study and asceticism. Here also he laid the foundations of his wide knowledge of sacred and profane authors so evident in his later writings.[8] An unconfirmed tradition names Theodore of Mopsuestia and St. John Chrysostom as his teachers, and Nestorius and John of Antioch as his fellow students.

In 423, much against his own will, he was raised to the episcopate of Cyrus,[9] a town in the province of Euphratensis in Syria, and he ruled this see of eight hundred churches with great diligence and ability. Not the least of his pastoral cares was the eradication of heresy, for Cyrus was a stronghold of Arians, Eunomians, Marcionites, and Encratites, as well as of Jews and pagans. By 449 he could claim[10] that not a single heretic was to be found in his diocese.

In the same year, 449, Theodoret was condemned at the instigation of the Monophysites by the Robber Synod, the so-called *Latrocinium*, at Ephesus on the charge of teaching the doctrine of "two sons."[11] Forced into exile, he appealed to Pope Leo I, who said the decision of the *Latrocinium* was null and void. At the Council of Chalcedon, in 451, he met at first with great opposition. A special session considered the case and insisted on his pronouncing anathema against Nestorius. With great reluctance he finally did so: "Anathema to Nestorius and to all who do not confess that the Blessed Virgin Mary is the Mother of God and divide into two the only Son, the only-Begotten." Then he was formally reinstalled in his episcopal dignity

I

and was recognized as "an orthodox teacher." Theodoret ruled the Church at Cyrus for some years yet, and died about 460.[12] We know nothing of this later period. But there is every reason to believe Theodoret's declaration at the Council, for he cannot be accused of simply changing his views under pressure, which would not agree with what we know of his character and personal integrity.

Some writers see in this rather inglorious end a resemblance between Theodoret and St. Gregory Nazianzus. Both were loveable, though somewhat too impulsive, churchmen; both had stormy episcopates and were brought to their knees by councils of the Church; both were spiritual scholars and orators who wrote in admirable Greek. Gregory, however, alone of the two is a canonized saint and a Doctor of the Church.

So much attention has already been paid to Theodoret's controversial works that his exegetical and oratorical talents, his wide culture, and his personal charm have been almost entirely lost sight of. By temperament he was a scholar rather than a practical man of affairs. Cardinal Newman, a kindred spirit, writes of him: "I am tempted to wish he had never been a bishop; he was a great preacher, and his own native place, Antioch, was the natural stage for the exercise of his gift."[13] Tillemont says[14] that he was loved and esteemed throughout Syria as an oracle.

DATE AND PLACE OF DELIVERY

That Theodoret was author of *De providentia* has never been seriously questioned. He mentions it himself on a number of occasions, particularly in his letter to Pope Leo which contains a useful checklist of some of his works: *Sunt enim mihi, quae partim ante annos viginti, partim ante quindecim, partim ante duodecim scripsi, quaedam contra Arianos et Eunomianos, quaedam contra Judaeos et gentiles, quaedam contra magos qui sunt in Perside, alia de universali Providentia, et alia rursus de theologia deque divina incarnatione.*[15] This letter to Leo in 449 seems to assign a date twelve years previously, that is, 437, to *De providentia* but this has not always been accepted as conclusive.

Garnerius says it was written before 433,[16] the year in which the

Interpretatio in psalmos[17] was composed and in which it is mentioned. This would make it belong to that class of books which Theodoret tells Leo he had written fifteen or eighteen years previously. Therefore, concludes Garnerius, it can be held to have been written, at least in part, immediately after the Council of Ephesus, after the Oriental bishops were ordered to return to their sees, and Theodoret engaged on the work as a sort of *consolatio*. Garnerius says "at least in part" for he believes that only the last two discourses were written immediately after the Council but that the first eight can probably be regarded as written before the Council.

Writers subsequent to Garnerius have not been happy about this division. Schulte, for instance, says[18] that it rests neither on the actual content of the work nor on chronological data, and that all the discourses were composed at the same time. He feels further that they were all written before the Council of Ephesus because there are no echoes of theological controversy to be found in them. Schulte is followed by Bardenhewer, Altaner and Da Mazzarino.[19]

The only internal evidence that might help to fix the date is concentrated in the last discourse where Theodoret touches on the doctrine of the Incarnation which was undergoing evolution in his mind. Bardy's testimony on this point is brief but decisive.[20] " . . . la doctrine qui y est exposée ne permet guère de supposer qu'il ait pu être écrit avant le concile d'Ephèse, comme on le dit ordinairement."

Recent writers, therefore, returning to the earlier view of Tillemont and Bertram, favor a date later than the Council of Ephesus and place composition after 435, most probably 437.[21]

It is probable that the discourses, if they were more than written exercises, were delivered in Antioch. Their style and logical order argue for a well formed and philosophically minded audience, which could hardly be expected in Cyrus.[22]

Sources and Style

De providentia is Theodoret's *haute vulgarisation* of a subject which is handled in more strictly philosophical terms, and with more explicit citations of profane authors, in the sixth chapter of his *Cur-*

atio. The arguments advanced in the present work are, for the most part, the stock-in-trade ones found in ecclesiastical and secular writers on providence. The work's claim to distinction is not based on the originality or profundity of the arguments, but on the cogency with which they are marshalled and the felicity with which they are expressed.

The Sacred Scriptures, as one expects in an exegete and preacher, provide Theodoret's primary sources. There are 130 Scriptural references in the ten discourses but, in marked contrast to the *Curatio* where over 100 classical authors are cited, there are only two references to profane sources, both possibly to Galen,[23] the productive 2nd century medical writer who commended himself to Christian writers because of his teleological approach to the study of anatomy. Old Testament quotations are culled in the main—sixty of them—from Genesis, the Psalms, and the Book of Isaiah. There is a single quotation, sometimes two, from each of ten of the remaining Old Testament books. From the New Testament, there are eight quotations each from the Gospels of St. Matthew and St. John, one from St. Luke, and none from St. Mark. Acts is quoted twice, and all of St. Paul's epistles are cited except 1 Thessalonians, Titus, and Philemon. From 1 Corinthians alone there are 12 quotations.

The tradition that St. John Chrysostom and Theodore of Mopsuestia were Theodoret's teachers helps to place the intellectual circle in which Theodoret was trained. At the center of that circle was Libanius, the well-known teacher of Chrysostom, who wrote: "Athens and Antioch held aloft the torch of rhetoric: the former illuminating Europe and the latter, Asia." Theodoret can be called the last great torchbearer of Christian rhetoric in Asia and *De providentia* is regarded by many as exhibiting his literary power in its highest form.[24]

DIVINE PROVIDENCE

For Theodoret, in common with the Greek Fathers,[25] providence is the divine action *ad extra* which sustains everything in existence. The divine government of the world is the execution of the eternal divine world-plan in time.

The question of the existence of divine providence troubled philosophers long before the coming of Christianity. Among those who were agreed on the existence of a god or gods there was the widest diversity of opinion on the forms of the gods, their place of abode, and the manner in which they employed their time. But, as Cicero remarked at the beginning of the *De Natura Deorum*,[26] "the most considerable part of the dispute is, whether they are wholly inactive, totally unemployed and free from all care and administration of affairs; or whether, on the contrary, all things were made and constituted by them from the beginning; and whether they will continue to be actuated and governed by them to eternity." This uncertainty persevered down to Theodoret's time, kept alive, in the main, by the dualistic philosophy of the Gnostics and Manichees, and the perennial discussions on the question by the Stoics and Epicureans.[27]

The doctrine of divine providence is partly Greek in origin, partly Semitic. Though the Hebrews had a highly developed appreciation of a directing providence, they had no single word to express it corresponding to the Greek πρόνοια. The idea runs through much of the Old Testament;[29] many of the psalms are veritable hymns in praise of providence, and it is explicitly mentioned in the Book of Wisdom.[30] It is one of the most frequently recurring themes in the New Testament.[31] Theodoret, in common with others, regards the Incarnation as the supreme manifestation of God's loving care for humankind.

Among the Greeks, Diogenes Laertes, citing Favorinus, says[32] that Plato was the first to use the term πρόνοια in philosophical discussion. Providence later became one of the chief doctrines of Neoplatonism, and was at the center of religious and philosophical speculation in the second and third centuries. E. R. Dodds, in his edition of Proclus, *Elements of Theology*, sums up the position admirably: "To deny that the gods exercise providence was for Plato a blasphemy meriting the severest punishment. Partly for this reason and partly because Stoicism and the Hellenistic religions had raised in an acute form the question of the relation between providence and fate . . . , the topic of πρόνοια bulks almost as large in Neoplatonism as does that of predestination and grace in the Christian theology of the period. The main lines of the neoplatonic doctrine, which makes fate distinct from, and subordinate to, providence, seem to have been already laid down by the second century."[33]

That Theodoret was familiar with this mainstream of Neoplatonism is obvious from the important position among philosophers that he assigns to Plotinus in his treatment of divine providence in his *Graecarum affectionum curatio.*[34]

The great extremes of wealth and poverty that prevailed in Antioch in the time of St. John Chrysostom and Theodoret, the extent of slavery, and manifest wickedness of many of the prosperous, gave the question of divine providence a special topicality and urgency. The skeptical had a ready breeding ground for arguments denying the existence of providence and the good-living poor were hard put to see how God could be provident and yet allow such anomalies to continue. The subject had already been treated by several Greek patristic writers,[35] but Theodoret's work is considered by many to be the finest on the subject in existence.

The testimony of Garnerius is well known: *Nihil hac elucubratione, quae decem sermonibus absolvitur, aut eloquentius aut admirabilius, non dicam a Theodoreto, sed ab alio ullo felicioris etiam Graeciae scriptore, in hanc rem editum est; ut in ipsa voluisse videatur auctor ostendere quantum in arte oratoria valeret, quamque posset eloquentissima quibusque invidiam movere; scribenti forsan indignatio sua auxiliata est.*[36] Majoranus (1545), Gualther (1571) and Ceillier (1747), all cited by Azéma,[37] are equally enthusiastic in their praise of the elegance, order, exactness, and psychological penetration displayed in these discourses.

In recent times, though the work continues to be admired,[38] the accolades have been modified. Bardy says:[39] "En dépit de certains détails d'un goût ou d'une valeur discutable, l'ensemble est fort beau; Théodoret manifeste à la fois l'étendue de son érudition et la profundeur de son sens chrétien, pour traiter un sujet difficile et toujours nouveau malgré les apparences."

Simonin,[40] also writing in *Dictionnaire de théologie catholique*, says that Theodoret aimed at a comprehensive treatment of the themes already outlined by St. John Chrysostom but never quite matched the brilliance of his predecessor. His style is characterized as dry, didactic, and having none of Chrysostom's inspiration. Even Scripture, Simonin says, is used with a somewhat chill sobriety. This latter criticism loses some of its cogency if it is remembered that *De providentia* is a work of apologetics as much as of homiletics and was directed at an audience which it hoped to convince primarily by arguments from reason and concrete experience. Simonin's last word on the work seems to damn it with faint pride: "On sent un exercice d'école, plutôt conventionnel, mais incontestablement brillant."

Azéma's verdict is altogether more balanced and just:[41] "Sans pretendre que tout, dans cette oeuvre, soit admirable et qu'elle soit absolument un chef-d'oeuvre, nous pensons neanmois qu'elle possede assez de qualites pour qu'on puisse la considerer comme l'une des belles oeuvres que nous a laissees l'antiquite."

The last word can be left to the only previous English translator, in a work (which is more a paraphrase than a translation) entitled *The Mirror of Divine Providence*, a copy of which is in the British Library.[42] He "thought good to publish it as a worke well worthy to be read and perused of all sorts of people at this time wherein Atheisme like an ill weed is growne to such height as it seemeth to overshadow the plants of true religion, while men attributing to nature what belongs properly to the Creator of Nature do both deprive God of his glory and also discover their impiety, to the danger of their owne soules, and the hurt of others."

* * *

I wish to record my gratitude to Susan Needham, Administrative Assistant, Department of Greek and Latin, The Catholic University of America, for skilled and generous assistance in preparing an untidy manuscript for publication.

DISCOURSE 1

DEMONSTRATION OF PROVIDENCE FROM THE HEAVENS, THE SUN, THE MOON, AND THE OTHER STARS

At Nature's Dictate, Children Seek to Defend Their Parents'
Interests
and Subjects Those of Their Masters

1. It is a law imposed on men by nature that children avenge the wrong done to their parents, and servants those done to their masters, that citizens run risks when their cities are under siege and, in a word, that those who have good done them repay their benefactors to the best of their ability. One can see a king, too, whose rule is right and just, and who tempers his power with gentleness, being zealously defended in wars by men with shields and swords. Let no one contradict me at the outset and accuse me of preaching falsehood, pointing to parricides, rogues, traitors, and tyrants. For the sermon is about people who keep the law; those others we usually style delinquents and criminals, and besides they pay penalties according to their misdeeds.

It Should Be the Same Between Us and God

2. Now if at nature's dictate children run risks for parents, and servants for masters, citizens for cities, and bodyguards for kings, how much more proper and just it is for those who have been created and redeemed not only to fight for Him in word, but even to choose the extremity of death for His sake. For He is nearer to us than fa-

9

thers; it is thanks to Him that these are called parents. And He is more powerful than masters. For it is nature's law and no mere chance that constitutes a man master of servants. And He is more steadfast than any wall. For a wall, however stout, is made by mortal hand and, even if it withstands the force of the engines of war, it will never weather the hand of time.

God's Claims On Us Are Infinitely Stronger

3. But God is everlasting and eternal, and is strong enough to afford every protection and safety, and He indicates His immeasurable superiority by surpassing kings as much in regal splendor as the eternal surpasses what is created and corruptible. For He is eternal and holds dominion born with eternity. The king, on the other hand, enjoys both existence and the power of ruling from Him, and only rules for a short time over a few people, not over all who share the same human nature.

We Should Oppose Those Who Blaspheme Him

4. Since, then, He is nearer to us than parents, more lordly than masters, more provident than any benefactor, more stable than any wall, and immeasurably more regal than any king, it is fitting that we who receive existence from Him and the good life as well, should offer the opposition of our words to those of people who dare to open their mouths in blasphemy against Him, and moreover that we should counter impious arguments with reverent ones.[1]

Not That God Needs Our Words

5. Not that we come forward as though God needed our help—for the Maker of all things wants for nothing, and does not need the assistance of a tongue of clay,[2] but He listens to its hymns of praise, requites its espousal of His cause, and rewards its refutation of falsehood. But to demonstrate our good will to Him let us put an end, if possible, to the impudence of our fellow slaves. If that is not possible,

at least let us thoroughly refute and expose it to those who do not realize its nature.

Errors of the Poets About the Notion of God

6. Many indeed and varied are the ranks of those who choose to speak impiously, and diverse are the weapons of blasphemy. For falsehood is multipronged and various, but truth is graced with simplicity. The band of poets, indeed, dissected the notion of God in their works, blended falsehood with the charm of fable, and served to mankind in cocktail form the heady drink of the error of polytheism.[3]

Philosophical Errors

7. But those who define philosophy in terms of a white cloak, a flowing beard, and long hair,[4] seeing how ridiculous the theology of the poets was, devised other paths of error leading to the same poetic abyss. For some cloaked the base language of poetry about the gods in refined language and subtle conceits;[5] others assigned the divine name to human passions, calling pleasure Aphrodite, anger Ares, drunkenness Dionysus, theft Hermes, and sagaciousness Athena, and preaching this with braggart wink and Attic elegance led many men astray into error of another kind.[6] And those who professed to be philosophers, and were commonly esteemed as such because of their appearance, and also professed to conquer the passions, made men worship the passions and foolishly persuaded reason, the director of the passions, to deify lust, anger, theft, drunkenness, and the other passions.

Errors About God's Existence and Nature

8. Others again, unable to conceive of anything supersensible and closing their mind to all but sense knowledge, made gods out of what met their eyes.[7] And that august name, which strikes the ear with awe, is applied by some of them to the elements[8] and by others

to their constituent parts.[9] Some said that the world came about spontaneously.[10]

Others have invented in their dreams a plurality of worlds[11] instead of just one. Likewise, certain ones have denied absolutely the existence of the divinity.[12] Others have declared that God indeed exists, but that He does not concern Himself with anything that exists.[13] Others admit that He does concern Himself but that He does so in a niggardly fashion and that He extends His providence only as far as the moon,[14] and that the rest of the universe is borne along according to chance[15] and is forced to submit to the necessity of destiny.[16]

9. There are also those who have the formal title of "Christians," but they are in utter conflict with the dogmas of truth. Some, in fact, divide into three[17] elements the being who is uncreated, calling one part Good, the second, Evil, and the third, Just. Others describe in their discourse two principles,[18] ungenerated and diametrically opposed to each other. Others still, who pride themselves on combatting these impious opinions, imagine another way which leads to impiety.

10. For, although confessing that God's son is the only begotten Word of God, they count Him among creation as creature[19] and so place the Creator on a level with His creation. And they strive to exclude the Holy Spirit[20] from the divine nature by their impious discourse. Others, completely abandoning the Right Road, and reluctant to follow in the footsteps of their predecessors, have departed very far past the truth. Of these, some have completely denied the divine economy that has taken place on our behalf.

Others agree that the divine logos became man, but that He only assumed a body.[21] Others call the body assumed an animated one, but say that there was no rational and intellectual soul in it, holding, I suppose, their own empty-headedness as a proof of this. We know that the only soul a man has is a rational and immortal one.[22] Let us leave aside, however, all these other views for the present. For the discourse, like an army set for battle, could not discharge argumentative volleys against all of them simultaneously.

The Opponents of Divine Providence

11. Accordingly, passing over in silence all the other arrays of heretics and bringing to the front the company of those who war on the providence of God, let us shatter it with counterblows, smash it in pieces, sunder its serried ranks, lead away our captives, and bring every thinking man into submission to Christ.[23] Let the remaining crowd of the impious fill the role of spectators witnessing the contest. For in all probability an individual engagement with each of these divisions would not be necessary, but all would capitulate to the truth after seeing the overthrow of these and taking into account the force of truth.

Getting Armed for the Contest

12. Now perhaps the words that follow, however tardy their progress, will touch both the present audience and those who happen on them later. Putting on, then, the armor of the spirit, the breastplate of justice, the shield of faith, and the helmet of salvation, and having the loins girt about with truth, and feet shod in readiness for the gospel of peace, and, above all, taking hold of the sword of the spirit which is the word of God,[24] let us enter the fray and let the divine trumpet sound and lend strength to our weakness.

What is Providence?

13. Let us at the very outset of the contest ask our adversaries why they object to the word "providence," particularly when they recognize a Creator. For it is against those that our discourse for the moment directs itself. Why do you direct impiety against it? What visible object seems to you to lack order? What phenomenon appears to be wanting in design? What part of creation is lacking in harmony? Or beauty? Or size? What object lacking harmony in its movement has given birth to this impiety in you? Consider now at least, if you have not done so before, the nature of visible objects, their position, order, situation, movement, rhythm, harmony, gracefulness,

beauty, splendor, utility, charm, variety, diversity, changeability, their regular return to the same place, their permanence in corrupt natures.[25]

Providence in the Heavens

14. Behold the providence of God itself breaking through each part of creation, manifesting and proclaiming itself and all but shouting through these elements, your mouths closed that are agape and your unbridled tongues bridled. Behold providence manifested in the heavens and in the heavenly bodies, the sun, the moon, and stars. Behold it also in the air and in the clouds, on land and in the sea, and in everything on the earth, in plants, grasses, and seeds; in animals, rational and irrational, footed and winged, swimming, creeping, and amphibian, tame and wild, domesticated and savage.

15. Think to yourselves who preserve the heavenly orbits, how in so many thousand years the heavens have not grown old and have not been changed by time although by nature they are liable to change. As blessed David teaches: *They shall perish but you remain, and all shall grow old like a garment. And as a vesture you shall change them and they shall become different. But you are the same; and your years shall not fail.*[26]

The Heavens, Although Liable to Destruction, Have Lasted Down the Years

16. And yet, although the nature of the heavens is passible and corrupt, it has remained as it was, maintained by the word of the Creator. For the word that created it keeps and conserves it, and freely gives it solidity and firmness for as long as He pleases. For this reason, although such a great fire revolves about it—the sun, I mean, and the moon and the other heavenly bodies—yet in all the circling through the years it is not melted or scorched, or consumed by fire, although fire has received such natural properties from the Creator.

The Normal Effects of Fire Are Suspended
in the Case of the Heavens

17. For gold and silver, iron and bronze, lead and tin, wax and tar, and all such substances are melted, dissolved, and liquified by fire. On the other hand, it scorches mud and marshy places, absorbing the moisture. It bakes stones, removes their solidity, and reduces their rigid nature to dust; firewood, grass, and straw it all too easily sets ablaze. But the heavens do not suffer a similar fate. Despite its nature, the fire does not dissolve the crystal-like heavens, nor does it injure their smoothness, nor does it interfere with their spherical shape.[27]

How the Creator Preserves Harmony
Between the Conflicting Elements in the Heavens

18. On the contrary, the heavens preserve to the end the form which they received at the beginning, for He who established them like a canopy and spread them like a tent to serve as a dwelling, has united those hostile natures into harmonious relationships.[28] And the fire is not quenched by the swell of the waters, and the fire, however intense, does not consume and destroy the crystalline, ethereal, nebulous quality of the heavens. Living like neighbors, they conceal their hostile properties and, in obedience to the Creator's word, have pledged lasting friendship; despite the fact they have no soul and lack a directing intelligence, they keep and preserve their initial shape.

The Creator Is At the Helm

19. For the Creator directs creation and has not left the ship of His making without a pilot, but is Himself both the shipwright and the One who planted the raw material, both causing it to grow and building the vessel, and He continues to hold the rudder.[29] And the proof of this is the circle of so many years and the vast span of time which, far from destroying the ship, has preserved it safe and sound, revealing it not only to primitive men but to recent generations.

The Sun

20. Now that you have seen, my friend, the providence of God manifested in the heavens, come, let us take you on a tour of the remaining parts of creation. And taking you by the right hand, like infants first beginning to walk,[30] let us prepare to inspect creation step by step. Descend, then, from the heavens to the sun as a first step, and do not be afraid of being burned, but step forward and look around. For it will not burn you so long as you are well disposed concerning the Maker, but it will show you the Creator ordering nature to use its powers in a manner opposite to its customary one.

21. For fire is used to be borne upwards in its normal manner, just as water has a downward motion.[31] Neither can water be borne up from the foot of a mountain to the summit, nor can fire be persuaded to send its flame downward. Even if one, holding a lamp or a torch, tries a thousand times to direct the flame downward with his hand, the flame again returns to an upward direction and resists the hand that confines it, and does not abandon its natural impulse but stays within its natural limits.[32]

22. With the Creator, however, all things are easy. What does not yield to your right hand yields to the wishes of the left. And it is possible to see the sun, the moon, the chorus of stars turning their backs on the heavens and sending down their beams. For they are the slaves of their Maker and their nature is to conform to their Maker's definition. The nature of fire does not obey your orders, and does not abandon its natural activity. For you and it are equally slaves. But in obedience to the wishes of the Creator fire changes its nature from tending upwards to downwards.[33]

Likewise water, which by nature is fluid and relaxed, the Creator leads and brings upward, and dragging it from below He places it between heaven and earth without support, but keeping it suspended aloft merely by His word.[34] But meanwhile you would not wish to hear anything about the clouds, or you would not want to run before you have learned to walk,[35] but gradually making your way through creation you learn the course of piety.

Consider, then, the providence of God which presides over the sun, the moon, and other luminaries, and which has bidden them by word, so to speak, to act as torchbearers for men and not simply to act as torchbearers, but also to be the measure of time.[36]

Day and Night

23. For the rising of the sun causes the day; its setting or virtual concealment brings night whose darkness the Maker tempers with the moon and stars. And day and night, like sisters,[37] can be seen borrowing time from each other to assist mankind, and paying it back gladly. When winter is spent, and spring breaks through, and most men get anxious about work, and about journeys and travels and voyages from ports, now that the sea has become smooth and free of its winter roughness, and the earth adorned with crops calls the farmer to tend them, and plants call the planter to cutting, clearing, irrigating, and digging, at that time day borrows from night and increases working hours for mankind.

Day Borrows From Night

24. The increase is provided in small installments lest it injure those using it all at once. For when work is suddenly greatly increased it causes great injuries to those bodies which have remained inactive for a long period. That is why the increase is gradual. About midsummer day ceases borrowing and immediately begins paying back, without postponing the refund for a single day. Nevertheless it pays back what it received bit by bit, as it received it. And so about midsummer, at the equinox, day is not ashamed that she is on the decrease, nor does she dare to deprive her sister of her due, but she continues on the wane until she has paid back the whole debt and provides a long respite for men.[38]

The Advantages of Night

25. Night is more pleasing to us than day at a time when we are confined to the house by frost and rain, and mud and mire.[39] Indeed

some, despite the length of the night, do not get sufficient rest and are annoyed when they see the glimmer of dawn. There again night, when she has received her due, does not beg a loan.

Thus our whole life is a journey through these stages and night no less than day is a benefactor to mankind. In the first place the alternation of darkness and light is very agreeable to us and makes the light all the more pleasing. That is why we find dawn more desirable than the middle of the day.

Night Provides Rest for the Weary

26. When we get too much of the light of day we want the quiet of night. And when we get this, we get enough of it too and light in turn becomes the object of our desire. Thus too, when we get our fill of work in the daytime we also rest our wearied body at night. And after giving ourselves this good service on a couch, in sleep and quiet, we face work at dawn like new men.[40] Such is the extent and quality of the service that night renders us. Thanks to it the hireling gains pause and the slave gets rest from labor. For the darkness of night checks those who are too anxious for work. Men engaged in fighting are often glad when night comes, both the victors and those pursuing the enemy. When they perceive its arrival they break off the pursuit and allow those escaping a more leisurely flight.

And Feeding Time for Wild Beasts

27. Night conducts men home and provides them with sweet sleep; it also draws out the wild beasts to feeding and gives them freedom to graze. Wherefore the mighty David, in singing the praises of the God of the universe, exclaimed: *He has made the moon for seasons; the sun recognized his going down. You have appointed darkness, and night was made; in it shall all the beasts of the wood roam, the young lions howling after prey and seeking their food from God. The sun rises and they are gathered together and shall lie down in their dens. Man shall go forth to his work and to his labor until evening.*[41]

An Objection About Wild Beasts

28. Thus night has this much use; it gives men rest and gives wild beasts a chance to seek their prey in peace.[42] Perhaps one of those who deny providence may say: Why were wild beasts created? But let the answer to that objection wait until we come to treat of wild beasts.[43] Meantime let the sermon continue its course. Even what we have said already is proof enough, I think, that night is useful, necessary, and profitable to man. Let us add a few points, however, to corroborate what has been said.

Night Alternating With Day Is a Measure of Time

29. Since our nature was mortal and our life circumscribed, we have also to learn the measures of time.[44] Night, occurring as it does between days, constitutes a measure of time. For, if light remained in unbroken succession, we would not have learned the cycles of years, or the number of months, but one day would seem to be the measure of the everpresent age as we believe will be the case in eternity. For we have learned that that will have no evening and will be completely without interruption.[45] For such an age suits people destined to live forever. At the present time, however, with all its shortcomings, for we are both mortal and perishable, a knowledge of the measures of time was necessary so that, observing its flight, we might take care of ourselves and make ourselves ready for the last journey. Night, then, alternating with day became a measure of time, and seven such periods produce a week.

The Monthly Changes in the Moon and the Circuit of the Sun

30. The measurement of the month we get from the moon; from it, too, it got its name. For they call the moon μήνη. It takes thirty days all but a few hours for the moon to wax and wane, becoming crescent-shaped, then a half-moon, then gibbous, then completely full, then gibbous again, then half-moon, and finally crescent-shaped.[46] We learn the yearly circle from the days as well as from the months. When spring begins to shine, the sun journeys through the

middle of the heavens, making day and night about equal in length. Reaching from there to the more northerly part of the Orient,[47] and rising from there, it shortens the nights and lengthens the days; by raising the earth's temperature, it ripens its crops.

The Sun's Course in Autumn and Winter

31. Continuing its course to its usual limits, it returns from northern to southern regions and again it sees that day and night are equal in autumn, and, proceeding in a more southerly direction, pays back to the nights what it has taken from them and given to the days. It also allows the air to become humid and to fill the clouds, and to rain on the whole mainland. From there it returns to the spring equinox and completes the annual circuit.[48]

The Seasons Are Arranged So as to Avoid Sudden Changes in Temperature

32. Now that you have seen the utility of sun and moon, the regular successions of night and day, and the benefits that accrue to men from them, consider next the very delightful and beneficial succession of the seasons of the year.[49] The Creator did not just divide the circle of the year into two, giving us winter and summer simply. We do not go from one extreme to another without any intermediate stage. Instead, spring and autumn afford us a mean temperature between the icy cold and the burning heat.

Spring Marks the Transition From Winter to Summer

33. An excessively wet, cold winter does not succeed a very dry, warm summer, but spring, which participates in the heat of one and the cold of the other, effects the best mixture of the extremes and taking in hand, so to speak, these contrary elements—the cold of winter and the heat of summer—brings complete enemies into friendly agreement.[50] As a result, our transition from winter to summer is made without difficulty. In a short time we get away from the cold

of winter and approach the heat of summer without experiencing any injury from the rapid transition.

Autumn Does the Same Between Summer and Winter

34. Likewise in changing from summer to winter, autumn intervenes to prevent us from reaching the extreme of winter all at once and also to temper the extremes of heat and cold, providing another mean temperature and conducting us to this extreme by easy stages.[51] Such is the care of the Creator for us. And thus He makes the changes of the seasons pleasant as well as endurable for us.

The Seasons Bring Manifold Blessings in Nature

35. But perhaps some ungrateful creature will rise to criticize these excellent provisions and blame this wise, beneficent economy in these terms: Why, pray, these changes at all? What use to us are those changes of season? I ask you, my smart, clever critic of providence, what blessings come to us without the seasons?

Winter on the Land

36. For at the beginning of winter we sow the seeds.[52] He who taught us how to do so nourishes them, raining on them from the clouds, drawing up sea water by His word, carrying it aloft and gently changing its briny nature, distilling it, and letting it down at one time in small drops and at another in a downpour of big drops as if He were separating these products of the clouds with a sieve. Accordingly the season of winter exists to provide you, you wretch, with nourishment, and to supply you, you ungrateful creature, with your needs.

Spring, Summer, and Harvest

37. When spring comes round again, some of the farmers cut the vines, others plant new ones, and the shoots that are burst by the

heat of the atmosphere are forced to put forth their buds. At the peak of summer, when the sun causes a steep rise in temperature, the wheat calls the farmer to reaping, grapes turn black, olives in full bloom ripen as do the various kinds of fruit.[53] Then the harvest comes and offers these in full maturity to the harvesters. And they, as soon as the harvest is done, prepare once more for the sowing.

Stop being ungrateful, then, stop using His gifts in an attempt to slander providence, stop throwing back His gifts in His face. Recognize in all that has been said the providence of God directing and governing you, and ensuring for you an abundance of every blessing.

Providence is Manifested in the Stars

38. Consider the nature of the stars,[54] their position, order, variety of shape, beauty, utility, harmonious movement, their risings and settings. The Maker of the universe has made them not merely to brighten the darkness of night and to take the place of a light for men on a moonless night, but also to guide men on journeys and to lead sailors to shore.[55] For sailors, keeping them in view, make their pathless way and, guided by their position, direct the ship and bring it into whatever harbor they want to reach.

Stars Are Guiding Points

39. Since water does not support horses, donkeys, mules, the tracks of wheels, and the marks of wagons and chariots which are an unmistakable guide to travellers by land, the Maker of the universe has given to the broad seas the disposition of the stars like road tracks on land.

Praise the wonders of divine providence!
Oh! ineffable love! Oh! unspeakable wisdom!

Who could marvel enough at the goodness of divine providence, at its power, its nobility in difficulties, its ease in managing awkward situations, its magnificence, its resourcefulness? Truly your knowledge was wonderful to me: *I was overwhelmed, and could not reach to it.*[56] That is my exclamation, too. If you listen to me, you too will recite these words with me, praise the Benefactor with all your might, and render grateful words of thanks for His countless blessings.

Lest we should cause you pain and you now only learning to walk and unprepared to make a long journey, we will rest you here, and leave you to contemplate the providence of God manifested in the heavens and the heavenly bodies. For you will probably both develop for yourself this meditation, after being conducted this far, fill in what has been omitted from the discourse for the sake of brevity, and exclaim with the prophet: *How great are Your works, O Lord! You have made all things in wisdom.*[57] To You be glory, honor and adoration forever and ever. Amen.[58]

DISCOURSE 2

Demonstrations From the Air, the Earth, the Sea, Rivers, and Fountains

1. Those who disbelieve in the reins of providence and are foolish enough to maintain that the universe, consisting of heavens and earth, for all its ordered arrangement, is without a guiding hand, seem to me to resemble a man sitting in a ship traversing the sea who watches the pilot take the tillers and move the rudders as required, bearing now right and now left, and directing his ship into his ports of call.[1]

2. Now that man would be a manifest liar, obviously resisting the truth, if he said that there was no helmsman at the poop, that the vessel had no rudders, that it was not directed by the movement of the tillers, but that it was carried along automatically, that it overcame the force of the waves on its own, that it struggled of itself with the impact of the winds, and that it was in no need of help of sailors or of a helmsman to issue orders for the common good to the crew.

Providence Is Apparent Even in the Minutest Parts of Creation

3. For it is plain and obvious to these that God directs the universe of His creation and conducts everything in an orderly and harmonious manner. They see the conspicuous harmony of everything that exists, the beauty and utility of every created object manifested in every part of creation, yet they deliberately close their eyes to all this, or rather they see it and behave disgracefully, reviling providence with the gifts they have received from him and warring on the Guardian with the blessings they enjoy. What we said yesterday[2]

24

about the firmament, the sun, the moon, and the other heavenly bodies was enough to persuade them, if only they listened with an unbiased ear, to exercise restraint and sing the praises of their Benefactor.

Lest the shortness of that discourse should afford a pretext for blasphemy to those who place a limit to providence at the moon[3] and say that thus far only does it extend, thereby minimizing it unduly, come, dearly beloved, let us descend from there again via the air to the earth and, conducting you by slow stages as we did yesterday, let us show that even in the minutest parts of creation providence is apparent and obvious to those who are willing to notice it, and, in a word, that it continuously presides over every phase of its existence.

An Examination of the Air

4. Proceeding on the way, then, let us examine the air, its rarefied nature, its evanescence, the ease with which it disappears, its need of solid bodies to contain it.[4] That is why the Creator of the universe, when He created heaven and earth, diffused the air in the intervening space, erecting with it an unbreakable wall between these two bodies and making it the stay of life for creatures living in between.

In breathing it we sustain our mortal lives. Likewise the irrational animals, whether they are winged, or creeping, or amphibian, make it their support in life.[5] When in motion it provides us with the winds' breezes; when it becomes dense it transmits rain to the earth from the clouds. Light travels by it to delight the eyes of the beholders. Midway between sun and earth it regulates the excessive brightness of the sun, moderates its dryness and heat with its own moisture and coolness, and makes our enjoyment of its light innocuous.

We Should Not Make Exaggerated Claims for the Air

5. And in case you think the air is the cause of these benefits, notice that the heat of the sun moderates the excessive cold of the air; for no one could bear the unmodified cold of the air. Winter is proof of this. In winter the sun traverses the more southern regions of the

sky, abandoning the more northern and intermediate regions and giving the air freedom to make its nature felt.[6] For this reason the air, no longer absorbed in the same way by the heat of the sun, becomes thick and dense, and issues in violent rainfall; this, in turn, the air changes into mist by the rather vehement impact of the winds, condenses it into snow and hail, freezing the dew distilling in the clear upper air with the cool breeze, and producing snow because of the cold.[7] And although the sun is far away when these things occur, it nevertheless makes its presence felt on the air.

6. The providence of God can also be clearly seen in this. For, since the utility of the elements is manifold and great and, apart from their utility, their beauty is impressive and their splendor ineffable, the all-wise God has arranged that apparent troubles should be caused by them so that we might not mistake them for gods, but should treat them as His creatures, ruled and directed by Him.[8]

7. Therefore the air, which is our support in life, which we breathe to sustain life, this treasure common to all, to the poor and those who plume themselves on their wealth, to employees and employers, private citizens and kings, which is breathed no less by the poor man than by those who are clad in purple, every single nature being favored by an equitable distribution according to individual needs, not only gladdens us with inhalations, and breezes, and a plentiful supply of rain, but also distresses us with icy cold, teaching us that of itself it is not able to produce life and sustain living beings. Likewise the sun not only delights us with the beam of its rays and helps us to distinguish between the sizes and colors of visible objects, but also distresses us with the excessive heat of these rays.[9]

8. And unless the Guide of the universe by moving the air produced cool breezes for us, this sun that is worshipped by foolish men would completely burn up everything and terminate the lives of its worshippers.[10] None of the elements on its own, then, is able to cause life, nor indeed could all of them blended together be the cause of any good apart from the governing power of the universe. And even when the air is temperate, and the rain falls beneficially on the earth, and the sun shines without excess, and the winds' breezes are ordered in movement, and the farmers till the land at their ease, scattering the seeds as usual, you can see that the earth yields its fruits grudgingly and also that human life does not remain free of disease. The Lord of

the universe does this to persuade us not to place our confidence in creation, nor to regard it as the cause of blessings, but to put our trust in its Creator.

The Earth

9. Since, then, you have seen even the air enjoying the guidance of God and lasting because of that for so many thousand years without being exhausted by mortals breathing it, or disappearing beyond the substances that contain it, let us now lead you here to the earth, the common nurse, mother, and grave,[11] from which you have received your body of clay and your mouth which, according to the vision of Daniel, *utters great things*[12] against the Maker.

10. Consider in the first place the earth's situation and the variety of its contours. For it is neither completely even nor steep, but it is divided into mountains, valleys, and plains. In the middle of great plains can be seen hills rising on high and between mountains places that are as smooth and level as gulfs of the sea. Besides, the Creator has allocated the mountains themselves for the utility of mankind.[13] He has separated them into steep crags, thus arranging modes of conveyance for the waters of winter and devising for man roads that give easy access to difficult places. The mountains also afford raw materials for the art of house building; the plains provide a supply of wheat for the mountain dwellers.[14] And the diversity of creation not merely supplies man's bodily needs but is a source of delight to his eyes. For one is likely to tire quickly of monotony.

11. Who, pray, arranged all these things? Who endowed them with such power that so many cycles of years did not exhaust the treasure?[15] Who keeps things in their position? Who directs the flow of rivers? Who causes fountains to rush forth? Behold them, on the one hand, gushing forth on the tops of the mountains and pouring their waters downwards; on the other hand, not appearing at the foot of the mountains but providing springs for mankind from very deep wells. Lest you think that it is natural for water to shoot up of its own accord, the Creator teaches you by these examples that water, at the divine bidding, occupies even mountain ridges without any effort, and does not come forth to the surface of the plains even when forced

by artificial means. You, however, dig and sink wells, and enjoy the waters drawn up from below.[16] For you are a fellow slave of the elements, not their Creator.

Mineral Waters Have Their Uses

12. It is easy, however, for the Creator to draw up water not merely to mountain crags but even to the middle of the air, and also to sweeten its bitter taste, change its nature from fluid to solid and from solid to fluid, dissolve its density, arrest its flow, reveal it running upwards although its natural movement is downwards, and heat it without fire. And He does this for your sake, you thankless creature, that you may be able to enjoy natural hot springs, so that you can make them serve your bodily ailments. And these in turn He has provided in variety for you, suited to your different needs. For some relax the stiffness of the sinews; others tighten and brace those that are slack. Others again make war on inflammation and on black bile. Others, finally, dry up running sores. Such is the benefit that your Guardian has provided in hot springs.[17]

Those Who Deny Divine Providence Allege That God Is Unable To Conserve His Creation, or Is Uninterested in It, or Is Jealous of It; the Absurdity of Such Views

13. Nothing, however, can dissuade you from blasphemy; you persist in your ingratitude and reviling; you are a victim of the error of the Manichees who enjoy food and drink but abuse the reapers and bakers who provide those things, and curse those who cut the bread, do not venture to cut it themselves, but eat it when it is cut.[18] Likewise, while you enjoy so many countless blessings daily granted you by the Creator through His creation, your only return to Him is ingratitude for His favor, and you revile and abuse Him, saying that He has no care for what He has made.

14. But see what an injury you do Him in slandering Him like this. For why should He create what He had no mind to conserve? Why should He not care? Is it that He is able but unwilling? Or willing but unable?[19] Now the whole of creation testifies to His

ability. For how could He endow visible things with size, beauty, and proportion if His power of conservation were not equal to His original conception? How could He bring into communion and relationship opposites like water and fire, day and night, and devise from them all an ordered harmony if He was not able to provide for them? For it is greater by a long stretch to bring things from nonexistence into existence than to conserve them when once in existence.

15. But creation testifies to His ability and also to His willingness. For He was under no constraint to create. It was *not because He needed anything* that He undertook creation, but because He was good and possessed goodness in a superlative degree, and wished to bestow existence on nonexistent things.[20] How could He who exercised such goodness in respect of nonexistent things neglect them when they came into existence? Neither is it possible to say that He envied His works.[21] For His nature is without envy and free of all passion. To expose fully how ill-founded their impiety is, let us put them a few further questions.

16. For what reason, would you say, did He envy the creation which received existence from Him? Because of its size? But He is uncreated and without limit; He had no beginning and will never have an end; He embraces all things and is in no way circumscribed, for *in His hand are the ends of the earth*,[22] and *He has measured the sea with His hand and the heavens with His finger span, and the whole earth with the flat of His hand.*[23] Is it because of its beauty? But it was made by Him. Now nobody, not even the most envious of men, after building a stately, imposing house, would ever envy it, but would rather be conceited and preen himself, and in his happiness would show them through it who had not seen it already. And what words could describe how far the beauty of creation falls short of the light of intelligence which has created all things? You see, then, where their impiety has led them.

17. Now seeing that the greatest wretches do not envy the houses built by themselves but even take great pride in them, is it not the height of blasphemy to attribute envy to Him who is the fount of goodness and whose nature is perturbed by no passion? If He is able to hold the steering of creation and wishes it to enjoy every blessing, it is obvious that He also cares for, and presides over it, and with the

reins in hand directs every created nature, and leaves nothing un-
cared for.

The Sea Is Another Proof of Divine Providence

18. To convince you of this, return again to the sea,[24] and observe its depths, its extent, its division into bays, its shores, its ports,
the islands in its midst, the kinds of fishes in it and their species,
shapes, variety, and fondness for the shore.[25] Observe, too, the
bound of the waves, the bridle of providence resting on them, keeping them from overflowing the mainland.[26] When they rush against
the sand, they fear the boundary, seeing the divine law engraved
there.[27] So, like a spirited horse throttled by his trainer, the waves
bend the neck and retire, as if they repented of having touched the
sand.

19. By means of the sea, divided mainlands that are situated far
from one another can be seen being brought into intimate relationship. For the Creator, wishing to instill harmony into human beings,
made them depend on one another for various needs. For this reason
we make long voyages on sea, seek our needs from others, and bring
back cargoes of what we want; nor has providence allocated to each
section of the earth all the needs of mankind lest self-sufficiency
should militate against friendship. For satiety makes people pre-
sumptuous and begets disorder. Accordingly the sea lies in the center
of the earth, divided into countless bays like the market place of a
huge city, providing an abundance of every necessity, and receives
many sellers and buyers and brings them from one place to another
and back again.[28]

20. Since journeying by land is fraught with difficulty and the
satisfaction of all our needs on such journeys is not only difficult but impossible, the surface of the sea is there to take vessels, small and large,
and to provide much necessary cargo for those in short supply. A single
frigate can be seen taking as much as many thousand beasts. To ease the
burden for seafarers the Creator made islands as ports in which they
could call, rest, buy their needs, and then set sail again for their desti-
nation. *Be ashamed* then *at this multitude of blessings, said the sea.*[29]

21. For the words of the Prophet apply more to you than to Si-

don.[30] For Sidon, ignoring the Creator, divided the Divinity into many gods, mutilated the monotheistic form of worship and extended it to nonexistent deities, not indeed denying providence but ascribing it to these false gods also. For it would not offer sacrifice to these false gods unless it had fully persuaded itself that they provide assistance and avert disaster. But you who have been delivered from the error of polytheism and agree that all visible things are created, you, who adore their Creator, banish Him from His creatures, set Him completely outside His creation, assert that such an ordered universe is without a pilot and is borne about aimlessly like a ship without ballast. Be ashamed, then, at the blessings received from the sea, from the earth, from the air, from the sun, and the sky which affords a roof over our heads. Respect the tribute you receive from Creation.

The Blessings You Receive from All Those Sources Come From Providence

22. For each of the blessings enumerated makes a contribution to you, offering services as a sort of tribute. The sun gives its light and heat and ripens the fruits of the earth. The moon is your lamp at night. On land stars show you the night time; they also signify the changes of the seasons; on the sea they are guides to the mainland.[31] Air when inhaled cools your natural heat. When it freezes it checks the outer blossoming of plants and seeds but sends the power of growth down to the roots lashing down what tries to come to the top; it also destroys worms and bodies injurious to plants and seeds. It supplies you with various kinds of game bird.

23. And why speak of the fruits of the earth and the products of streams, rivers, and the sea? In your enjoyment of these can you forget their Giver? And reaping the fruits of Creation do you make war on the Creator, displaying your anger and taking leave of your senses? Do you not perceive these gifts which you carry around in your hands, and are you torn with contradiction?

Now I know your objections but I shall not raise them in this discourse or undertake their solution. But, with the help of another sermon, I propose to fashion an argument with them in support of the providence which you assail. Leaving you, then, with the injunction to meditate with pleasure on what I have said, and to derive benefit from it in every way, I shall sing the praises of Him who governs the universe.

To Him be glory forever and ever. Amen.

DISCOURSE 3

DEMONSTRATIONS FROM THE COMPOSITION OF THE HUMAN BODY

A Third Treatment Is Offered Those Afflicted with the Disease of Denial of Divine Providence

1. Those indeed who are sound in body are in no need of the physicians' care. Unimpaired health does not need the assistance of drugs. But those who are attacked by disease are accustomed to call on the assistance of doctors, and avail themselves of the help of the weapons of medical science against sufferings as if they were trying to repel enemies from the human body. For medical skill protects bodies and wars on diseases. Likewise, those who are sound in soul and enjoy a healthy spiritual life do not need doctrinal remedies. Those, however, who are hidebound by some wretched preconception and are victims of loathsome doctrines, having contracted the disease over a period, are in need of many purgations[1] potent to their soul. They also need many remedies capable by their action of closing and blocking up its productive pores,[2] and of putting an end to the wretched sufferings.

This Treatment Is Compounded of Human Nature Itself

2. Dangerous, indeed, and difficult to deal with is the disease of those who try to deprive creation of Providence. Accordingly, we have already applied two treatments to them compounded from the elements of creation.[3] To eradicate the disease and rid them completely of this troublesome malady, let us try to apply a third preparation for them. The materials for this treatment[4] we shall take, not

from the heavens, land, and sea, nor from the sun, moon, and other heavenly bodies, nor from the air, clouds, and winds, nor from the rivers, fountains, and springs, but from the very composition of those people who try to blaspheme.

Human Speech

3. Although they have obtained a mouth from the Creator to pour forth praise to the Giver for the benefits they enjoy, they are not merely reluctant to sing His praises, but they even defile the tongue with blasphemies,[5] and bring the instrument of reason into disrepute. Yet this one organ is sufficient to demonstrate not only the wisdom of the Creator but also His immense goodness.[6]

For it resembles an organ, composed of bronze reeds pumped up by bellows,[7] set in motion by the artist's fingers and rendering harmonious sound. Now nature did not learn this from science, but science was taught how to contrive this delightful sound by nature. For nature is an archetype of science, and science a replica of nature.[8]

Voice Production Has Affinities With Organ Playing

4. You, then, who have the gift of speech and dishonor the One who so honors you, consider how the lungs resemble bellows, which the muscles surrounding the thorax press upon, corresponding to the action of the feet in organ blowing, causing it to contract and expand. This transmits the breath through the windpipe,[9] and when compressed, opens the epiglottis and is borne through the throat to the mouth. Speech, then, manipulates the teeth like so many bronze reeds with the tongue[10] and makes them run up and down and glide without effort and with perfect ease.

5. The salivary gland also helps to facilitate this movement, resembling, as it does, a fount gushing forth moisture. When the constant movement parches the tongue, it needs saliva in moderation to moisten it, make it smooth, and give it freedom of movement.[11] This is how articulate voice comes about: When speech comes in contact with the teeth by means of the tongue, and breath is exhaled, as I have said, and the lips contract, and the air is smitten harmoniously

by the emission of the breath, the exhaled breath becomes the vehicle of speech while nature expels the smoky substance as superfluous.[12]

The Function of the Lungs and Windpipe

6. Now since the Creator has constituted the heart the source of natural heat,[13] and the whole body takes the quality of its heat from this part, and since the heart encompassed by so much heat needed some slight process of cooling, the Maker of nature has caused it to be ventilated through the lungs.[14] They receive pure air from outside through the windpipe and send it through the left lung to the left cavity of the heart. From there, according to those who deal scientifically with these matters,[15] respiration originates. The lungs send the pure air to the heart, lay hold of what is impure, and expel it again as superfluous through the windpipe, and this air, though superfluous and quite useless, becomes the vehicle of speech, if the mind wills it and moves the tongue in rhythm and harmony.

We Should Praise God for This Gift of Speech

7. And what is discharged by the heart as injurious, and expelled by the lungs, becomes an auxiliary of articulate speech. Truly we can exclaim—*O the depth of the riches, of the wisdom, and of the knowledge of God.*[16] Truly *who shall declare the powers of the Lord? Who shall make all His praises heard?*[17] Truly *how great are Your works, O Lord! You have made all things in wisdom.*[18] What tongue could sing the praises of the Creator sufficiently? What discourse could do justice to our own composition? What speech could adequately describe the organs of speech? Who is so wise as to discern fully the wisdom of the Creator?

The Production of the Human Voice Surpasses in Ingenuity the Production of Sounds By Musical Instruments

8. You see these things and enjoy them, yet you are reluctant to praise their cause, but accuse Him of not caring for the creation

which He cares for so well. And indeed this one part of the anatomy should be sufficient to demonstrate the care of the Maker for men. For, having made him with a capacity for speech, He made the appropriate organs of speech.[19] Technology, in imitation of nature, has invented wind instruments, lyres, and lutes. In place of teeth it has extended strings, and in place of lips it has put brass. The plectrum is the tongue for the strings.[20] The hand, changing to treble and bass, imitates reason preparing the tongue to run up and down.

The Musician Cannot Make His Instrument
Produce Articulate Speech

9. Now, when such precision appears in music, listeners marvel at the rhythm and harmony of the strain, yet they do not appreciate human articulation. Art, however, imitates nature, but it is nature that makes the voice articulate. The voice is the creation of God, who is the Maker of all things. Just as art uses as a model a living being in fashioning bronze or stone into a human likeness, giving it eyes, a nose, a mouth, ears, a throat, hands, a chest, an abdomen, thighs, legs, and feet without being able to endow it with perception, reasoning, and voluntary movement,[21] so the lyre, lute, and bronze-reeded instrument omit harmonious sound and rhythm through inflation or percussion, but only the human organ, the archetype, produces articulate speech.

Human Speech Is the Work of the Creator

10. For speech is the handiwork of the Creator Himself, but all these things are the work of the image of the Creator. As man is the image[22] of the Creator he strives to imitate the Creator. And the things he makes are like shadows contending with the truth;[23] they are true to their forms but lack their native energy. Seeing such divine providence manifested in human organs, then, stop calling it want of care. In order that you may learn from the rest of the anatomy the care of our Maker for us, come, let us lead you to an examination of the heart itself.

The Heart

11. This is the most important part[24] of man and since it is entrusted with the rule of the body it is protected on all sides like a king,[25] and is fortified by a strong thorax so that it cannot be easily injured from outside accidents. Since it is in continuous motion[26] (for it is the source of the arteries) He has covered it with the loose, spongy, porous and arterial texture of the lungs, like a soft blanket,[27] on the bottom, while on the top He has strengthened its conical shape and surrounded it with tissue that is membranous, but dense and strong. Both air and blood supply it with nourishment; it draws the blood from parts of the liver through a sort of canal, the vena cava.[28] The liver draws this matter from the abdomen.

The Alimentary System; the Purifying Process in the Liver

12. The abdomen derives nourishment through the gullet after the teeth have cut up the nourishment, and the molars changed it into tiny particles.[29] When it has drawn in the nourishment, it first retains it, converts it into juice, alters, transforms, and assimilates it.[30] Then, after thoroughly digesting and altering it, it effects an equitable division, passing some on to the liver to strain and retain what is pure, and rejecting what is superfluous, sending it to the intestines with the assistance of the evacuative power.

The liver, when it receives the pure part of the nourishment, is not satisfied with the purgation and scrutiny it has undergone, but cleanses and separates it further with what I might term strainers.[31] The spleen draws the sediment, so to speak, and very thick lees through ducts and transforms this into nourishment.

The Supply of Nourishment

13. What has been overdigested and has contracted a bilious quality, and become wan in color, is received in the gall bladder. The fluid matter that is very thin and devoid of nourishment goes into the receptacle for urine. The vena cava takes the nourishment, completely purified, assimilated to the liver, and changed into blood, and

brings a supply to the heart,[32] and on its way up it branches into many veins and gives nourishment to the breast, shoulders, and hands; it extends as far as the nails and twines around the throat, it reaches the head, it enters into the buttocks, thighs, knees, legs, and feet; in a word, it circulates through the body and leaves none of the bodily organs without its moisture.[33]

Veins

14. The veins are like channels and conduits whose task is to supply the body with moisture. For this reason they have a loose, porous covering so that the adjacent parts of the body may draw off nourishment easily. The arteries, however, have not only thick but double coverings. For arteries are air vessels, not blood vessels,[34] and air has a smooth and easy flow. This is another manifestation of the providence of God. He made the veins, which were to provide blood for the various parts of the body, from fine membranes and covered their openings with porous matter. For blood is dense and needs large pores for secretion. To keep it from being all secreted, and to provide a sort of moisture for the adjacent parts, He has constructed the blood vessels in this way.

Arteries

15. The Creator did not create in the same way the arteries, whose function is to provide air everywhere (air is less dense, easily disappears, and is easily secreted through the tiniest pores). And the Maker has not constructed them in the same way nor made them from one covering, but from two thick, very tight ones. He also placed the arteries beside the veins so that the blood might be propelled by the movement of the hot air and circulate everywhere, for it is apt to clot when stationary.[35]

The Circulation of the Blood Resembles
a Domestic Water Supply

16. For this reason He has grafted them to one another in certain places with minute perforations so that the blood might get a little air to drive it on and force it to move, and also that the air might enjoy moisture to keep it damp and soft and not allow it to dry up altogether. What inventive, resourceful man in building a house ever made such provision that it had a water supply, devising a supply of well-heads, and procuring tanks and sinks for his good pleasure[36] as did the Creator of the universe in constructing this edifice of human reason and in equipping it with vessels of such quality and quantity to supply its need?

The Respiratory System Resembles Good Ventilation

17. What architect who wishes the west wind to blow on houses leaves vents for the wind in the same way as the Supreme Architect, God, has planned that the breath which is smoky and sooty might gain an exit, and that pure air might enter and run into all the arteries? What gardener channels water and applies moisture to the roots of the plants in the way that He, who planted human nature and made all creation, silently applies moisture through the veins to the limbs of the body?[37] In the matter of nourishment our needs are no different from those of trees that do not have souls. We are just as much in need of it as they are. If the tree does not get nourishment it becomes dry and withered; likewise, a man overcome by hunger loses all moisture and is condemned to die.

Human Beings Are Nourished Much As Trees

18. Just as trees derive their moisture through the roots either from the rainfall of clouds or from the flowing water of rivers and fountains, and this nourishes the shoots, the bark, and the piths, and brings on leaves, makes them bloom, and ripens the fruits, so too the human being receives nourishment in the mouth, which corresponds to a fountain, the esophagus, which we usually call the gullet,[38] tak-

ing the place of a channel. The stomach receives the nourishment and transmits it to the liver, just as the roots send it to the bottom of the shoots.[39]

Growth and Nourishment Are Provided for by Our Maker

19. The liver not merely retains what is necessary for its own use, but transmits this moisture through the veins for the other parts of the body.[40] Bodily nourishment causes young people to grow, become tall and stout, and reach in a short time proper size. When the normal size is reached, further growth stops and nourishment alone continues. Thus the Maker of all things takes care of our nature, and not merely fashions us but continually looks after our nourishment and all our other needs. Words, however, fail me in praising my Maker. The diversity of His care for us surpasses understanding, and no amount of talk could do justice to the wisdom of His handiwork, and no one could arrive at a proper appreciation of the make up of human bodies.

Man Alone Is Made Vertical

20. The following consideration should be enough to make you praise the Creator. You are not bent to the ground like irrational animals, you do not trail your stomach on the ground like pigs.[41] Only look up and you behold providence. Alone of living beings He has made you upright, borne on two feet, and has pivoted each of these, not on one limb, but on three, and has fitted it into three joints.[42] The first articulation is at the hip joint; the second is at the knees; and the third is assigned to the ankles. He bound these joints with strong sinews and endowed the muscles with voluntary movement. He made the joints neither too loose nor too tight, for in the latter case movement would be rendered quite impossible and excessive looseness would cause the joints to escape from one another and become dislocated. Thanks to this providence of His you walk and run when you please, and you have the power to stand and sit.

The Buttocks Provide Man a Natural Seat

21. Mark another manifestation of His providence. The body provides the natural couch of the buttocks[43] so that you can make a seat out of the ground or a stone and not be hurt by sitting on bare limbs. You are ungrateful notwithstanding. You fail to recognize the gifts, and rave and rant against this wisdom that makes such provision for you.

A Dog Recognizes His Master

22. A dog recognizes the one that feeds him; he sits beside him when he is at home, and misses him when he is away. He shows delight at his return by shaking his ears, wagging the tail, showing his obedience, recognizing his inferiority, making plain his anxiety to please, and doing all this despite the fact that he lacks reason and is bereft of any speech, but has discovered through time, habit, and frequent kindnesses the difference between stranger and familiar, between friend and enemy.[44]

But Man, Endowed with Reason, Fails To Recognize God

23. But you, with the help of speech, and with reason as your guide, reason, more winged and penetrating than any visible object[45] (The sun completes the circuit of the earth in a day, but the human mind can form a concept of it in a moment; it reaches the heavens in imagination and transcends them; it beholds God as best it can in a mirror and sees the countless myriads of angels and the thousands of archangels; it busies itself with what is under the earth and strives to penetrate beyond it but to no avail, for an image is limited to what is known to exist) with such a guide, such a pilot, such a trainer, you fail to recognize the divine gifts. You do not add the number of benefits but are steadfast in your ingratitude. You are reluctant to learn the elements of providence, although there are so many things at hand to teach you. Take heed lest He abandon you completely to

your own devices and force you to learn by experience the difference between the care of providence and the want of it.

The Spine

24. Come, friend, now, and let us lead you to another part of the anatomy. Consider now the spine, which extends from the sacrum near the buttocks to the neck and resembles a stout pillar,[46] composed of many vertebrae, supporting the abdomen, shoulders, hands, neck, and head. Since the Creator has placed no bone near the abdomen on the outside so that it may easily be distended when it receives nourishment and may provide sufficient space for the food, the spine supports it at the back. The Creator has constructed it from numerous bones so that it easily bends, if a person wishes to bend, without any break resulting from bending. The spinal marrow nourishes it, with its source in the brain.[47]

The Neck

25. Why should I speak of the hands whose utility is proclaimed by crafts of all kinds? We shall in any case be talking about them in our next discourse; we refrain until then from going into their various uses. Let us come next to the neck and examine its formation. Imagine aqueducts that are pierced top and bottom and have many similar perforations including one very great central one through which the water pipes draw off most water, distributing it and forcing it to go through other pipes conveying it to the south, east, west, and north of the city. The neck serves a similar function for the body. Science imitates nature, as I have said already, and incorporates its devices in its own works.

The Esophagus and Spinal Marrow

26. The neck contains the mouthpiece of the esophagus, and transmits food and drink to the stomach. Besides it contains the trachea reaching from the lungs to the larynx, and also veins and fine

arteries through which the brain receives blood and air.[48] When nourished and developed it sends the spinal marrow through the bones next to it to the backbone. This is the source of nourishment for all the bones; it produces very strong tendons, some thick and smooth, others broad and rounded, which serve to bind together the joints and provide the muscles with the power of movement.

The Cranium Is a Protection for the Brain

27. Now that we have come to the head, imagine it as the acropolis of the body,[49] raised aloft, and protecting the brain like a rich treasure in a very strong fortification. For the cranium is a sort of protective helmet;[50] the Greeks call a helmet *kranos* because of its similarity in shape to the cranium. The cranium surrounds the brain and protects it as far as possible from external injury.

The Pia Mater

28. To prevent the bones which are hard and rigid from piercing and injuring the brain which is very soft and quite porous, the brain is surrounded with two coverings for which the medical term is the membrane.[51] The finest covering is placed next to the brain and is called the pia mater;[52] it is made so as to touch the brain and hold it firmly without injuring it because of its extreme fineness. The composition of the second covering is thick and strong, and it is placed between the brain and cranium in such a way that it neither injures the brain by its rather tough texture nor suffers injury from the bones which are harder than it. The brain, then, as I said, is protected in the head like a rich man in a stronghold.

The Eyes Are Protected by the Eyebrows

29. Since the custodian of the stronghold—the mind, I mean—needed observers to see both friend and foe, the Creator has also provided these, and has not left it to one, but has appointed two guards, one on the right and the other on the left, to watch and observe. And

since these needed protection—a defense and bulwark and palisade[53]—the Creator of this city has not been negligent in this regard either. For the eyes, entrusted as they are with the faculty of sight, are provided with prominent eyebrows, which act as defenses and bulwarks and which shield the eyes and enable them to observe far-distant objects. To shield them from the downpours of rain He causes fine hairs to grow on these defenses, and also on the surface of the face and these hairs retain the perspiration rolling down from the forehead diverting it and letting it drop from the temples, thus keeping the eyes free of this discomfort.[54]

The Protective Role of the Eyelids and Eyelashes

30. Since the guards needed armor, He gave them the eyelids as tunics and the eyelashes as swords and javelins. These latter have not the same position as the eyebrows lest they be more of a hindrance than a help. They are not arranged in a straight line so as not to rub against each other in the closing of the eyelids, but they are slightly forward to prevent injury from tiny bodies.

31. When a rather strong wind is blowing it sets in motion not only fine dust but also coarser articles, motes, and the like. Similarly, gnats and such creatures attack the eyes but take to flight at the sight of the eyelids, as if they were palisades.[55] Ears of corn are defended in the same way by the Creator of the universe. By placing awns over the blades of wheat He prevents granivorous birds from doing too much harm to the crop.[56] He frightens them off with the swordlike edges and puts them to flight.

32. But perhaps some ungrateful wretch may say: What more has he conferred on me than on the ears of corn? But, you foolish one, He has made the ears of corn in that way for your use. Why should you be ungrateful if he has fortified what belongs to you with your weapons and on your account. You sow the wheat, most ungrateful wretch. He waters it, gives it heat, nourishes it, guards and watches it, and ripens it for you. You reap it, bring it to the threshing floor, skillfully separate the chaff, grind it, and, when the wheat is separated, knead it, put it in a pan or oven, enjoy the bread, and yet fail to recognize the Benefactor.

The Structure of the Eye

33. But let us return to the eye. Examine its structure well. Note the number of coverings it has. Look at its external symmetry. Look at the delicacy of the pupil, the surrounding halo which we call the iris, the circular cornea, the choroid membrane, the crystalline ball resting below it and looking through it, the transparent fluid enveloping it, the net-like retina, the glandular cavity on which the whole structure is seated, the nourishment which is provided from the brain through a very tiny vessel, the efflux of secretion at the corners.[57]

Changes of Color in the Blood

34. Consider also how many changes of color the blood undergoes. At first it was nourishment, masticated by the teeth, and transmitted to the stomach. The stomach changed it to its own color making it white. The liver, when it receives it, changes it again to its own color. Blood is such that on reaching the brain it becomes white again, and part of it is transferred into bones, and part of it is transformed into tough, another part into flexible, tendons.

The Sense of Smell

35. But perhaps I am acting like those who try to count the sands of the sea[58] when I strive to track down the manifestations of divine providence in the human body. Go through the other faculties for yourselves: taste, smell, hearing. See how the nose apprehends odors, admits what is pleasant, repels what is unpleasant, and ejects what is secreted from the head.[59]

The Nose and the Ear

36. Because of its situation in the upper portion of the body and because it receives vapors sent up from below, the rise of which might do great injury to the most important part of the body—I mean the

brain—the Creator has not been negligent in this regard either. He has made certain ducts, spongy and porous, through which the humors and moist excretions descend to the palate and nostrils, and has assigned two ducts to expedite the discharge. With regard to the vaporous, discolored excretion, He has caused it to be borne and expelled through the sutures of the skull.[60]

37. Consider also the faculty of hearing. However many impressions it receives, it is never overwhelmed or overpowered; it does not register them all in the same way, but recognizes the difference between treble and bass;[61] it enjoys harmony and avoids its opposite.

The faculty of hearing is our mode of reception of the divine oracles; it is nature's way of learning every human skill: grammar, rhetoric, logic, arithmetic, medicine, engineering, and all the other discoveries of man. Use this hearing for our discourses, then, take it as a remedy to purge the soul and free it from wretched blasphemy.

Establish on the foundation of hearing the gate of reason and the fear of God as gatekeeper, and examine in fairness the discourses offered you. Let the gatekeeper open the gates to pious people, but let him turn away blasphemers, wretches, and haters of God. Let him close the gates and place on them the strength of faith like an unbreakable bar.

The Rewards for Listening Sympathetically

38. Thus it can come about that those who regard the sermons as friendly and useful will be freed from their enemies and enjoy health of soul, these who have, in St. Paul's words, *not itching ears*[62] and do not listen to discourses which, though delightful, are injurious. Such people will form a just estimate of what they hear and only choose what is useful, seeing God, as the prophet says,[63] in everything, by night and by day, walking or sitting, in everything they do or suffer.

To Him be honor, glory, and adoration for all ages. Amen.

DISCOURSE 4

DEMONSTRATION FROM HUMAN HANDS AND FROM DISCOVERY OF CRAFTS

1. I have heard the voice of the prophet chant and exclaim: *The heavens proclaim the glory of God and the firmament declares the work of His hands.*[1] No one indeed on this earth has ever heard a voice from heaven like the voice which is produced by the passage of air through the windpipe to the mouth,[2] by speech harmoniously applying the tongue to the teeth, by the contraction of the lips and the vibration of the resisting air.[3] No, but by displaying grandeur, and manifesting beauty, and affording to man the benefit of shelter, it silently proclaims the Creator and moves the tongues of all to sing His praises.

A Well-built House Makes Us Think of the Architect

2. When we see a house that has been well-made architecturally, built on a firm foundation, finished with even gables, made broad, spacious, lofty and well-proportioned, with windows inserted in ordered symmetry and all the other fittings which usually adorn such houses, we immediately marvel at the architect, try in his absence to make a mental picture of him, and refer all its proportion to his art.

Similarly the Heavens Should Remind Us of the Divine Architect

3. Likewise,[4] when we look at the heavens and the beneficial motion of the heavenly bodies it is not these we reverence, but we

47

celebrate their Maker as best we can in songs of praise, and by analogy *we visualize the Creator from the grandeur and beauty of created objects.*[5] For we argue rightly and justly: if created objects are so great, how great must the Creator be? And if such be the beauty of the things that are made, what must be the beauty of the supreme Architect[6] and Maker of the universe? *For the heavens proclaim the glory of God and the firmament declares the work of His hands.* Again, *day unto day utters speech, and night unto night reports knowledge,*[7] not by release of the voice, nor by utterance through the tongue, but by continually succeeding one another and by being increased at one another's expense[8] for the service of mankind.

4. And so loud is their proclamation that the whole human race hears their voice. *There are no speeches or utterances where their voices are not heard.*[9] For every race and every tongue hears the proclamations of day and night. Tongue differs from tongue, but nature is one and derives the same lesson from day and night. Thus the same author, singing the praises of the Creator in another Psalm, says: *Your knowledge was wonderful to me, I was overwhelmed and I could not reach to it.*[10]

5. Withdrawing, he means, into myself, alone and away from all external disturbances, I wished to contemplate my own nature and discern clearly the reasoning power of the soul, the knowledge it is capable of receiving, the crafts with which it has filled life and which make life more pleasant and delightful, the abundance of words it produces and the unlimited number which it listens to, the manner in which it stows away the memory of these things and preserves them carefully, the ease with which it recalls whatever stored-up matter it wishes, how it directs the body, appointing the eyes to determine weights and colors, the tongue to discern tastes as well as to attend to its proper function, the production of speech, the nose to discriminate odors, the ears to receive communications from outside, while the rest of the body is entrusted with the faculty of touch, giving these organs the power of perception and receiving from them sensations of pleasure and pain.

6. Revolving, he means, such considerations in my mind and seeing the formation of a single body result from this meeting of opposites, and the union and concord between mortal and immortal,[11] I am overcome by wonder and, failing to comprehend it, I admit defeat[12] and, proclaiming the victory of the wisdom of the Creator,

I sing the praises of my Maker, exclaiming: *Your knowledge was wonderful to me: I was overwhelmed and could not reach to it.* These words indeed are an apt description of us also in the present circumstances, trying to see wisdom manifest itself in the parts of the human body and discovering our shortcomings in the attempt.

Providence in the Most Insignificant Parts of the Body

7. Our contemplation, though dim, has been very profitable, for even in the least part of the body we have seen the resplendent providence of God. For what is more worthless than hairs?[13] What part of the body is so lacking in perception? Yet our discourse has shown their use and necessity. Eyebrows and eyelids show this as well; likewise the hair which both ornaments and covers the head.[14] Even those who are bald teach us the use of hair. First, bald men blush as if despoiled of beauty. Secondly, they devise wigs to take the place of hair.

The Growth of a Beard in Adolescence

8. And it is for this reason, it seems, that the Creator has allowed some heads to be without hair, so that we may learn that the Creator fashioned the whole being with the same provident care with which He fashioned hair. Thus He also adorns with the beard, covering part of the cheeks and the lower chin, those who are coming to manhood[15] after leaving their boyhood days behind. First the down sprouts, then a moderate amount of hair covers the cheeks to inculcate the difference of ages by the growth, and to persuade them by the change of appearance to abandon childish delights and to undertake serious pursuits. Since the pains of childbirth are sufficient to teach this lesson to women, He has bearded the cheeks of men alone.[16]

9. And if one of those who have learned only to contradict the truth objects that there are growths of hair on other parts of the body, let him learn that he has no grounds for ingratitude in this regard either. For nature by self-growth has provided a covering which we

try to provide artificially. So it is that nature does not give the girdle of hairs to those who cannot yet distinguish between good and evil,[17] but has well and becomingly adorned with this girdle those with incipient knowledge who have learned the purpose of the several parts of the body, as if to conceal their unnecessary blushing.

This Sense of Shame Is a Consequence of the Fall

10. Adam, our first parent, had not this shame in paradise. *For the two of them, Adam and his wife, were naked and were not ashamed.*[18] But after the transgression of the law, becoming ashamed of their transgressions and hearing the divine Voice, they plucked fig leaves and made girdles[19] for themselves. Come, then, you who chafe at the Creator and despise providence, recognize the providence of the Creator in these limbs. He rejoices at creating these parts, mere mention of which causes you to blush. *And God saw all the things He had made and they were good.*[20] And *let us make a help like unto himself.*[21] And God's first blessing: *Increase and multiply and fill the earth and subdue it.*[22]

11. Since our discourse has touched on the parts of the body which in Paul's language are somewhat dishonorable[23]—I do not know what forced me to digress—notice once more the ineffable beneficence of the Creator. The mouth, which is entrusted with attending to speech, receiving nourishment, and transferring it to the stomach, He has placed near the eyes. The place of excretion, on the other hand, which can annoy the eyes, produce aversion to food, and fill one with nausea, He has placed far from the eyes and has in fact made it quite invisible to them, by directing the large intestine backwards, opening a passage between the buttocks, and with their projection providing it with a natural concealment.[24]

12. Bow your head, then, before the boundless love of God for man. Tremble at His ineffable care, seeing that it created what you are ashamed to speak of and caring for what you blush to mention. Since what is visible of man is mortal, and being mortal needs nourishment, He had to provide him with a mouth and places of excretion, and He created the convoluted coils of intestines[25] to contain the impure part of the nourishment so that there might not be im-

mediate evacuation, for in that case constant eating[26] to replace the constant evacuation would become troublesome.

An Examination of the Hands

13. Why speak of all the wonders of nature? It is time now to speak of the hands which we passed over yesterday with a promise to explain their usefulness today.[27] Look at them, then. In construction they are no longer than necessary, lest they become a superfluous burden for the rest of the body, and, again, they are no shorter than necessary, but their size is rather proportioned to the purpose for which they were made.

14. To serve these needs the Creator has made them in three parts. He has inserted the first joint[28] at the shoulders, then fitted the arm and forearm to the elbow, then joined the rest of the forearm to the carpus, and added the metacarpal bones, inserting in them the five fingers. He also fashioned each finger from three phalanges, making the extremities of some of them hollow and of the others spherical, and inserting the spherical part in the hollow. Then He bound them in tight tendons and gave the muscles the power of voluntary contraction. He covered them with soft skin lest hardness might impede digital contraction. He made the extremities of the fingers porous on the inside but gave them external protection by placing on them fine, broad nails projecting over the edges.[29]

15. He made them fine so that they might not weigh down the tender flesh of the extremities and so become too much of a burden, and made them broad so as to be resilient in heavy work while affording external protection to the porous flesh underneath. He made the tops of the nails round, for this shape left them less liable to injury, because corners of triangular and rectangular forms are easily injured in fragile bodies.

Man Is Not Provided with Talons or Hooves

16. The Creator provided lions, bears, leopards, and the other wild beasts with paws that are sharp, broad, long, and very strong,

thus giving them natural armor,[30] for they cannot, being irrational, help themselves with artificial weapons. Man, on the other hand, is created rational and as his intellectual nature helps him to discover many sciences and techniques He has made him without this natural armor. He has not given him the paws of wild beasts, nor has He covered his feet with hooves.[31] For if He did, how could he climb ladders? How could he stand on narrow walls whilst working in stone and mortar, in the building of houses? How could he stand on the roofs of houses if he had hooves or cloven feet?[32]

But as it is, the softness and shape of the feet and the flexibility of the nails make movement easy for him and his carriage safe. He can easily walk on planks in his bare feet, and dart up steep ladders, and do countless things of that sort with the greatest of ease.

Shoes Serve the Purpose of Hooves

17. Man, however, derives the usefulness of hooves from a different source. For taking the skin of the lower animals, and with the assistance of the art of the tanner and the shoemaker,[33] he makes an imitation of feet in arrangement, size, length, and breadth and puts these on to ward off injury from hard bodies in walking and to dull the edge of the cold.

The Various Uses of Hands

18. This is why the Creator has given hands to man only, the organs, as it were, befitting a rational animal.[34] With them men till the earth, cut furrows, scatter seeds, with spade or hoe in hand dig pits,[35] plant trees, and with sharpened scythes at one time cut the vines when they see them coming to maturity, and remove what is superfluous, while at another they cut the standing crops and reap the wages of their work with the help of their hands, binding the sheaves, bringing the loads to the threshing floor, and separating the grain from the chaff. They consign the chaff to heaps and put the grain in barns with the help of their hands. They gather in the vine crop, collect the olives, press the wine, tend all kinds of vegetables,

collect countless varieties of fruits by their skill, and gather and distribute them to those who wish to enjoy them.

Hands Help Man to Cross the Sea, Thanks to Shipbuilding

19. With hands man not only adorns the mainland with ripe
meadows, waving crops, and spreading groves, but has also fur-
nished the sea with many roads and has provided with many travelers
what was impassible to human feet. For with his God-given brain
man derived the art of shipbuilding[36] from the smith's craft, which
had already originated through the discovery of the axe, the saw, the
adze, and the other tools of carpentry, and also from its older sister,
agriculture. Cutting the timber of non-fruit trees with these tools,
and putting the keel under the ship as a foundation, he fitted planks
to it for walls, joining it thoroughly with bolts, greasing it with pitch,
in this way fortifying it against the inroad of water. That is how the
ship,[37] the vehicle of the sea, originated.

The Pilot Uses Hands to Steer the Ship

20. Now since this chariot needed horses and mules, so to
speak, and yet could not have these since it was seagoing, the pilot of
the ship also made wise provision for this and again used hands to
help. Raising the mast in place of a pole and fitting the sails to it in
place of a yoke, he used the impact of the winds' breezes instead of
horses and mules and drove them, like ponies, with the rudder. And
since the vessel needed reins, their place was taken by the rudders,
and the pilot, taking the rudder bar like a charioteer with the prow
as the outer edge of the chariot, leads the ship here and there at his
ease.

21. He knows, too, not only how to direct his ship intelligently
when a favorable wind is blowing, but he can also break up the attack
of disorderly winds and can bridle them as if they were unbroken,
unmanageable, young horses. Such are the inventions of the mind of
man, using hands to help. With them the sailor traverses the sea, the
pilot directs the ship, the merchant unloads the cargo of provisions

he has purchased, and every fisherman plies his rod and tries to catch the invisible prey in the well-devised folds of nets.[38]

The Reciprocal Benefits of Human Crafts

22. But come, let us leave the sea for the land. We have not sufficient time to deal minutely with each pursuit. Behold, then, all the crafts borrowing something useful from one another:[39] the contractor gets his tools from the smith; the smith gets his house from the contractor; both get food from the farmer; the farmer gets the equipment for his house from them and also what can help him in his agricultural pursuits.

The Creator Taught Man to Mine Minerals

23. Better still, consider how from the beginning the Creator showed the necessary uses of things to man. From what did he learn to mine iron, bronze, black lead, and tin? Who showed him veins of silver?[40] Who taught him how to dig for gold and showed him how to collect the tiny gold dust?[41] Where did he learn the nature of glass?[42] Who taught him how to refine clay? Who taught him to put such clay in fire, in what manner to do this, and for how long? And how to make separate parts of a continuum, and a continuum of separate parts? How did he learn that, with the help of fire and air, he could fashion from this material countless kinds of drinking vessels, bowls, flagons, crofts, tiny jars, utensils, and other necessary equipment for every phase of eating and drinking?[43] It is surely obvious that he received a knowledge of all these things from his Maker, and that the Creator implanted in his nature the faculty of invention and of discovering the crafts.

The Art of Weaving

24. So too He said in conversation to mighty Job: *Who has given the wisdom of weaving to women and the knowledge of embroidery?*[44] Truly this beautiful art also is a gift of God. With time it has been made

little of[45] and knowledge of the invention has taken away the reputation of the inventors. If, however, one took careful stock he would
assuredly marvel at this craft. For the fleece is sheared and washed
with water. It is first sorted and carded into fine shreds, then the
thread is made into a skein. The next stage is the actual spinning, and
in this stage the weaver takes threads that are entire and have the appearance, so to speak, of straight lines and separates these from the
rest. When the rest is separated the warp is prepared for the weft.

25. Next, women take it in hand and weave the fine yarns. First
they place the warp like strings in order on the looms and pass the
weft through them, separating the threads with the combs, loosening
some of the broken lines and tightening others; then they thrust and
compress the weft with the instruments made for this purpose and
in that way complete the web. Who would not justly marvel at this
wisdom given to mortals? Notice how on a single color of underlying
threads, woolen or silken, imitations of all kinds of living things are
embroidered, the forms of men, hunters, worshipers, and the images
of trees and countless other objects.[46]

With reason you say: *Praise the Lord, all you nations,*[47] you who
are deemed worthy of such wisdom and revel in such blessings. Who
has revealed that fish of the sea provides a dye for woolens?[48] Who,
too, was the inventor of that craft and dyes woolens in many different
colors?

An Objection: Worms Spin Even Better Than Humans

26. Now perhaps one suffering from ingratitude may say that
worms spin more delicate yarns than men.[49] This again is brought
about by divine providence. Lest you become arrogant at knowing
all kinds of techniques, or act wantonly with your supply of wealth,
providence teaches you through the worms that these things are not
your own doing but are the gifts of divine beneficence.

Man Is Superior to the Worms

27. Yet in teaching you this He has a word of comfort for you
also, lest you be pained at being surpassed by worms. He offers what

they spin to you and subordinates their work to your rule. Alone of all things living you have built beautiful cities, fortified them with turrets and ramparts, and you alone have built beautiful inns and dwelling houses, and joined sea to land by means of harbors.

God Has Given Men the Science of Medicine to Fight Disease

28. Since God made you mortal in the present life and knew that you would be afflicted by ailments (for sickness is part of the lot of mortals), He also taught you medicine[50] and equipped you with it to fight disease. You have learned in medicine to know the different kinds of internal diseases, to recognize the ebb and flow of fever by the beat of the pulse, to see its beginning, crisis, and decline, to foresee the signs of death, to identify the nature of troublesome matter, and to apply the proper remedies to combat it, to dry up humors, to reduce temperature, to heat up and evaporate a cold, to carry away refuse either by emetics or evacuative medicines, or by bloodletting.[51] It would require a long list to name every disease and every remedy, for the enemies of human health are numerous, but the remedies are just as numerous.

Nonedible Plants Have Medicinal Uses

29. Research has discovered several treatments for each disease. So it is that the Creator has arranged it that many plants grow on the earth, nonedible as well as edible, since we men need treatment as well as nourishment. We eat some of these plants, the herb-eating animals eat others, while others still are collected by medical practitioners and those that are harmful to eat thus become preventive drugs.[52] This should not move you to revile providence. For each of these things invites the tongue of well-disposed men to praise.

Grammar

30. But I resemble creatures which swim in the sea and, being buffetted on all sides by the waves, desire to reach the mainland;[53]

having ventured on the sea of the wisdom of the crafts, and endeavored to escape the impact of the waves of arguments which assailed me, I now want to run to the end and reach the shore. Leaving behind all other pursuits, I will treat next of the science of grammar which has more for speech than any of the other sciences, and is the distinguishing mark of man,[54] endowed as he is with the use of speech.

The Spoken and Written Word

31. Grammar invented the alphabet[55] and limited it in number. Then it joined letters to one another and produced the combination of syllables. By fitting two or three syllables together, a knowledge of words was arrived at. By combining and interweaving these a single harmony of speech came about. The next step was to fill books, thousands of them, with the wisdom of the ancients. Some contained wisdom concerning the gods, or religious observances, or mysteries, and others contained secular wisdom in which the variety of meter, the beauty of diction, and harmony of composition, disguised their mythical nature, afforded enjoyment to the ear, and provided pious people with arguments against those nurtured on impiety.

Writing Letters is a Link with Far-distant Friends

32. Thanks to writing, we can communicate with absent friends, even those who are several days' journey away,[56] and despite the many miles intervening, we nevertheless transmit our thoughts by hand. The tongue, the primary organ of speech, is powerless, but the right hand facilitates communication and, taking up the pen, corresponds with a friend.

The Hand Is Specially Formed to Hold a Pen

33. The vehicle of speech is no longer the tongue and mouth, but the right hand once it has practiced its art for a time and got a thorough grasp of the formation of the alphabet. It was for this reason that the Creator made our hands the way He did, divided into five

fingers, one of the five being a thumb. For if all the fingers were of equal length they could not do every kind of work. But now that one is different from the others we can easily hold a pen, a spade, a hoe, a saw, an adze, a hammer, a pair of fire-tongs, and all such artisan tools.[57]

These Considerations Should Lead You to Grateful Prayer

34. You see from what we have said, then, what providential care you enjoy, what arts and sciences God has bequeathed to you to help you not only to live but to live well, what zeal He has employed in serving your needs, what a supply of blessings He has showered on you that with the help of these blessings He might make life agreeable for you, seeing that He has contrived not only a sufficiency for you, but also that superfluous blessings should flow from all sides.

Dismiss ingratitude from your tongue, then, teach it to sing praises, to submit to the Lord, and to supplicate Him. Learn to exclaim with the prophet: *Your knowledge has become wonderful to me: I was overwhelmed and could not reach it.*[58] To Him be glory, now and forever and ever. Amen.

DISCOURSE 5

DEMONSTRATION FROM MAN'S CONTROL OVER
IRRATIONAL ANIMALS

1. You are well aware, dearly beloved brethren, how great is the care of the Maker of the universe for us and you do not need to be instructed by sermons. For you are continually drawing from the fountains of His beneficence and singing His praises with all your might. But since some men suffer from such insensibility that they fail to recognize the gifts of God and, while continuing to enjoy God-given blessings, utter words of ingratitude against the Maker, it was necessary for us to demonstrate in our sermon, by a rapid survey of creation and by dealing with the composition of man, that the providence of God is very clearly manifest in every part of creation and of man's nature. It has also revealed the wisdom and utility of some of the devices invented by human skill.

Consideration of Certain Skills Has Been Deliberately Omitted From our Discourse

2. It has purposely omitted consideration of other skills which promote emulation and refinement such as painting and the plastic arts, sculpture, the art of the goldsmith, cookery and the manufacture of various kinds of pastries. Also, it has left untouched of set purpose those activities that go beyond the limit of curiosity; I mean astronomy, geometry, arithmetic, and music,[1] whose function is to charm and transport the ear, modify the dispositions of the soul in any way it pleases, resolve sadness into mirth and produce firmness and manliness in a dissipated soul.[2] In this way it avoids prolixity, aims at brevity, and leaves the contemplation of each art to the intelligence

59

of the audience. For it is easy to make what we have said the starting point for a study of what we have omitted.

An Objection: Bees Surpass Man in Inventive Skill

3. Those who do not know how to praise God, having learned to revile Him instead, may perhaps say: God has not restricted the gift of invention to human nature, since even the smallest species of winged creatures, the bees, can be seen leading a social and community life,[3] armed with a sting on account of their weakness,[4] setting out from the hives in due rotation,[5] making their journey by air, flying around groves, meadows, and cornfields, settling on blossoms, leaves, and fruits, collecting the useful, downy substance, loading themselves, putting their burdens in their folds and on their necks, and thus making the journey back to the hives.

Bees Master the Art of Making Honey Without Taking Lessons

4. Then in constructing the honeycombs[6] they need neither rule nor square,[7] either in making the angles equal to one another in a way surpassing all geometrical skill, or in constructing the fabrics of the walls and the very fine, porous partitions of the honey, or in packing the moist honey well within those fine, compact walls, and thus filling the receptacles with the sweet flow of honey.

Men Have to Undergo Long Periods of Apprenticeship to Master Human Crafts

5. Why then, they urge, is mankind so constituted, divided into teachers and taught, that he masters his craft after much toil and time, while the bees, a hardworking, progressive race, have no division into teachers and taught, do not learn their skill with the help of straps and rods,[8] but, with an innate, self-acquired knowledge[9] of their difficult work, make the honeycombs, fill the containers, and have no need of rules or compasses or set squares?[10] And they fill the containers without squeezing out the grapes or by doing injury to any

other fruit, but by drawing off the dewy substance and producing the honey.

It Is for the Benefit of Mankind
That Bees Have This Skill

6. Come now, let us fashion the answer from the actual charge, for the case quite simply condemns itself. The bees place this arduous, spontaneous, activity and its excellent, most delightful fruits at the disposal of mankind.[11] And, like servants on the call of their masters, they go out from the hives, collect what is useful, keep carrying their loads, eagerly make the honeycombs, and imprint their seals and signets on the streams of honey brought in as on a treasure, and they continue to pay this tax or tribute to men as if they were kings.[12] Why, then, you wretch, do you misrepresent the situation and, while enjoying the tribute, revile its Maker, treat wantonly the labors of other creatures, and release the slings of ingratitude at the One who provides these things?

Life in a Beehive Is a Model of Harmony for You

7. You not only reap the fruits of their toil but you also derive another blessing from the same source. In the first place, you learn what blessings are conferred on man through living in harmony with his fellows and what fruits come the way of the worker. For community life is modeled on the life in a beehive.[13]

8. Nothing is owned privately there; riches are held in common; possession is undivided. They have no lawsuits or courts of law. They do no injury to one another, look for no more than their share, and steadfastly pursue a common object in their toil. Accordingly, they expel the drones who do not want to work, preferring to live idly on the toil of others. They hate rule by many, or democratic rule; they have but one leader[14] whom it is their pleasure to obey. And for all that they do, or undergo, they do not listen to instructions or read laws or go to teachers. None of them is wiser than another; young and old are equally well-informed. All have the same share in what we have spoken of, not by intellectual knowledge, but by having im-

planted in their nature by the Maker of the universe this industrious and noble activity.

9. Each of these considerations can be a source of profit for you. You, a rational creature, learn from the irrational creatures to abhor an idle life as dangerous, pursue works of virtue with zeal, and collect this treasure from every source; not to seek for power that does not become you, but administer what you have with integrity and justice, bear in mind that what exists is common property, and extend its enjoyment to those who stand in need of it.

The Well-Ordered Life of the Bees Is a Particular Reproach to Wrongdoers

10. To those who are well-disposed and who have kept their natural virtues intact, innate reason is a sufficient teacher, but the well-ordered community life of irrational creatures is a veritable reproach to those who have corrupted their nature and chosen an undisciplined life of plunder and destruction. It was, then, with an eye to your welfare that the Creator has adorned the irrational animals with certain natural advantages so that you may also derive benefit from that source.

The Testimony of Scripture on Similarities Between Animals and Men

11. Solomon also testifies to this when he exclaims: *Go to the ant, O sluggard, and emulate its ways.*[15] Or go to the bee,[16] and note how industrious it is, and how it seems to regard work as a vocation. Kings as well as private individuals use the fruits of its toil for the good of their health. But the God of the universe Himself testifies, speaking through the prophet: *The turtledove, the grasshopper, the swallow, and sparrow of the field have observed the times of their comings; but my people have not known the judgments of the Lord.*[17] And again through Isaias: *The ox has known his owner, and the ass his master's crib, but Israel has not known me, and my people have not understood me.*[18]

The natural advantages of animals are thus a rebuke to those endowed with reason. Wherefore, the prophet, bewailing and bemoaning men's relapse to the animal state, exclaims: *Man when he was in honor did not understand; he was compared to senseless beasts and was become like to them.*[19] For this reason the prophets call some men wolves, others lions lying in wait, others dogs that bark at their master, others again heifers in a frenzy, others snakes and the offspring of vipers, others cobras that stuff their ears and do not listen to soothing strains.[20]

12. And just as wicked characters get the names of wild beasts, so too souls that are simple and without guile get the names of animals that are held in esteem. Examples could be found of a soul adorned with simple faith being called a dove or a turtledove. The spouse uses this name of the Church in the mystical book of the Canticles,[21] and the name sheep is given by Christ to souls who are docile and love the shepherd. *My sheep*, He says, *hear My voice, and I know Mine and mine know Me.*[22] And again: *I am the good shepherd. The good shepherd lays down His life for the sheep.*[23] And in another place: *He shall set the sheep on his right hand, but the goats on his left.*[24] And again those are called lofty eagles in the holy Gospels who rise above the things of earth, the eye of whose soul[25] is pure and who desire to shed the things of the flesh. Speaking of the saints being taken up to heaven at the time of the resurrection, it says: *Where the dead body is, there will the eagles be gathered.*[26]

We Can Learn Modesty from the Bees

13. It is plain then from what has been said that the Creator has allotted and assigned natural advantages to the bees and all other irrational creatures for our sake, so that we may derive profit from every source. We can also derive another profitable lesson from the bees. We learn from them not to swagger, or get ideas about ourselves, or forget our nature, just because of the discovery of sciences and arts, but rather to recognize the Maker and refer all blessings to Him as Cause.

The Honey Which They Make Is for Us

14. Lest we be distraught and annoyed at having to share our skill, and at being no better than the brute creation, the Creator has given us the fruit of the bees' toil, so that He might bend our proud

necks in humility by this sharing of skill and might allay grief by persuading us that those who shared it are our slaves. Why, man, do you grieve then at the sight of the industry of the bees? For their toil is your gain. They do the work, but you enjoy the fruit of the labors.

The Spider's Web Inspired the Invention of Hunting Nets

15. Again, the Creator has taught the spider the art of spinning fine, invisible webs, in order to teach you how to catch certain kinds of birds.[27] The spider, in fashioning his webs, is taught by instinct, and has not learned his craft by reason. With reason residing in you and a model placed before your eyes, you have made countless different kinds of nets. This insignificant, irrational creature, the spider, in showing you the use of a model, keeps you from becoming conceited and boastful.

16. And again, the variety of nets is a source of consolation to you, for there is only one model, but countless imitations. For birds you have contrived nets the color of clouds, or air, and, having made them fast in thickly wooded places, you camouflage them from the birds by their resemblance to the air. You use the fear of pursuit as an ally in fowling. You drive the hunted birds from every direction, forcing them towards the nets: they are in dread of their pursuers, cannot see straight in front of them, then head straight into the invisible nets, and are caught in the toils. With these suspended in air you hunt for birds.

17. You have other devices, and surer ones, for the same pursuit of these creatures, ones which you spread on the ground, digging a trench, filling it with water, and putting tame birds in the nets so that comrades may be attracted when they see and hear them. When they see the water, and hear the sound of a bird, or see one, they fly towards the place and you artfully succeed in snaring them in your nets. You have yet another device for hunting four-footed animals. Cords, snares, and foot-traps are used for deer; hunters' nets are used for wild boars, gazelles, and hares; pits and devices of that sort are used for the more savage sort of game.[28]

18. Birds and beasts do not satisfy your quest of game: you also pursue creatures in the sea, and utilize traps, landing nets, casting

nets, and dragnets in your search for the variety that swim, while those that live under the water you skillfully bring to the surface. You hunt the creatures that live on water and, though you live on land yourself, you provide yourself with the inhabitants of the deep, which afford millions of fish for your enjoyment, thanks to the art of fishing.

19. Do not be annoyed, then, because a spider spins fine webs. Rather learn from this not to be arrogant but to praise the One who made you both. It is a consolation to you, too, to see the spider hunting gnats, mosquitoes, and such insects while you, by your skill, overcome the swiftest of winged creatures, and creatures in water and under water are forced to yield to your schemes, and everything that goes on foot has to obey your commands.

Your Mind Ensures Your Superiority
Over the Animal World

20. Do not then bewail the fact that you have not got wings. You have got wisdom, which gives you command over winged nature. You have also a mind that is swifter than any bird, much swifter even than the winds themselves.[29] In a moment it can be wherever you wish. Though your body be an impediment and your feet be tied to earth, your mind ranges the heavens and the heavenly beauties. It transcends the heavens and forms a concept of what is beyond them. It journeys around the entire globe and has dealings with countless races, and holds converse with far-distant friends.

The Ox, Despite His Strength, Obeys You.
Also the Ass, Mule, and Camel

21. Why, then, should the want of visible wings trouble and distress you, seeing that you possess mental wings so obviously superior to the wings of birds? Your body is not made for flight, yet your wisdom enables you to pursue the birds of the air. With the help of your intelligence you yoke the ox despite his strength and the fact that he has horns, and compel him to be your servant, and submit him to continuous toils: plowing, carting, drawing loads too heavy

for other beasts, and bringing materials for the building of houses. You give the orders and he submits to the yoke, lets the straps be put on him, forgets the usefulness of his horns, fears your voice, is unaware of his superior strength, but chooses to be the slave of a very inferior being.[30] Such is the superiority of mind over muscle.

22. A man makes an ass, a mule, or a camel carry a load and the animal crouches at his command and rises again when bidden, laden with his burdens. Even though the animal is worn out by long journeys, he puts up with the hardships, obeys those who burden him, takes his fodder when he gets it, and does not cry out against his owners even when he is hungry. From nature he has learned the definition of the state of servility. For that reason, the mere voice of their owners terrifies even the strongest of animals. You, however, despise the Lord of the entire creation, and in spite of the useful lesson which the example of animals affords you, are reluctant to obey the Lord and to supplicate Him; you do not submit with graciousness to the burden of virtue (for it is a burden, imposed on you by the Master).

In Contrast to the Submissive Animals
You Refuse to Submit

23. Instead, you rebel and become imperious, you fly from the yoke like an unbroken young horse, you refuse to take the bit but, bursting from it, run away, bear down from the heights, and dethrone the driver seated on you. On the other hand, all who have loved this delightful state of subjection, and who have been consumed with a noble and burning love for their master, have derived much profit from irrational animals. One voice speaks for them all in the Psalms: *I am become as a dumb beast before you and I am always with you.*[31]

24. I follow You, he means, like an obedient animal, not troubling about the nature of the road You lead me along or inquiring whether it is short or long or hard. It does not trouble me whether it is narrow or steep or precipitous. For I tell myself that, since You are good, You will guide me well. On the strength of this, though in all other matters I am given to inquiry, and seek for reasons, and am quick on deciding what is necessary, and know well how to avoid

unpleasantness, with You in the lead I abandon this reasoning, and I imitate the obedience of the beast. I reason in other matters, but I become like a mute beast in Your presence.

25. Therefore I am never separated from Your company but am always with You, following in Your footsteps, obeying the reins and going where You lead whether the way is smooth or rough, broad or narrow. For I take courage from Your wisdom and rely on Your goodness. I know that whatever You will is really noble and good. Such, I say, is the benefit that can be derived from irrational creation by those who know how to take their lesson. Do you, then, when you see the dumb animals obeying you, obey Him who has made them to serve you.

The Horse and the Elephant Obey You

26. He has made the herds of horses subject to you. You get a horse that prances around and has yet to be ridden into proper shape by training and you break his high spirits, check his rearing, bend his high neck, get him to look straight in front of him, teach him the rhythm of walking and the way to let down his hooves properly, and to make a quick spurt when necessary, tame this gregarious creature, and teach him to respond to voice and hand. An animal, superior to you in strength and speed, submits to you and the lash. He puts up with your threats and, by his actions, timidly acquiesces in his state of service. He accompanies you when you go hunting, and enters the fray with you in war, going with a rush against the enemy.[32] And if you have a mind to flee, he becomes afraid, forgets his daring, takes to his heels, flees, and shakes off his pursuers with all speed. He does not disobey if he is ordered to rush in the face of a phalanx, nor does he demur when commanded to retreat. He knows but one definition of safety, the bidding of his rider.

27. Why speak of the horse, the donkey, and the camel? Even the elephant, the greatest of land animals,[33] is willing to obey you, yet he can take up by the roots even the mightiest of trees with his trunk. Forgetting his power and ignoring his strength, he fails to see that his body is as big as a mountain, but he accepts you as master. And when you are seated on him—by you I mean anyone—and issue

an order, he carries it out. If he gets money from spectators for a look at him, he uses his trunk as a holder and transfers it to you.[34]

28. He also enters the fray with you in war and takes many archers on his back who use him as a tower from which to fire on the enemy,[35] and as he advances on the columns he terrifies them, easily breaks through their lines, and scatters the heavily armed troops.

Reason Makes up for Man's Small Body

29. The fact that you have a small body should not upset you. Rather you should consider the size of the animals that are subject to you, ardently praise the One who placed you over them, and in this way show your gratitude to the Maker. He had your soul's salvation in mind when He did not endow you with too large a body so that, excelling in both soul and body, you should not succumb to diabolical pride.

30. Seeing that, small as you are, you rave and rant against your Creator, what would you not do if you were bigger? As it is, the fact that you are small makes you practice moderation and recognize the Maker. The gift of reason makes up for the smallness of stature. By the aid of reason you lead and direct all kinds of animals, sheep, goats, swine, herds of horses, camels on pasture or those used for transport, birds of every kind, and mules. Some of them supply you with meals, giving your festive board a lavish appearance, affording you delicacies of many kinds, and also supplying you with all sorts of garments; others of them draw corn and carry wood, and keep you supplied with your other wants.

Dogs Lack Reason Yet Are Faithful to Their Masters

31. In the case of dogs, some hunt with you, some mind the sheep, some look after the house. Shepherds sleep knowing that the dogs will keep vigilant. A few men can tend many flocks with their help, for the dogs run risks for the sheep, as well as for their masters, do battle for the shepherds, and fight bravely against wolves. Even when wounded, they do not take to ignoble flight, but bark to call for help from the shepherds. All this the dog does although he has

no reason to learn, but only a certain natural gift with which he is adorned.

32. When bidden by the hunter to follow the trail he takes up the scent and carefully uses that to guide him, not stopping until he runs down his quarry. And when he gets the game, he holds it in his teeth and claws and does not partake of it, but keeps it safe for the men who sent him and, though the slave of unreason, he recognizes his state of subjection and does not attempt to take a share of the quarry from the owner. If his quarry proves too big for him—a wild boar, for instance, or a bear or the like—he avoids the impact of tusks, but he puts up a brave fight.[36] He keeps jumping up on their backs, tries to hold his quarry without harm to himself, and gives it no chance of escaping from his constant attentions. With such close attention he keeps the animal turning this way and that, and makes him stay in the same place and await the hunter. The hunter, when he comes, quickly dispatches it with the weapons of his art.

Such Animals as Rebel Against You Do So Only After Provocation

33. And let none of you, quick with counterargument, introduce dogs that bark and asses that kick up their heels, camels that bite, and bulls that hit with the horns.[37] Only a few out of many are subject to such passions and then it results from plenty of provocation. Besides, such outbursts show you that it is not in the nature of things that they should be subject to you, but only through obedience to the will of the Maker. Such rebellions too against your rule—a camel that bites or a bull that butts—are a proof of this. They would all resist your rule in the same way if a divine law did not restrain them.[38] It follows that their disorder helps to keep you in order, their restiveness keeps you at rest, their tyranny teaches you not to be tyrannical but to acknowledge the Creator.

34. Therefore the Creator created wild beasts[39] and reptiles[40] to educate your young and daring spirit in virtue that, through fear of wild beasts, He might bring you to a knowledge of your need of the divine assistance. While fear of them hangs over you as a constant threat and spur, it rouses you to prayer and makes you call on Him

for help and assistance. Compelled by necessity to seek aid, you are glad to be the servant of One who can come to your assistance. You are forced to sit by and watch so as to escape injury from those who plot against you. You look up and seek your guardian, desiring a reversal of misfortunes. This fear, too, directs your steps to God.

God Does Not Allow the Wild Beasts to Cause Unlimited Fear

35. Lest constant fear, however, should make your life miserable, He has made the animals dwell at a distance from you. Venomous reptiles He has concealed in holes and made to live in caverns beneath the earth. He does not leave them free to go against men, but bids them keep hidden always, appear but seldom, disappear at the sight of men in that they are their absolute masters, harm very few and that rarely, and avoid starting the encounter but act only in self-defense. For we would never experience fear if we never had any experience of them. As for four-footed beasts, the Lord of the universe has also told them to inhabit thickets, rocky beaches, places full of caves without a soul living in them.[41]

36. He has set aside night as a special time for them for feeding: *You have appointed darkness,* Scripture says, *and it was night: in it shall all the beasts of the woods go about. The young lions roaring after their prey and seeking their meal from God. The sun arose and they were gathered together: and they shall lie down in their dens. Man shall go forth to his work and to his labor until evening.*[42] Then, marvelling at the divine economy, the prophet exclaims: *How great are Your works, O Lord! You have made all things in wisdom.*[43]

Animals Have Always Been Subject to God-fearing Men: Adam, Noah, Daniel, St. Paul

37. That it was after the entrance of sin[44] that these animals, which had been subject beforehand and had acknowledged the state of servility, refused to serve man, is attested by Adam, the founder of the human race, who put names on them all, and neither feared, nor fled, nor suffered any injury from them.[45] The second head of men, the spark of the whole race, the blessed Noah, testified to the

same thing. He looked after the animals in the ark, the very wildest as well as the tame ones, tending both types in the same place for a whole year, and compelling the carniverous animals to eat grass.[46] The number of clean animals kept safe and sound bears the same testimony.

38. The great Daniel testifies to this, too, when, given as a feast to the lions, he terrified them with the splendor of his virtue and frightened them exceedingly with the stamp of the divine likeness. When they saw in the likeness a very true and genuine imitation of the archetype, they admitted inferiority, laid aside ferocity, and thought it was Adam that was before their eyes who had named them before the fall.[47]

39. It was the same with the blessed Paul, applying a piece of wood for fuel to the flames and tempering the cold of the atmosphere with the help of a fire. A viper concealed in the wood, in avoiding destruction by fire, clung to the apostle's hand as if defending himself against what he was destined to endure. When he discovered no laxity or weakness of sin but the stout, unbroken armor of virtue, the viper straightway left him like a missile rebounding off a shield and fell into the fire as if purchasing for himself the punishment of his own daring, seeing that he had attacked in wrath the hand of his master.[48]

Wild Beasts Act as a Useful Discipline on Men

40. The various kinds of animals, then, are like straps, canes, and teachers' disciplines.[49] They are very readily despised by those who have come to man's estate and have left childhood behind them, but they are very necessary and useful for those who are still undeveloped in understanding. And just as *the law is not made for the just man*, as the great Apostle says, *but for the unjust and the disobedient, for the ungodly and for sinners, for the wicked and defiled, for murderers of fathers*[50] and all such, so wild beasts exist as a discipline for men. They terrify and frighten those disposed to sin, while those who lead an upright life regard them as lightly as playthings.

41. When you thus experience God's loving care, then, and become fully acquainted with His all-embracing providence, cease,

dear brethren, your calumnies and requite the Benefactor with hymns of praise. Would it not be out of place to praise the teacher who uses the rod on his pupils for their good, dispelling laziness with the stick and implanting a sound knowledge of the rudiments with its help, or to be grateful to a doctor not only when he prescribes foods and drinks for a patient but even when he operates, cauterizes, wars on disease and keeps it from spreading, and at the same time to blaspheme against God who cares for souls with greater wisdom and more concern, and by abundance of blessings and by fear of punishments inculcates the elements of virtue, eradicates the disease of sin, and is concerned about purity and health of the soul?[51]

Keep your tongue from evil and your lips from speaking blasphemy. Turn away from evil and do good.[52] Behold His care for you, sing a hymn of praise for His providence so that, seeing your gratitude for the favors, He may deem you worthy of the blessings He has promised, which may we received in Christ Jesus, our Lord, to whom be honor forever and ever, Amen.

DISCOURSE 6

That Wealth and Poverty Both Have Their Uses in Life

Previous Arguments Have Not Convinced Our Adversaries

1. To the wicked I have often quoted the words of the prophet: *Do not act wickedly*, and to sinners: *Lift not up the horn. Lift not up your horn on high, speak not iniquity against God*[1] by saying that God has created the world but has left it to look after itself. These utterly senseless people are not convinced by the heavens which, according to the prophet, *proclaim the glory of God*,[2] nor by the sun *setting out like a bridegroom from its bridal chamber*[3] and reaching the ends of the earth with its brightness and heat.

They Find the Inequalities in Life a Stumbling Block

2. Nor are they convinced by the moon which regulates the measurement of time by its changes; the rising and setting of the stars, which act as a guide to sailors and a call to farmers to harvesting and sowing; the succession of seasons; the changes of solstices; the opportune and successive risings of clouds; the harmony between land and sea; the running of rivers; the flow of streams; the abundance of crops; the variety and usefulness of animals; the composition of the body in keeping with the endowment of reason; the immortality of the soul and its wise guidance of the body; the countless and manifold techniques that satisfy our needs and also supply us with something over and above; the numerous other gifts which a beneficent donor daily gives to mankind.

3. Now such people, while enjoying these manifold blessings,

73

rebel and rave, calling all this care a want of care, throwing aside riches and poverty and complaining about the inequalities of life.[4] Come now and, with the wise pilot of the world to help our discourse, let us meet their difficulties, answer the objections, and show how thinly spun are their gossamer arguments.[5]

First Objection: Why Are Sinners Wealthy and the Virtuous Poor?

4. Why, they object, do men who are utterly depraved possess riches and a superabundance of blessings, why do they sail through life with a favorable wind[6] and with a steady flow of money to cover the expenses of their wickedness? For abundance feeds the fire of greed for more: wickedness, joined to wealth, sets off a mighty blaze, and opportunity, joined to desire, is an intolerable evil. Devotees of virtue, on the other hand, live in poverty, and submit to hardship; they are short the very necessities of life; they live in squalor and dirt; they are hounded down to earth, treated with violence, trampled in the mire, and forced to put up with countless hardships of a similar nature.

What Constitutes Happiness, Wealth or Virtue?

5. The first question, then, we put to our objectors is: what is their definition of happiness? And if they say wealth, we shall instantly refute their falsehood. For how could what on their own admission helps in wrongdoing constitute happiness? How could wealth be the definition of happiness and the foundation of good fortune if it is the means by which wicked men become supercilious and puffed up, strutting through the marketplace on horseback or in carriages, despising others in so far as it is seemly for them to look down on them, wronging, grasping, appropriating what does not belong to them, coveting what is unbecoming, taking their neighbors' belongings, enjoying other people's good fortune, trading on the misfortunes of the poor, and so on?

6. But if they admit that virtue is the supreme blessing and that the one who loves it ardently and cultivates it eagerly reaches the summit of good fortune, why, pray, should we look up to riches and

say that those who possess them are to be envied? For great wealth and heroic good conduct are diametrically opposed.

An Analysis of Virtue and Its Species

7. Let us inquire then, making our search together, and taking the torch of truth as guide, what are the species of virtue and how can one acquire them with ease. Now we define as virtue prudence, temperance, fortitude and justice,[7] together with what derives from these or the philosophical parts inhering in them. Let us examine, then, what each of those mentioned signifies, what is its meaning, interpretation, or function.

8. Prudence is an innate watchfulness of reason, as opposed to folly and sensuality which is reason intoxicated by passion, clouded, darkened, obscured, and prevented from observing what it should. Sound reasoning, then, is called prudence. We define temperance as freedom from the domination of the passions. For when intellect was and is possessed of sound and perfect wisdom, the passions abate, recede, subside, cool down, and the intellect rides securely in the saddle. This ordering of the passions and the soundness of the ruling mental faculty we call temperance.

Fortitude we define as the due movement of passion; on the other hand, unlawful and uncontrolled passion is called audacity. Justice is the right ordering of the soul and the due subordination of the passions. For the possession of justice results to us when concupiscence and anger are harmonized with reason and there is no conflict between them. Now that we have learned the constituent parts of virtue, and the meaning and function of each, let us next inquire how one so inclined may acquire virtue, utilizing either wealth or poverty in his quest.

Wealth Can Be a Hindrance to Virtue

9. Now wealth brings troubles and cares of all sorts in its surge, and many a mighty breaker. It is the enemy rather than the friend of virtue. For how could one lead an upright, temperate life if he is constantly gorging himself, carousing and banqueting, with his mind on

soft couches and dining tables, forever thinking of bakers, confec-
tioners, and makers of pastries, of wines with a fine bouquet, tumblers, goblets, all kinds of drinking glasses,[8] and a variety of luxuries,
if he swallows his drinks neat and puts no curb on his appetite, if he
quenches the spark of reason, heaps up the fires of passion, kindles
unrestrained indulgence, whets the edge of anger against attendants,
turns the master of the passions into a slave, puts what should be the
ruler of the appetite at its beck and call, reduces to slavery what has
received the direction of life from the Creator, delivers the ruler in
chains to the subjects, prepares to unseat the rider from his mount,
leaves the pilot rudderless and no longer in command of the entire
ship, but with a vessel abandoned to the waves of passion which lash
it and try to submerge it?[9] Far from prudence having any part with
such a person he is a prey to all kinds of excess; not only is he without
a shred of fortitude, but he is in slavery to his enemy, the passions.

10. It is scarcely necessary to speak about justice, since even our
adversaries admit that the man who covets increased possessions is
reluctant to recognize the distinction between right and wrong. For
such persons everything is disordered, undefined, and confused.
Even the most argumentative will see from what we have said that it
is difficult for those who rely on riches to keep to the way of virtue.

Poverty Is a Help to Virtue. The Wicked Admit This, and Also Pagan Philosophers

11. But poverty is a help to the good life, and the only sure road
to perfect virtue, as we shall presently learn. In the first place, if the
necessities of life are in short supply the passions are compelled to be
subject to reason, and are not allowed to flare up and bolt from the
driver, as happens to those who live in luxury and for their stomachs'
sake. Secondly, the soul when loosed from superfluous burdens,
freed from external cares,[10] and enjoying complete quiet and calm,
returns to itself, sees its own worth, and recognizes the slavery of the
subject passions, it takes command, lays down the law for its subjects, and checks one warring against another. At one time it causes
concupiscence to revolt under the impetus of anger, and dissolves its
vehemence with its own gentleness. At another time it changes its

tactics of vengeance against it, and with the lash of anger checks its forward bearing.[11] Work, finally, helps reason to regulate the passions, for compelling want is a spur to industry and a shortage of the necessaries of life encourages activity, while hardship resulting from toil quenches the passions, prevents them from flaring up, and spends their fuel.

12. Why, then, are you ungracious at seeing upright men saddled with poverty, why do you abuse an instrument of virtue, behaving like a man who praises thrones, benches, couches, doors, and objects of beauty made by builders, but scoffs at the instruments of the mason and architect and criticizes his adze, gimlet, and the other tools with which each of these things is made? But that it is much easier to lead a virtuous life in poverty than in wealth, even the children of wickedness themselves attest.

13. So, too, do the philosophers among the Greeks and in this they are following merely the law of nature. For it is in poverty that all men have acquired moral virtue and that without hearing the divine oracles which clearly proclaim: *Unless one renounce all that he possesses . . . he cannot be My disciple.*[12] Nature, however, was a teacher large enough for them. For the divine law does not introduce new enactments, but recalls to mind the laws of nature to publish them which time, through the negligence of man, has destroyed.

14. Since Socrates, Diogenes, Anaxarchus,[13] and their like in their desire to possess moral virtue renounced the possession of wealth and took poverty as their ally in the pursuit of goodness, and even though they were blind to the truth of dogma and had no expectation of the kingdom of heaven or accurate knowledge of the true good, why then, my friend, do you criticize poverty which makes the path of virtue easy to follow and makes the rough and steep way smooth and easy for those who enter upon it?

Not That Wealth Is Intrinsically Evil

15. Now we say this not in accusing wealth or curing evil by evil. For if riches were evil, the fault would redound to their Giver. What we maintain is that wealth and poverty, like raw materials or instruments,[14] are given to men by the Creator and that with these,

men, like sculptors, either fashion the statue of virtue or strike the figure of evil. With riches, however, only a very few can fashion even a few parts of virtue while with poverty it is possible for many to make them all. Let us not scoff, then, at poverty, the mother of virtue; and let us not slander wealth, but let us blame those who do not use them for the proper end.

16. Iron was given to man as a help for builders, farmers, and sailors, and to assist in the other techniques in life. Those, however, who make war on one another do not allow iron merely to minister to their essential needs, but contrive the slaughter of one another with it. Surely we do not find fault with iron[15] on this account; rather we should blame the wretchedness of men in abusing it. Similarly, the use of wine was given to man to gladden the heart, not to set it mad. But those who hold excess in honor, and are slaves to drunkenness, turn the sire of gladness into the father of madness. We, however, with correct discernment, call those who abuse a God-given gift drunken, tippling scoundrels, but we reverence the wine as a God-given gift.[16] Let us judge riches and those who use them in a similar manner, acquitting riches of blame and giving those who possess them the greatest praise if they husband them properly. If, however, inverting the order, they seem to be the slaves of wealth, heeding its every behest and perpetrating every wickedness in its service, let us indict them for wickedness, because, while constituted masters of wealth, they destroyed their dominion and exchanged mastery for slavery.

A Second Objection: Why Are Riches Not Distributed Among All Men Equally

17. Perhaps some of those who specialize in contradicting the truth may say: Why has the Creator not given the gift of wealth to all men instead of allotting wealth to some and poverty to others, leaving life full of anomalies? I would like to ask a man such as they why has the Creator not given the same faculty to all the members of the body, but has entrusted the eyes with the task of discerning colors and shapes, the ears with recognizing voices and sounds, the nose with apprehending odors and distinguishing between pleasant and

unpleasant, the tongue with judging the taste of things and recognizing the difference between sweet and sour, pungent, bitter, and
fatty?[17] Why has He given the faculty of walking to the feet, and to
the hands manipulation of all sorts? Why is the stomach the receptacle of nourishment; the liver, its purifier; the head, the storehouse
of the marrow; the heart the source of heat; the arteries, the containers of air; the veins, the channels of blood; and so on, each part
having its own faculty?

Answer: Different Degrees of Wealth Among Individuals Contribute to the Good of the Whole Community

18. The reason is that all these parts we have mentioned, as well
as those we have passed over in silence, contribute to the perfection
of the one body. Although each is entrusted with its proper function,
it contributes to the good of the whole. For sight guides the feet,
shows them the smooth way, and diverts them from the rougher
places, whereas the feet do the actual walking. The ear hears noises
and stimulates the eye to sight; the eye perceives the causes of the
noises. And to corroborate what we have said here is the testimony
of the apostle: *The eye cannot say to the hand: I need not your help. Nor
again the head to the feet I have no need of you. Yes, much more those that
seem to be the more feeble members of the body are more necessary. And such
as we think to be the less honorable members of the body about these we put
more abundant honor.*[18]

19. No one ever felt annoyed at perceiving that there were different faculties in the members unless he had completely lost his wits.
On the contrary, such a one loves and admires the Maker for so
wisely disposing every part, for assigning an appropriate function to
each, and for making what is proper to each to the advantage of all.
For the eye is not alone in its enjoyment of things seen, or the ear of
things heard, or the mouth of things tasted, or the nose of things
scented, or the feet of walking, or the hands of working, or the stomach of nourishment, or the heart of heat, or the brain of sensation.

20. No, every member has its proper function and also makes
its contribution to the common fund. It is the function of one to provide heat for the entire body, of a second to look after its entire nour-

ishment, of a third to make some other contribution to the whole organism. Various functions have been assigned to all parts of the body, the benefits of which accrue to each, and a common fund results. The ear is not annoyed because it cannot see, nor is the eye annoyed because it cannot hear; each accepts the limits of nature and makes its own contribution which was assessed from the time of creation.

21. You are very indignant, however, because all men are not swimming in riches, do not live in grand houses and deck themselves in splendid apparel, do not all ride on horses and chariots and have people to order around, both retainers and a swarm of servants to attend to their needs, because they all have not gilded couches and a soft, comfortable bed, and wonders of cookery, and devices for pleasure, and luxury served from every quarter to inflame their desires.[19] How could such a man possess prudence after overwhelming the reasoning faculty with such encumbrances? Why speak of temperance, justice, fortitude and prudence, the very names of which they cannot bear to hear? How could wealth be possessed by everyone if all enjoyed the same rank?

If All Were Equally Wealthy, Life Would Be Impossible

22. If there were perfect equality and all were equally well provided with money, how could they enjoy the necessities of life? Or who would put up with serving, being equally well off? Who would look after the fire and prepare the meals, if want did not compel him? Who would bake bread or grind the grain in the mill, separate the meal with a sieve, knead, cook, and stand over a blazing fire? Who would lead the oxen under the yoke to plow, renew the land, sow the seeds, reap the grain when it sprouts in full bloom, deliver it to the thresher and separate the chaff, if poverty did not spur him on to toil? Who would work in quarries, carry loads of stones for masons, and build fine, well-designed houses, unless want goaded him and moved him to work? Who would become a sailor? Who a mariner? Who would risk the perils of the sea? Who would become a weaver? A shoemaker? A potter? A worker in bronze?

23. If all were equally well-off, nobody would ever be another

person's servant. One of two things would happen. Either everybody would eagerly take to every kind of work through necessity, or we would all perish simultaneously through lack of the necessities of life. It is unnecessary to prove that one man cannot master every human craft;[20] anyone who has tried has failed. For if a man wants to learn two things simultaneously he fails in both, making them mutually destructive. The mind, with its attention divided between two things, and unable to comprehend both, learns a part of each but fails to get a clear, accurate knowledge of even one. If there were equal provision of wealth, the result would be that all would face annihilation, and would be in the same position as those who destroy their appetite by excessive indulgence in food. For those who are continually eating delicacies take the edge off their appetites, and those with an inordinate love of money are willing to do without the necessities of life, preferring to die rich than live in poverty.

24. Let us leave these, however, to their folly, and let us proceed to demonstrate from this the loving care of God, and let us show that what they call inequality is the starting point of a pleasant life and the foundation of the best economy. It will be shown that providence, which directs the universe, ensures equality in this.

Inequality in Wealth Is the Foundation of a Sound Economy. Besides, Basically We Are All Equal

25. In the first place, He has given the earth as a foundation common to all, a common hearth, nurse, mother, and burial-place,[21] one principle of formation, first parental dust, and He has given us a common roof, the sky. He has left us the sun, moon, and the other heavenly bodies, like lamps, as our common possession. The air which He diffused between heaven and earth is a source of wealth common to all. The rich do not breathe in more than the poor; the poor get an equal share, in fact more. For the poor are more plentiful, possess stronger sense organs, and are free from superfluous burdens. Rivers, too, and fountains provide a supply of running water for everybody.

26. Besides, He has provided rich and poor with the same sort of bodies, or, rather, the poor have an advantage in that their bodies

are stronger. For "want is the mother of health," according to the wisest of medical men, and "toil and exercise are the attendants of health," according to this same authority.[22] The souls of the rich and poor have the same nature. There is the same starting point of conception for both; marriage is their common basis of procreation; the months of pregnancy are the same. Time does not fear the power of money, nor does it allow reverence of wealth to make it yield up the infant before the allotted time, or to lengthen the period of gestation. No. Rich and poor alike reach the same term.

27. Both are produced in travail, and, to judge by experience, birth in poor circumstances is easier, and travail less difficult. Those inured to hardship bear it the readier. It is for this reason that gynecologists impose compulsory work on their well-off patients in the days preceding childbirth. Pregnancy is the same for all, but it is not so with the actual delivery. The comfort of riches make some people all the more discontented; others, lacking the necessities of life, are comforted by nature. Or rather, the Author of nature, having mingled inequalities in this way, applies the comfort of doctors and druggists to a case that is difficult when the person concerned is well-off; on the other hand, He affords the comforts of nature to a poor case that cannot afford this assistance. Observe the balance of the just judge and move your tongue to praise.

28. Look at infants. They are all brought forth in nakedness; the rich man's baby is not clad in purple or the poor man's in rags; both come forth naked, since the Creator has proclaimed equality. Both breathe the same air; both are nursed in the same way. There are not two kinds of milk, one for the rich and one for the poor. No. Both enjoy the same nourishment.

Death Is the End of All

29. Not only do we all enter into the world in one and the same way; we leave it in the same way, too. It is the one death that awaits us. Death is in no dread of the rich man: it does not fear bodyguards; it does not stand in awe before purple; it is undaunted by walls, or towers, or palaces of kings; it penetrates into bedrooms; it is unmoved by tears; it does not heed entreaties; it is not corrupted by bribes; it

is not impeded by medical skill; it shows that the preparations of druggists are of no avail; often it does not wait for the dying person to give his last instructions or name his heirs, but it snatches, drags, sunders the body from the soul.[23] Those who pride themselves on their riches and those who live in poverty have the same end, and after death there is the same road before them.

30. Decay and corruption follow for all; the worms come forth, the awful eye becomes extinct and melts away; the insatiable mouth and the raging tongue become the waste-ground of worms. The proud neck is not only bent but broken, the swollen cheek not merely contracted but ground into a little powder. The bloom of the cheek withers and vanishes. The fingers which write obscenity lie utterly deprived of harmony. These things all await rich and poor alike.[24]

Rich and Poor Have Complementary Needs

31. It remains now to show that poverty and wealth, which you think belong to individuals, are common to all, and this will presently, with God's help, become clear. Those who live in poverty derive their equal share of enjoyment from the wealth of the rich. For God who created both classes equipped the poor with all kinds of crafts which cause the rich to come to their doors and give them money to get what they want from them. And since their wants are proportioned to their wealth, they are in need of every necessity of life. From some they buy bread, from others, meat; some put shoes on their feet, others put clothes on their backs, others make carpets, chaplets, and spreads for them; some men build houses for them; others make couches and chairs; others look after the vegetables and various kinds of fruits; others tend the wheat, barley, and the farm crops, without which life would be impossible even if one possessed the gold of Croesus and Midas.[25] Bread, kneaded of millet, or even of bran,[26] is sufficient for the poor man and common sauce satisfies him.

32. Judging the matter fairly and justly, which would you call needy, poor, and in want, the man who has few needs or the man who has many? The man who has the resources of life in his hands or the man who trusts in fickle gold, which seals and stamps fail to detain, which takes leave of bolts and doors and reaches the hands of robbers?

Now no thief would steal his trade from a poor man, but a sycophant, not to mention a thief, would deprive a rich man of his possessions.

33. The poor man sits in the marketplace, be he shoemaker, goldsmith, silversmith, tailor, or trader in any other of the necessities of life. The man who prides himself on his riches, who holds his head too high and gesticulates, approaches, surrounded with many attendants. The poor man in all likelihood sits stitching his leather or engraving his silver, or doing whatever his craft requires. The rich man stands talking to him and indicates his needs by his presence. Why, then, are you disturbed and blame the state of poverty, seeing that the wealthy are in great need of it and cannot live without it? You should marvel, rather, at the One who guides things so wisely and who, by giving money to some and crafts to others, unites them by their needs in harmonious friendship. For the rich men supply money, the poor provide the fruits of their trade.

34. Poverty is moved to rivalry against wealth and surpasses it in its gifts, for what wealth regards as useless, poverty transforms by its skill, showing its necessity and utility for every need. Indeed, if one must know the whole truth, poverty collects the very raw materials of wealth. For it mines the gold, silver, bronze, and iron which sustain the wealthy man. Riches borrow from every craft possessed by the poor. The poor take the shapeless raw materials, give them design and form, and produce rings, earrings, necklaces, bracelets, necklets, goblets, and all the other objects which cause the wealthy to become puffed up.

35. Since, then, wealth depends on poverty, and the poor man has a source of wealth in crafts, why tax such equality with inequality? Why call friends enemies? Why slander the state of things which makes life more pleasant for rich and poor alike? For both get what they want from one another, thus satisfying their needs.

A Third Objection: Why Do the Majority of the Wealthy Live Immoral Lives?

36. But perhaps you will say: Why do the majority of the rich live in injustice?[27] Why do they not all cherish justice? There again you forget that man has free will, you deprive him of the glory given

him by the Maker. Besides, evildoers would have great ground for
self-defence if the judge distributed wealth only to the just in the
present life. They would say the same as their master said to Job: *You
have made a fence for everything inside and outside their house. Their crops
and vines you have multiplied. Only stretch forth your hand and touch all
they have and verily will they bless you to your face.*[28] That is what hard-
ened sinners would say if those who cultivated virtue were the only
ones to receive the gift of riches.

37. The Creator, however, placed at man's disposal poverty and
riches like raw materials: certain men used them to acquire virtue,
others made them the foundation of wickedness, but neither wealth
nor poverty is in itself an excuse for evil living. Those who husband
their riches properly, and do not increase them at the expense of other
people's misfortunes, but rather share all they have with those in
need, are a sufficient reproach to those who spend their wealth on
wickedness and in a spirit of selfishness. Those, too, who accept their
poverty philosophically and endure its attacks with courage and pa-
tience, are standing reproaches to those who have learned evil doing
while living in poverty.

Poverty Has Many Advantages, Especially Good Health and Endurance in Illness

38. Mark another provision of the Ruler that you may sing His
praises with greater fervor. When He saw the amount of attention
paid to rich people, He gave health to the poor as their special portion. The rich man is carried in a litter while the poor man walks on
his own two feet. The rich man desires the poor man's health; the
poor man pities the rich man's weakness.

39. When he is ill you can notice the rich man attended by an
army; he is in terrible suffering and cannot bear the painful attack.
In winter he keeps to his heated apartments, reclining on soft
couches, wrapped in warm clothes, with fires laid to counteract the
cold and countless drugs at hand to fight the disease. He listens grate-
fully to the assurances of the doctors, and derives consolation from
the presence of friends who put an end to the throbs of pain by their
conversation.

40. If the season is summer other houses soon open their doors to him, open-air verandas that allow the breezes easy access. When the breezes stop, the servants devise ventilation with fans.[29] Young shoots are everywhere around, creating an imaginary garden and giving the house the appearance of a grove. Water fountains are devised on the top story, in the hope of enticing sleep on his eyelids. Despite all this attention, the rich man is just as much in pain, throws off the bedclothes and tosses from side to side, signifying the concealed inflammation by the agitation of his hands.

41. The poor man, on the other hand, has only a single hovel, generally a rented one. Indeed some who cannot pay the rent live in the marketplace with the ground as a bed and chaff as a mattress. No doctor stands by them, no cook to carry out the doctor's orders, no housekeeper, no maid, maybe not even a wife. The providence of God does all for him, blunting the darts of suffering, deadening the pains, quenching the inflammation without any drug, affording protection from the cold and heat and damp underneath. No one tells him what food nourishes disease, what favors good health: he eats what he gets without picking or choosing; what is harmful does him good; a drink of cold water takes the place of medicine; dry bread quenches his inflammation, and he does not need emetics or enemas. Nature satisfies his needs and takes the place of doctors when he is ill. You will notice that a man lying in the open endures illness more readily than those who enjoy all the attentions I have spoken about.[30]

Take Everything as Coming from Divine Providence

42. Regard, then, everything that happens as coming from the providence of God, and do not worry about any individual happening. If you wish to make a close inquiry, do it in a spirit of reverence. Let this spirit lead you in your journey, guiding you to the solution of your pursuit. Fortified by it, take every opportunity to praise the Creator. Imitate those three youths who, when committed to the furnace, called the inanimate creation to join in their hymn of praise. They dragged to this marvelous spectacle the tyrant who had cruelly committed them to the furnace, and, by virtue of this miracle, compelled him to reverence the God he had outraged. No furnace could

turn their tongues to blasphemy; committed to such a fire they celebrated God in song.[31]

43. Neither furnace nor lions urge you to blaspheme, but you fail to recognize the gifts which you enjoy from a beneficent God. If, then, you listen to me, you will adorn your tongue with piety and praise creation, singing a hymn to the Creator and adoring His all-embracing providence, because to Him is glory and power now, always, and forever. Amen.

DISCOURSE 7

THAT THE DIVISION INTO SLAVES AND MASTERS IS AN ADVANTAGE IN LIFE

1. The Creator of the universe does not need mortal tongue to chorus His praise. Nor does He listen to the chant of angels as though He needed it; but when He sees creatures well disposed He treats them with indulgence. When people made their customary offerings to God they did so, of course, not as if they fulfilled some need on God's part, but in thanksgiving for countless benefits received, an attempt to make an adequate return. It can be observed that all did not offer one and the same sacrifice. One man sacrificed a calf; another, a lamb; another, a young goat. The number of their offerings varied, too. A man who through poverty lacked these sacrificed a pair of turtledoves, or the young of doves. If he had not even these, he could offer a little fine meal or some incense.[1] From this, then, we learn that the just Judge looks to the intention of the giver rather than to the size of the gifts.

2. And we offer our worthless sermons, not in the hope of adding to the depths of wisdom with our tiny drop, but in an attempt to show slaves how thankful they should be, and also to reprimand fellow slaves for their rashness, and to make them submissive to the yoke of their master. For we are thoroughly distressed at seeing the all-directing wisdom of God misrepresented by them. It is for that reason we have labored over our present discourse, and we try by our arguments to put an end to such blasphemy.

Our Opponents Object to Slavery as Well as Poverty

3. The previous discourse adequately demonstrated the extreme folly of their complaints against the apparent inequalities of life

88

and their failure to take into account the relevant facts. It showed that poverty has its uses and it disproved the necessity of wealth. Since they are not satisfied with complaining about poverty but also bewail slavery and lament about imperial taxes and the other things which fit only too well into this life, let us now deal briefly with these points, imitating the best doctors who, when they notice their patients off their food and loathing everything offered them, well and truly outwit their revulsion with the aid of medical artifices. For, by sweetening foods that are too dry or too sour,[2] they bring it about that the sick man's repugnance is changed to a great relish.

4. Those who blame everything they see and experience resemble sick men. The sick, however, are smitten by disease against their will and they refuse food because of grievous pain: they desire to eat, but are hindered by illness. The others are preyed on by sufferings that are voluntary and self-chosen; they are difficult, not in matters of food and drink, but in everything that is arranged by the wisdom and justice of divine providence.

Such People are Impossible to Please

5. When they are putting in the crops they long for showers, but if they have to go on a journey they grumble if it is raining. They wish for the warmer rays of sunshine to ripen the crops, and then they complain and find fault with the heat.[3] They endure all sorts of hardship for their stomach's sake, tilling fields, making voyages by sea and long journeys over land. And again they turn to scathing criticism of providence, as if it had been ordained that the stomach, instead of obeying the wishes of the soul, should rule it instead.

6. They find fault with thunderbolts, hailstones, and all such scourges and again blame the forbearance of God. They have no regard for His justice or His forbearance, but pray that they may enjoy the forbearance while transgressing grievously. Yet they wish those who have offended themselves to pay the full penalty of justice. They see a poor man: immediately their tongues are set in motion against providence, and many criticisms are heaped on poverty. They see a rich man strutting along on tiptoe, glaring like a lion, swinging his shoulders from side to side, or borne in a carriage, surrounded by

numerous slaves and guards:[4] immediately they turn their blasphemies on riches. They are annoyed that life is full of inequalities, yet they hate death which puts an end to inequalities and assigns equal honor to all.

7. Assuredly those who dislike death should admire life, or those who find fault with life should have nothing but good to say of death. For life and death are diametrically opposed. These people, however, rail indiscriminately against both and speak equally amiss of everything. In childhood they regard man's estate as happy, but when they grow up they say that children are to be envied. But why speak more about all the misrepresentations of this wretched disease? Nothing has escaped the torrent of abuse discharged by their tongues. Come now and, following the medical approach, let us show that what has hitherto revolted them is really extremely pleasant. We have said enough in the preceding discourse about wealth and poverty and the apparent lack of equality between them, and we have demonstrated the utility of both.

In the Beginning All Men Were Equal. Class Distinction is a Consequence of Sin

8. Let us now show that the division of mankind into rulers and the ruled is foreign to the Creator's original design. Look back at our first formation, and notice that man was formed from the earth, but that woman was not formed in the same way. The Creator took a rib from man and fashioned the female from it, lest it might seem to be different in nature because of its difference in appearance. Thus man was fashioned from the earth, woman from the man, and from the two came the whole human race.[5]

9. The Creator, then, did not from the beginning assign slavery to one class and rule to others, but created a single race of them all. He commanded Noah to fit out the ark, and saved him as a reward for his integrity. He ordered himself, his wife, his children and their wives to enter the ark when it was ready, but no slave set foot in it.[6] For nature had not yet received this distinction, apart from the only real slaves—irrational animals—which the Creator of the universe had brought into this life to serve mankind.

There was Need of Rulers to Preserve the Social Order

10. Later, when He saw great disorder arise among them because of lack of control and all sorts of lawlessness perpetrated with complacency, He divided mankind into rulers and the ruled, so that fear of rulers might lessen the volume of crime. For fear can bridle the onrush of irrational passions and reduce the soul's downward inclination toward evil, and often fear has triumphed where reason has failed. When nature was driven headlong to evil, and the mind was lashed on all sides by passions and became submerged like a ship without ballast, leaving the body to founder without direction, laws became absolutely necessary to act as an anchor to hold the ship in position and prevent it from being carried away, and to allow the pilot to emerge and take hold of the tiller. The establishment of these laws would have been impossible if there were equality of power and of rule.

11. Even in democratic states, where the people had control of affairs, all were not equal. Some examined the laws, others revised them; some were generals, some filled the role of subjects, while the head of the state was over both rulers and the ruled. In oligarchies, the majority of the citizens belonged to the category of subjects while the minority, who excelled in wisdom and were conspicuous for virtue, attended to public affairs and held command. Some were ephors, others navarchs, others harmosts.[7] They led the people as they thought best.

It was wrongdoing, then, that introduced the need of laws. Laws presupposed the power of legislators, and not only of legislators but also of those with power to punish transgressors. Wrongdoing also introduced disorder. The Guide of the universe put order in place of disorder, and used laws as a bridle to check the impact of sin. He handed the reins of this bridle to the rulers, and they ruled cities, villages, and military settlements.

Fear of the Law Curbs Wrongdoers

12. Who would resist wrongdoers if fear of the laws did not check the impetus of their passionate greed? Like fish, the larger

would devour the smaller[8] if the law did not keep before their eyes the sharpened sword, the fire heaped up, and all the other means devised by rulers for punishing those living in wickedness. For if, where laws are binding and rulers have punitive powers, there are some who are wilder in disposition towards their neighbors than any wild beast, and act like scorpions, bite like snakes, fight like dogs, and gnash their teeth at their friends like lions fighting with other animals, what would happen if there were no laws and no rulers to inflict punishment?

13. Admittedly transgressions are attempted by some, but all the same those who attempt them try to escape notice through fear of the laws, and seek to conceal the wrongdoing by persuasive words. The victim of injustice gladly comes before the judges and enters a case for damages. He is not overawed by the might of the defendant, and he does not tremble before his display of riches; he runs to court as into harbor, outlines the forms of injury, asks the laws to be introduced, and begs the judge to give his decision accordingly. The judge gives his decision, and he orders the house, or the field, or the property that has been seized, to be restored to the injured party. Often he exacts a fine also from the man who dared to do wrong.

14. Because of this fear, housebreakers and footpads do their wicked deeds in secret and not openly, and in attempting to escape detection they proclaim their fear; otherwise they would have taken swords, slaughtered all persons they met, and seized their possessions. Through fear the majority hold their peace, but some who dare to perform evil either lay an ambush on the more deserted roads or do their evil work in the cities by night, using darkness, sleep, and the general quiet to help them in their wrongdoing.[9] If two or three of these are detected and punished in accordance with the laws, they become a sufficiently salutary example for the others who, when they see the punishment of those who act like themselves, hate evil as the mother of such deaths.

Now I do not know what led me to that disgression since my object was to deal with the cause of slavery. It is time for me to return to that subject.

*The Division Into Masters and Slaves is Natural and Necessary. It
Was Brought About by Man's Sinfulness and Not by God*

15. Sacred Scripture testifies that the Creator of the universe
contrived the unity of the human race from the beginning of time,
and from one man and one woman filled the whole world with people. Nature corroborates Scripture's testimony. People, whether
they live in the east, west, north, or south, or along the equator, all
have the same kind of composition, the same number of external
senses; they differ only in customs and color. Difference in ways of
life and in moral freedom makes for different customs. We can note
the same differences among ourselves. Different environment em-
phasizes difference in color. Those who live far from the sun's rays
have a whiter complexion, while those whose lot is to live toward the
more southern part of the globe in the east or west, being closer to
the rays of the sun, are black in body, just as blocks of wood are
burned to a cinder on too big a fire and assume a black color.

16. The nature of man, then, is one—ruler and ruled, subjects
and kings, slaves and masters. This unity of nature proclaims the justice of the Maker. In time nature, divided into slaves and masters
while preserving its unity, put a check on sin which had necessitated
this division.[10] In this is revealed the equity of the Creator. For He
preserved to the end the identity of essence, expelled the disorder of
sin by His ordered rule, and moderated its greed by the rule of law,
like a shipwright straightening planks with a plumb line and remov-
ing any unevenness.

17. Do not criticize the Creator when you see slavery, but
rather avoid wrongdoing and blasphemy, which caused the human
race to be divided into slaves and masters. When you see a ship borne
on favorable winds and the passengers sitting at ease while the sailors
ply the oars, or haul the sails, or carry out some other command, and
the man at the prow takes observations of rocks, shallows, and jagged
roughness, and brings them to the notice of the pilot, and the pilot is
overall and directs the ship with the rudders, you marvel at the order:
you do not demand that all be pilots; you do not entrust to them all
the command of the ship.

18. And looking at those who sit at ease and those who carry out
the commands—one man reporting his observations, another in com-

plete charge—you do not complain or upbraid it for lack of order; on the contrary, you cannot stop marvelling at the order of it all. Yet you do not wish houses to be run like ships: you are upset at seeing one man running the house and the rest of them carrying out his orders. Now the running of a house closely resembles the direction of a ship. The master of the house, like a pilot, once he takes possession of the keys of the house, is in charge of everything. The steward over the slaves, who is entrusted with caring for all the others, imitating the helmsman, tells the master what he considers to be in his best interests. Of the other slaves, some are like sailors with particular chores, doing what they are ordered. The rest, like passengers, are in the midst of these, being directed by them and having their requirements carried out. Why, then, praise a boat directed in this manner and keep criticizing a household which is managed along the same lines?

19. You would praise an army, I take it, in which the general issued the commands, the company officers looked after the companies, and the company sergeants led the ranks in good trim. The centurions and chiliarchs pass along the instructions received from the general; at one time they put the men in line; at another, in a hollow square; at another, in column. Sometimes they deploy either flank to the utmost and encircle the enemy without letting them take to flight; they discharge missiles on them from all sides and annihilate them. None of those things could have taken place if the army were not divided into generals and men. It would be most disastrous for an army if many took command, splintering the troops, upsetting the harmony, and the attempt to direct by many commands leading to harm rather than direction. Surely, then, it is absurd for you to approve the rule of one man on a ship, or to praise the discipline of an army where the orders of the generals are carried out, and yet to find fault with a house that is run in the same way?

An Objection: Slavery is Irksome. But a Slave's Life is Often More Enviable Than his Master's

20. But it is irksome, you say, to be a slave, to let the enjoyment of the necessaries of life depend on masters, and to be afflicted by continuous tribulations. If in the interests of truth you were prepared

to review all that we have said, leaving mere controversy aside, you would find that the role of master is fraught with care and that of slave has numerous advantages. The master of the house, beset by many worries, considers how to provide for the needs of the slaves, how to pay the state taxes,[11] how to sell what is over and above from his produce and buy what he needs. If the land is unkind to farmers, in this imitating the ingratitude of men to the Creator, the master is distressed, looks around his creditors, pays his accounts, and goes into voluntary slavery.

21. When the land gives a good yield and is laden with crops, covered with corn, and weighed down with fruit on the trees forcing the branches to bend to earth, he is again goaded by fresh troubles. For when he looks around for buyers, he finds none, and the good yield becomes more intolerable to him than any scarcity. Not only do worries crowd around the masters in daylight to besiege and disturb their soul, but by night the fight is intensified for the soul, when it is at rest and, away from external disturbances, can see more clearly whether its domestic affairs are in good shape or bad.

22. The slave, on the other hand, though a slave in body, enjoys freedom of soul and has none of these worries. He does not bewail the failure of the crops or lament the scarcity of buyers; he is not pained at the sight of a creditor nor does he fear a swarm of tax-collectors; he is not forced to sit on juries; he does not fear the voice of the herald, or the judge looking with awesome eye. He takes his food, rationed no doubt, but he has no worries.

23. He lies down to sleep on the pavement, but worry does not banish sleep: on the contrary, its sweetness on his eyelids keeps him from feeling the hardness of the ground. Wisdom, speaking in accordance with nature, said: *Sleep is sweet to the slave.*[12] He covers his body with a single garment, but his body is stronger than his master's. He eats rye bread, and never tastes anything dainty, but he enjoys his food better than his master does. His master is constantly bothered by indigestion: he takes more than enough, bolts his food, and forces it down. The slave consumes only what he needs, takes what is given to him with moderation, enjoys what he receives, digests it slowly, and it fortifies him for his work.

24. You consider only the slavery of this man; you do not consider his health. You see the work, but not the recompense involved; you complain of toil, but forget the happiness of a carefree life. You criticize his lowly state, but fail to notice how soundly he sleeps. You should see from that the providence of God and witness the equity of His rule. When sin necessitated the division of men into rulers and slaves, God joined cares to responsibility, allotting to the master sleepless nights and more than his share of sickness, whereas the slave received better health, greater zest for his food, pleasant and longer sleep calculated to free his body from fatigue and make it stronger for the toils of the morrow.

Toil is the Lot of All

25. See, therefore, not only the toils, but consider also their consolations, and sing an unceasing hymn of praise to the Governor of the universe. Why do you, who are so ready with your criticism of everything, find fault with toil? What human blessing is obtained without toil? What kind of good fortune would human nature enjoy without toils? We reap the blessings of the earth and the fruits of commerce through toils. We dwell in cities after building them with toil. As a result of toil we live in houses, clothe ourselves, put shoes on our feet, and partake of all kinds of food.

26. Must I catalogue all the needs of men which are satisfied by toil? You resemble a drone bee, reared in laziness, culling the fruits of the toil of others, making no individual contribution to life except using your tongue to heap abuse on everything. Laziness produces idle talk and a great amount of garrulity. The man engaged in work says little but does a great deal.

27. Since it is through toil, then, that each of these blessings is obtained, do not find fault, my friend, with slavery because of the labors. Note, instead, how many masters work no less hard than their slaves, far harder, in fact, if you count the worry as well as the work. Do you, then, look at those men of today who are energetic; I will show you the men of old who toiled more than the slaves.

Examples from Scripture of Masters Who Worked Harder Than Slaves

28. Behold the blessed Noah hewing wood, trimming it with an adze, shaping it with his joiner's square, getting ready the ark, as was ordered, from rectangular blocks, uniting the joints with bolts, thus completing the whole, then painting it with tar and pitch to protect it from the inroads of the waters.[13]

29. Behold mighty Abraham, the patriarch, master of three hundred and eighty slaves, doing his share of the work himself, attending to the guests, running to his herds, rounding up the calves, and getting his wife to bake. Behold her likewise kneading the flour, baking it in the ashes, and not leaving the tasks to the slaves. Look at that marvelous old man attending in person to his guests, and instead of joining them at table actually waiting on them.[14]

30. Behold Rebecca, the daughter of Bathuel and granddaughter of Nachor, marriageable and beautiful; yet instead of being content to remain in her boudoir she works herself, carrying water from the well on the outskirts of the city. She not only brings the water home but waits on the visitors herself, giving the spring water to them and their camels, preserving the precious possession of her continence, keeping her virginity untouched, going about her tasks with the greatest zeal, preferring to shine at these than to display her own beauty.[15]

31. Her son, the mighty Jacob, as befitted a son of hers, spent twenty years working as a shepherd and wrestling with wild beasts, enduring the scorching sun and unable to get sufficient sleep at night.[16] We find, too, in the Scriptures that his wives also, for whom he endured these tribulations, tended flocks as well. Their children also tended flocks as laborers and shepherds, subject to all the toils of slaves.

32. And the God-like man, Moses, spent forty years of his life in this way. His wife, a daughter of a priest, tended flocks and joined him in marriage after he had helped to liberate her from wicked shepherds.[17] It would be superfluous to expand on this and bring forward all those of whom Scripture tells us that their race was run with toil.

33. If work, then, is common to masters and slaves, why do you

criticize slavery on the score of toil? Slaves share in the toils of their masters, but they do not share in their worries. If toil is common to masters and slaves, but only masters shoulder the worry, surely we should judge those who are free from care as happy, and not class them among the wretched.

Since the providence of the Ruler of the universe is clearly revealed in all this, let us now bring together each of our arguments, summarize them, and make them easier to understand.

Recapitulation

34. We have shown, then, that the Creator gave one and the same nature to mankind at the beginning and dignified it with free will; furthermore, that nature, abusing this very freedom of the will, fell into evil and failed in all sorts of wrongdoing. Laws accordingly became necessary to check the impact of sin, and laws presupposed legislators. Of necessity the human race was divided into two classes, some to rule, the rest to obey the rulers. Thus it was hoped to arrest the rapid advance of evil through respect of the laws and fear of the rulers. Archons rule the cities; guardians, the towns; and generals, the armies: overall are the kings. The pilot rules the ship; the trainers, the athletes; the teacher, the pupils; the shoemaker, his assistants; the worker in bronze, his apprentices. In the same way the master rules the house. No house could be properly run without a master, as houses without them, being all but deserted, testify.

35. Likewise there are beings higher than angels, for we learn from Sacred Scripture that the heavens above us are inhabited by both angels and archangels.[18] The archangels give the orders, the angels obey. You see that their habitation is free of transgression, and their nature incorporeal and superior to passion, and yet they do not reject this arrangement whereby the angels obey cheerfully and the archangels rule with moderation. Why, then, do you complain at the division into ruler and the ruled of human beings where the inclination to evil is great? Our Maker has given us the rule of masters as a sort of preventative cure for the ulcers of sin.

36. A father rules his family, correcting the children that are

unruly and praising those that are well-behaved. The teacher rules his pupils, and the husband his wife. The master rules his slaves, regarding the better-disposed as worthy of honor, encouragement, and often of freedom. On the other hand, he corrects those who are slothful and inclined to do wrong, and he teaches them manners. The God of the universe has established this same order in the priesthood. Some He has deemed worthy to be priests, and he has appointed others to rule them. He has also set up other orders of inferior clergy.

37. If you are offended at the sight of some masters who are excessively cruel and lacking in restraint, and some who barter away justice for bribes and bring forth objections on these scores, I shall forestall this wicked thought at its conception and assert that it was not God who entrusted leadership to such men, but that it is the wickedness of subjects that has brought the rule of such men on themselves. Those who refused to derive any benefit from good administrators but disregarded their discipline by the depravity of their conduct, deprived themselves of God's loving care. Bereft of divine direction, they got rulers of this type so that by experiencing worse ones they might be reminded of the better ones, and might recall their wise and admirable direction.[19]

38. We find the God of the universe often giving rein to man because of the excess of man's wickedness, and He allows the human race to be borne where it will. Of this He has warned us speaking through His prophet to Israel: *And I said: I will not tend you. That which dies, let it die, and that which perishes, let it perish; and for the rest let each devour the flesh of his neighbor.*[20] When wicked rulers are in control, then, and cruel, harsh masters rule households, we should implore the One who directs the universe and, by conversion of life and a change in our ways, make supplication, rousing Him to help us and fervently begging Him to give us better times.

39. For He is easy of access to those who entreat Him with a pure heart, since He is good, and it is His nature to show mercy, or rather He is the fount of mercy as He testifies Himself promising those who make supplication: *You will call and I shall hear you; as you are yet speaking I will answer. Lo, I shall be at hand.*[21] We will show in our next discourse, please God, that those who flagrantly transgress

the law and strive to outstrip all others in impiety are unable to injure those who follow sound reason and cherish virtue.

But for the present let us chant the praises of Him who bestows gifts on men individually and collectively, and surrounds our nature with countless blessings. To Him be glory forever and ever. Amen.

DISCOURSE 8

That Upright Slaves Suffer No Corruption Through Service to Wicked Masters

1. I am well aware that a man who undertakes to speak on this subject needs great powers of eloquence and of intellect, for facts are apt to lose luster when translated into words, and the weakness or strength of the description is taken as the measure of the facts by those who judge things not on their real merits but by the skill with which they are described.

2. I took courage, however, from the importance of the subject, for I did not measure it by vain concepts of thought or place any value on the petty, miserable product of my brain. My sole consideration has been that the light of truth is manifest to those who want to see it, just as the sun is visible to those whose eyesight is sound.[1] Even if there were no one to plead for it, the providence of our Creator and Saviour proclaims itself. Therefore I did not think that I would be doing anything unreasonable or reprehensible in lending the support of my voice to this testimony that is borne from all sides, making the stuffed ears of those ungrateful men resound with my words.

3. We have amply demonstrated, aided by God's grace, that poverty and wealth are necessary and useful in life, and that the Physician of souls has applied slavery and rule, like drugs, to the wounds of sin. Our present purpose is to show with God's help that slavery does not harm those in that state but it is, on the contrary, a great blessing to them if they so wish it. We promised yesterday to speak of this today.

The Problem: Can Slaves Lead Virtuous Lives?

4. One could, if one wished, without resorting to examples from history, examine slaves about us and see that many of them lead a virtuous life, gracing slavery with equanimity, not needing to be forced, doing their duty conscientiously, freely choosing to serve their masters, as a result of which they obtain their freedom and a handsome sum of money, reaping the reward of their good services. Nonetheless, it is not, I hope, irrelevant to introduce a few examples of slaves from history, and show the treasure of sanctity which they accumulated by way of refuting those who try to attack slavery and make this the basis of a further attack, and they dare to hurl their weapons against the providence of God.

The Example of Abraham's Servant

5. Let us first of all summon the servant of the patriarch Abraham.[2] When he saw old age coming on the patriarch and knew that the end was near (for old age is a prelude to death), he got instructions to get a wife for Abraham's son from his own people and avoid a matrimonial alliance with the Canaanites, and those instructions were surrounded with the traditional oaths and benedictions. The first thing this admirable servant did was to check all of the words of his master, fearing the oath by which he was bound, and shrinking from the all-searching eye; his first thought was, if the woman chosen refused to leave her country, should he bring the son there? Abraham answered that it would be unnecessary to bring him, that he was to trust in God who called him, and to rely on His guidance.

Abraham's Servant Prays that he may Choose the Right Wife for Abraham's Son

6. The slave set out from his master's house and got to Charan late that day after covering many miles. He mounted camels to make the going easier and then, bidding a long farewell to the gifts he was offered and to all the trappings of wealth, he raised his hands to

heaven and begged God to make a match for the son of his master and to give him a daughter-in-law suited to his master in character. It is worth hearing his venerable words: *O Lord God of my master, Abraham, behold I stand nigh the spring of water and the daughters of the inhabitants of this city will come out to draw water. Now therefore the maid to whom I shall say: Let down your pitcher that I may drink. And she shall answer: Drink and I will give your camels drink also until their thirst is quenched: Let it be the same whom you have provided for your servant Isaac and by this I shall understand that you have shown kindness to my master,*[3] Abraham.

7. Who but would admire the man for his piety? Or rather who could find adequate praise for his every single word? His prayer, you can see, is graced with faith, wisdom, and piety. Is it not supreme piety and wisdom to turn one's back on everybody and depend on the providence of God for the success of one's journey? Does it not exceed the limits of faith for him to rely on the justice of his master, to call the God of all things *his* God, hoping thereby to receive the answer to his prayer and to have his petition granted.

The Character of Rebecca

8. To get what he asked is a sign of God's favor. He would not obtain it so easily if he were not on intimate terms with the Benefactor. Moral worth ensures this intimate relationship. That such is, and always was, the case is the lesson of history. Before he had finished his prayer, Rebecca showed signs of hospitality. She was asked for a little water and was eager to give drink to all the camels. With an effort she drew the water and relieved the thirst of men and beasts, showing both courage and kindness, and appearing as the archetype of the maiden depicted in the words of the prayer, worthy of the house of Abraham in that she had a hospitable disposition resembling that of her future father-in-law.

9. This was the object of the trusty servant's quest, not beauty, nor poise, nor a fresh complexion, nor lovely eyes, nor well-lined eyebrows, nor illustrious parentage, nor a big dowry, but a hospitable disposition, a gentle manner, a calm, measured voice, a capable,

generous character, worthy of the master's house where there was an open door for visitors of all sorts, and everyone got what he wanted. That was the object of his quest, and that is what he got.

10. He did not take her without examination, but he went over everything that had happened to see whether the Lord had really blessed his way. When he discovered all the signs he sought, he thought of thanksgiving before producing the tokens of a suitor and did not in his delight forget his Benefactor. Looking at the gift, he saw, with the eyes of faith, the Benefactor, and he accepted the gift after praising Him with all his might. He learned on inquiry about her and her family, that she was the daughter of Bethuel, and he got a stable and fodder for his camels.

11. *He bowed down and adored, saying: Blessed be the Lord God of my master Abraham who has not taken away His mercy and truth from my master and has brought me the straight way into the house of my master's brother.*[4] When he had received more than he sought—for the maiden not only gave him water but freely promised to give him lodging and food for himself and his camels—when he had received friendship unsought in addition to what he did seek, he returned thanks to the best of his ability and bore testimony to the truth of the divine promises: *Blessed be the Lord God of my master Abraham who has not taken away His mercy and truth from my master,* Abraham. You are just, he means, in being more than provident to those who reverence you and in regarding your well-disposed servant—my good master—as worthy of every attention. Events prove the truth of your words. You confirm in children the promises you gave my master.

12. Praising the beneficent God in these terms, he gave the suitor's tokens to the maiden, and she adorned her ears with golden rings to show that she had favorably and readily understood the requests of the strangers. Likewise she adorned her hands, too, in perfect submission to the generous impulse of her heart. When he entered the house and saw her parents, and revealed his master's wishes, did he, recognizing the assistance of God in this, and conscious of all the help he had received, forget his master, or overlook him in his preoccupation with his own thoughts, or put his own pleasure before duty? By no means. When her father and mother, and he who had brought the sorrows on them,[5] were prevailing on her to stay that they might

have the pleasure of her company, at least for a few days, the slave said: *Stay me not, because the Lord has prospered my way. Send me away that I may go to my master.*[6]

13. He embellished his speech with frequent mention of the name of God, attributing the abundance of blessings he received to Him, and gave the credit to providence for what he had done himself. Tell me, what harm did slavery do this man? What man brought up in freedom, and priding himself on the independence of his ancestors, would make such a display of virtue? What higher virtue could there be than this? Some one may say perhaps, however, some of those who are skilled at contriving calumny and are critical of what is good, that his master's wisdom trained him in this way, that in contemplating him like a mirror he derived from him the marks of virtue, and that those who have evil masters receive their imprint from the archetype, learning from them the first elements of wrongdoing, then becoming experts in evil and reproducing in themselves the image of those who have taught them. Come now, let us refute the falsehood of those men and show that a life of virtue or vice is freely chosen, and that a master, however wretched, cannot compel a slave to lead a bad life if he does not wish to do so himself.

Joseph Is Sold Into Slavery By His Brothers. He Resists the Seductiveness of Potiphar's Wife

14. Behold that God-like man, Joseph,[7] grandson of Rebecca, and great-grandson of the patriarch, Abraham. In the springtime of his life, at his full vigor, in the bloom of his youth (for spring is especially the season of bloom), in the springtime of his youth as I say, and in the bloom of life he had great physical splendor and even greater splendor of soul. His father loved him and regarded him as the favorite, not only because he was born to him in his old age,[8] but his character resembled the old man's and he imitated his father's virtue. This son, whenever he had dreams,[9] recounted them to his father in the hearing of his brothers. He immediately became the target of their envy, and envy led to slanderous abuse. After some time, when they saw their young brother coming to them, they were un-

able to bear the tidings promised by the dreams, and they pounced on him like wild animals on a lamb separated from the fold and deprived of the protection of the shepherd.

15. They neither respected the grey hairs of their father nor pitied him who regarded Joseph as the staff of his old age. The law of nature did not stay them, or the bond of relationship, or their common origin, or the tender years of their brother and his freedom from sin, or the leadership that had been forced on him in his dreams and had hitherto been the merest shadow of rule. They tried to kill him on the spot and thus defile their hands with a brother's blood.

16. When Ruben dissuaded them from murder and bade them avoid this defilement, they hid him for some time in a cistern, and then they sold him a little later to Ismaelite traders, reducing the penalty from death to slavery, since they could not bear the sight of one whom a dream had made king.

17. Joseph paid in this way for his dreams. He was led into Egypt and sold to Potiphar, the chief cook of the Pharaoh. While there he upheld his family pride, kept the good name of his ancestors untarnished, and did not trim his sails to the wind. No change in morals resulted from his change in fortune; he did not change his conscience with his color. No, although his state had changed from freedom to slavery he remained loyal to his principles in word and action, and his integrity was reflected in his countenance.

18. This won him the highest regard, and he was entrusted with the management of his master's house. He was always kind to his master and impartial to his fellow slaves. He was gracious to those who thus honored him and was suitably solicitous for those under his direction. He was loved by masters and subjects alike. God rewarded his virtue with corresponding grace; indeed he reaped rewards far in excess of his toils. Whatever he put his hand to, the Lord prospered. Soon, however, another storm caught him up and a tempest more stormy than slavery again pursued him. After the temporary calm came another gale. Making his way through waves and gales, he managed to keep his head above water.

19. He was, as was said, a young man in the bloom of his youth, like a bud just come to flower with the first growth of down on his cheeks crowning his face. He radiated splendor, mingled with comeliness and an air of freedom, with modesty resting on his brow and

winning persuasiveness on his lips. These traits were frequently no-
ticed by Potiphar's wife[10] and, instead of deriving some good from
them, she fell into the depths of passion. The sight of him only added
fuel to her burning desire, and no amount of reasoning could quench
the fire which she had allowed to kindle too much. So she took
shamelessness to help her and tried to ensnare the young man in conversation.

20. He proved too elusive for her bait and easily escaped the
nets she laid for him, neither responding to nor heeding her seductive
and wheedling words. So she abandoned words and turned to action.
When she had the house to herself, she embraced the young man,
thinking that he was a slave to passion and not its master.

21. But he derived no courage from the fact that the house was
empty; he was aware of the all-seeing eye of God. He took no account
of his own status, nor was he cowed by the fact that she was his superior. He had no desire to relax the reins of passion as a compen-
sation for the trials he had already endured, or under the pretext that
no one would notice his human frailty or would punish wrongdoers.
He reasoned against such extenuating circumstances as his inferior
position, his reversal of fortune, the upsurge of passion, his burning
youth, the coaxing blandishments of a mistress to a slave, the absence
of accusers, the threat of calumnies, and a thousand misfortunes that
were bound to result.

22. His first act was to drop the role of servant and assume the
role of adviser and guide; he defends purity and attacks license. As a
young man to a mature woman, as a slave to a mistress (a married
woman at that, who could gratify her desires in a legitimate manner),
he who was still unmarried and a prey to concupiscence sets out to
champion chastity. It is worth repeating the noble words of this pure
youth: *My master does not know what he has in his own house only for me;
he has delivered all things into my hands and there is nothing in this house
which he has not given over to me but you, since you are his wife. How then
can I do this wicked thing, and sin against my God.*[11]

23. You do not see, he means, the One I see. You are intoxicated
by passion, but I am in my sober senses, and I see the Lord of all who
sees everything that happens. No roof, wall, or closed doors can keep
that eye from seeing what it wants to see: the darkness of night does
not impede His vision. He knows clearly what is in our minds and

observes what we are going to say before we have uttered it. At the sight of Him I am in fear and terror, and I cannot violate marriage which is nature's fountain, the entrance gate to life, God's way of preserving the human race from extinction, of planting where death strikes down, of overcoming by birth the destroying hand of death and the sickle of the reaper. In this way it is like spring succeeding to a ravaging winter, and clothing where winter has laid bare.

24. You have entered the bond of matrimony, my good lady. Cherish it. Do not break the partnership. Do not look beyond that. Cleave to your husband. Your lot is to plow the furrow with him. Do not bring dishonor on the laws of marriage or of nature. Do not defile the union blessed by God. You have slaves under you; do not become the slave of pleasures, do not bring your authority into disrepute by such a wretched slavery. Do not let such abject desires enslave your soul. Do not invert the order, abandoning the rule of reason and giving rein to the passions. I would that you, too, were free of passion. You may not heed me, you may not want to be free of this delirium, but at any rate I cannot consent to do wrong. A slave in body I am, but not in soul.[12]

25. Besides, I detest the injustice of this deed. I have received, my mistress, many blessings from both of you. Could I think of returning evil for good to my master? Although I was a bought slave, I was preferred to the home-born ones. Only yesterday or the day before I came to your house, and now I have received complete control. The master has given me charge of everything in the house; he has appointed the last slave bought to rule the others. He has made you supreme in all domestic affairs in deference to the laws of marriage. How could I look him in the face again if this were the return I made him for heaping such honors on me? I should be a wretch, dear mistress, an utter wretch, if I forgot his kindness and overlooked his goodness. Greater than all others, nay, greatest of all, is the injustice done a benefactor. I was appointed to protect his possessions, not to deprive him of them. I am not going to change from a trusted guardian into a thief. I am not going to encroach on what has remained outside my domain. I am not going to imitate Adam, our first parent. He had power over all the trees but one, and he reached for that. In his desire for the one, he lost all the others.[13]

26. Some such words this slave addressed to his evil mistress.

The fact that he was a slave and that his mistress was corrupt did him no harm, but only enhanced his golden, superior qualities. His words had no effect on her: he fled her attentions but she snatched his garment, leaving him with nothing but the covering of modesty.[14] He did not feel ashamed as did Adam after the fall, however, but felt as Adam did about his nakedness in his state of original innocence, and departed.[15] Immediately, the lady falsely accused him to her credulous husband of attempting to seduce her, although he had championed her virtue.[16]

27. In silence he listened to his master's reproof and he refused to expose the guile of the mistress. His silence only served to make his guilt more certain, but he preferred this to relating the tragic circumstances of the plot and exposing the infidelity of his mistress. He employed the necessary deliberation, but did not put forward a case against her as he might. As if caught barehanded, and without standing trial, or hearing the charge, he accepted the penalty brought against him, went to jail, was chained with criminals alongside, and accepted all his misfortunes smiling.

28. The weight of this cruel reverse did not break his strength of soul or turn its courage into cowardice. So joyful and happy was he in his troubles that he was a source of inspiration to his fellow prisoners, whom he frequently comforted when he saw them downhearted. Often a person's state of soul is reflected in the countenance which is affected by the movements of one's thoughts, and this is true of the color of the face, the motion of the eyes, and the blinking of the eyelids.[17] A grim expression indicates the rise of anger; drooping lids reveal despondency; the eyelids furrow in the act of smiling and become quite contracted in the act of thought. When the eyes are arched, it is a sign of conceit.

29. Well, since most of the inclinations of the soul are revealed on the countenance, this great champion, when we judge men's dispositions from their countenances, constantly inspired their drooping spirits. When he saw two of the Pharaoh's servants looking disconsolate,[18] the chief cupbearer and the chief baker who were with him in custody for some crime or other, he approached them and asked the cause of their despondency.

30. Although he was surrounded by such troubles and was the great-grandson of Abraham, the grandson of Isaac, and son of Ja-

cob, the most dearly beloved of his brethren, regarded as a shining light, the soul of mirth, now turned into a slave, and enduring this calamity not through being captured by fierce barbarians, but because he was enslaved through his brothers' envy, and for no display of wrongdoing, but because his dreams nourished their enmity, he took none of those things into account, not even the events subsequent to his slavery—the struggles to keep continent, the adverse judgment given after the trial, punishment instead of garlands, and prison instead of applause—no, he advances to those others in distress to console them and he asks his fellow prisoners: *Why is your countenance sadder today?*[19]

31. When they tell him that they had dreams and were perturbed because they could not interpret them, this saintly man did not groan at the mention of dreams or raise a cry at the memory of his own misfortunes. He did not shed an ignoble tear, or lament, or pour out the tragic story of his sufferings. Neither did he utter a loud laugh at the mention of dreams which he knew were false. He did not say to those prisoners: You seem unaware, my friends, of the falsehood of dreams; apparently you have not experienced how deceitful they are, and you wish to have them interpreted. I have learned from experience, and my advice to you is to laugh at them. They contain no secret truth; in fact, they are quite at variance with the truth. I entertained hopes of ruling my brothers and taking control in my father's house. Dreams led me to believe as much. Far from getting command, however, I lost my freedom and became a wretched slave. And even my slavery has not been plain sailing. After being buffeted by many a breaker, I am now confined to jail. Do not let these fantasies of night disturb you. Dreams are nothing but lies.

32. He said none of these things at all. They did not even enter his noble mind. Instead he said to them: *Does not interpretation of them belong to God? Tell me what you have dreamed.*[20] He repeatedly employed the name of God, using it to adorn his soul and speech. In saying that interpretation belonged to God, he trusted in it as if preparing himself to be a temple of God. They told him the dreams. He did the interpreting and cleared up what was puzzling and obscure. When he was finished interpreting, he said to the chief cupbearer: *Only remember me when it shall be well with you. For I was stolen away out*

of the land of the Hebrews, and here without any fault I was cast into the
dungeon of this house.[21]

33. He did not feel constrained to lay bare his brothers'
crime, but covered up for them by the mention of stealing; he did
not dare to shower abuse on those who were responsible for his
slavery, but modestly cloaked over their injustice. Far from wishing to indict his brothers, he did not even reveal the unsuspected
wickedness of his mistress. Although he knew all about her intem-
perance, lust, lying, calumny, and plotting against him, he mentioned none of these things, but merely entered a simple plea in
his own defense: *I was stolen,* he says, *away out of the land of the*
Hebrews, and here without any fault I was cast into the dungeon of this
stronghold.

34. Mark the wisdom of the words, the magnanimity, the lib-
eral, undaunted spirit that always remained unchanged, neither
elated in prosperity nor downcast in adversity, but always welcom-
ing with a smile the sorrows as well as the joys of life, and ever regarding virtue as the only object worth admiring and striving to
obtain. In what way did the wickedness of his mistress injure this
man? What harm did her sinfulness do him? Do not say that the immorality of masters harms their slaves, for it is possible to serve even
evil masters without imitating their bad example.

35. As proof that masters do not teach immorality and that
riches do not make for evil ways, look at Joseph when he was released
from slavery and was next to the throne. He is not elated by his el-
evation, but wields his authority with gentleness and displays consideration in his rule.

36. He sees his brothers plotting to kill him, but he does not
put them to death. He remembers the dreams, but forgets the envy
they caused. For famine drove his brothers into Egypt and necessity compelled them, without recognizing him, to bend the knee to
him.[22] The dreams which had caused trouble were fulfilled by the
very ones who had fought against them. And those who had sold
their brother so as not to have to recognize his authority, as the
dreams had foretold, brought about their own submission by the
sale.

37. The sale made him a slave; as a slave he rejected the advances of his mistress; by rejecting her, he was accused in the

wrong; as a result of this, he was confined to jail; while in jail he interpreted the dreams for the Pharaoh's servants; this got to the Pharaoh's ears and he too is put at his ease after being disturbed by dreams; because of his wise interpretation and the plan of action he prescribed, he was himself chosen to put the plan into operation.[23] In good seasons he built up reserves for the times when it was anticipated that the crops would fail, and he kept the abundant harvests to help out in time of famine. Thus he was instrumental in feeding not only the Egyptians but also his brothers who had exposed him to destruction.[24] They were genuinely respectful to him now, though his dreams had earlier stirred their envy, and they now pay real court to him whom they could not see so honored in a mere dream.

38. He accepts the homage; he does not pay them back in their own coin; he even gives them nourishment, attention, and free food.[25] Finally, looking at the brother born of the same mother as himself,[26] he first lays the imaginary plot[27] and then, when he heard them urging the case of the younger, saw that they were less concerned about their own safety than about the service of their aged father,[28] he drops the threatening manner, orders everybody to leave the place of judgment, and says: *I am Joseph, your brother, whom you sold into Egypt*,[29] and, lest the shock should prove too much for them and leave them paralyzed, he immediately added: *Do not fear and let it not seem to you a hard case: for God sent me before you into Egypt for your preservation.*[30]

39. When he saw that they had not a word to say for themselves and were tongue-tied with shame, he did not blame them despite his manifold sufferings, but made an excuse for them: *God sent me before you for your preservation in order that many people might be nourished.*[31] It is not your doing, he means, but the work of God. Do not worry about my slavery, which was in the designs of God. Away with fear! No harm befell me as a result. The rule of all Egypt has been conferred on me through slavery. In consequence I am next to the Pharaoh, and am entrusted with the reins of the government of this nation. That was the sort of Joseph, as a slave and as a Pharaoh, in prosperity and adversity, when things went badly and when everything was well. It follows that sin is not caused by wealth or rule, or

poverty, or slavery, but everything is under the direction of free will.[32]

Abdias, the Slave of Achab and Jezabel

40. That the immorality of masters does no harm to the virtue of slaves is easy to see from other examples. Every student of Sacred Scripture knows of the wickedness of Achab, the impiety of Jezabel, and their rage against God. Abdias, however, was a slave with them:[33] they gave him a certain amount of responsibility, but he did not follow in their footsteps but took, in fact, the opposite direction. In their wrath with God's prophets they had attempted to put them all to death, thinking it fun to destroy the prophets of God, so eager were they to extinguish the last spark of religion.

41. But Abdias opposed their designs of profanity and strove to keep alive the torch of faith. He hid a hundred prophets in two caves[34] and kept them in food while the rest of the world was in the grip of a famine brought on mankind by Elias as an answer to their sins. Undaunted by the violent temper of his superiors, the slaughter of blameless men, the tyranny of hunger, or the shortage of supplies, he made light of his efforts to take care of the holy prophets. He hated intensely the cruelty of his superiors, and he brought sufficient food to the prophets, preferring their salvation to his own safety, and thinking that life without them would not be worth living.

42. He refused his masters no service that did not conflict with his divine obligations, but he regarded regulations levelled against the Maker of all things as ridiculous, despised those who laid them down, and pitied those who were forced to carry them out. Thinking it suicidal to obey them in such circumstances, he allowed the prophets to escape who were condemned to death, for he regarded it as more glorious to die doing good than to live in sin. Thus the depravity of superiors did him no harm; their wickedness merely served to set off his admirable virtue. Nothing is firmer than a conscience determined to do good; nothing is more powerful than a soul refusing to be a slave to sin. But how I digress. The

virtue of saintly men keeps me talking and forces me to exceed the limit. Come now, bear with me longer, and let us take another example.

Abimelech, the Slave of Sedecias

43. Sedecias was the last king of the Jews. He was steeped in vice and could not bear to hear the word of God. He put the saintly Jeremias, a contemporary prophet and bearer of God's message to man, into a cistern that stank and was dirty, because he had foretold very severe and painful penalties.[35] But Abimelech, an Ethiopian slave and a eunuch, took no account of the splendor of the court, or the prevailing immorality, or the fury which the prophet had provoked, or his own servile state. He reproached his master for the unjust sentence, blamed him for his criminal attempt to wrong the prophet, reminded him of the all-seeing eye of God, and terrified him with the threat of retribution justly deserved.

44. Thus a slave, a eunuch, an alien, an Ethiopian, a member of the race of Cham, becomes adviser to a king, a full-blooded man, native born, an Israelite, a prince sprung from the race of Sem.[36] He convinces the king with his inspired words, releases the prophet from his unpleasant, dark dismal captivity and gives him food during the time he is under siege.[37] God blessed him as a reward for his goodness, and when the city was captured and the king's retainers put to death, he came safe as God had promised.[38]

The Example of Ananias, Azarias, and Misael

45. It is plain then from what has been said that evil masters not only do not harm upright slaves but are often a source of great merit to them. This can be gathered from another example. When the city was destroyed for its many sins and many had perished of hunger, many more in conflict, the king of the Chaldeans led what was left off to Babylon as prisoners of war.[39] Selecting those of noble birth, of fine physique, and in the prime of youth, he ordered them to live in the palace and be numbered among his slaves. But first he bade them get rid of the evil condition in which they were as a result of

the siege and the journey. They were given the best of food and drink brought from the king's table.

46. Now mark the nobility of those blessed youths. Nothing could persuade them to falter in their loyalty or to transgress the moral law in the smallest degree, neither the capture of the city, nor the burning of the Holy Temple,[40] nor the despoliation of the sanctuaries and holy places,[41] nor the precious vessels fallen into barbarian hands,[42] nor the liquidation of kings, nor the slaughter of priests,[43] nor their distance from their places of worship, nor their stay in a strange land, nor the absence of doctors of the law, nor the impiety of their masters, nor the constraint of slavery, nor the harsh yoke of the king, nor their tender years, nor love of life, nor fear of death, nor any similar consideration.[44]

47. They called on the man who cared for them to provide cereals for them to eat. They spurned the king's banquet and detested the variety and luxury provided, for they saw it polluted by consecration to idols. Such was their courage, their love and confidence in the God of their fathers, that they assured their attendant that cereals would be more beneficial to them than if they consumed the viands of the king.

48. They were not disappointed in their hope, but reaped the fruits of their faith. For, as they had said, they appeared better nourished and better fed than any of those who had dined sumptuously, and were adorned with greater beauty and bodily strength.[45] After some time, when they came to manhood and had given proof of their virtue, the prisoners were put to govern the natives, and then a new chapter opened in their lives.

49. The arrogant prince, imitating his father's[46] blind folly, erected a huge statue made of wood and gold and ordered everyone to give it divine worship. Those who refused he threatened with the furnace, which he stoked up to the top in his insatiable rage.[47] Many carried out the command to curry favor with the king. Many more, as was their habit, worshipped it as they would any other idol. Some abandoned their scruples through fear of the fire, and in spite of pricks of conscience offered divine worship to the idol.

50. Those noble youths, Ananias, Azarias, and Misael, however, children of the law, inheritors of the faith of Abraham, champions of piety, precursors of grace, champions of faith, slaves in body

but free men in mind, prisoners of war but more magnanimous than kings, not merely refused to adore the idol but, when they were arraigned for failing to carry out orders, offered no excuse, condemned the adorations outright, and exclaimed with a loud voice: *The God we worship is in heaven and He is able to save us from the furnace of burning fire, and to deliver us out of your hands, O king. But if He will not, be it known to you, O king, that we will not worship your gods nor adore the golden statue which you have set up.*[48]

51. We do not serve our Maker for money. We do not buy salvation by piety. We do not wish to preserve life at all costs, but we love the Master's will. If He delivers us from evil, we give thanks, but if He allows it to befall us we bow down in adoration. We know well that He can make us rise superior to all your threats. Of that we have no doubt whatever. Whether He so wishes, we do not know, for the depths of divine providence cannot be sounded. Do not delay, then. Punish us as you have prepared, for death with a good conscience is dearer to us than life in sin.

52. When they said this, he delayed no longer, but committed the youths bound to the furnace. The fire severed the iron fetters, but their hair, so easily inflammable, was preserved. The fire did not dare to touch what was fed to it, but retired, turning its back, and attacked its own worshippers, leaving the servants of God unharmed. This caused a new and unexpected wonder. Those who were in the middle of the fire treading on coals experienced no sensation of burning, while those standing without, keeping fuel to the furnace, were turned into fuel themselves.[49] Being consumed by the flames they cried out, while those in the furnace continued their hymn of praise, invoking all creation to share their song, and commanding the elements worshipped by those senseless people to praise their Benefactor. The effect of this miracle was such that this ranting, furious tyrant ran to them, adored them for refusing to worship the idol, and ordered all his subjects to adore the God of the young men.[50]

The Example of Daniel

53. The mighty Daniel had the same experience. As a prisoner of war forced to live among barbarians, he observed the laws of his

father to the letter; in carrying out the function entrusted to him he kept his soul pure and untarnished and he displayed such magnificent virtue that the savage tyrant was terrified by its luster.

54. First, he interpreted dreams[51] which were puzzling the tyrant, then he directed and advised him about what he ought to do and what would be beneficial for the future. It is unnecessary for me to relate all his wonderful exploits: how the king forbade anyone to address prayers and supplications to God; how Daniel prayed as usual in secret; and then, when the impious law was promulgated, how he went on praying to God openly, laughing at the law, and despising the man who made it; how he was given up to the lions and how he terrified even these with the keys of his virtue, bridling, as it were, their savage mouths with the impress of the divine image; how he drew the impious king to behold this wonder; how he taught him that the God of the Hebrews is the Maker and Lord of all things; how he exposed the deceit of the idols.

55. All these things can be learned from Scripture, and go to show quite clearly that those who serve wicked masters need not suffer any harm thereby, but can reach the height of perfection, free their masters from error, conduct them to the truth, and be a model of salvation to many others.

An Objection: Why Do the Just Get the Same Treatment as the Wicked?

56. Let no one, then, find fault with slavery or think that a wicked master can overpower the virtue of slaves. Behold instead the providence of God everywhere. Now someone may say perhaps: Pray, why did the God of the universe allow the just also to be made prisoners when he handed over the wicked to the king of the Babylonians? What kind of providence was this? What kind of justice? Is it not rather disorder, pandemonium, and confusion?[52]

57. Those who are ignorant of the depths of divine providence try to say so, but the initiated, who have experienced the divine mysteries,[53] know the root cause of these things. For the loving Master cares for sinners, corrects them, and does not want to neglect anyone. For this reason, when He sends criminals to prison, with them He

sends pedagogues, so to speak, to teach them to live virtuously so that they may journey on the straight way without faltering, illuminated and guided by their word and example.[54] Scripture bears testimony that the captivity of such people has been a source of salvation not merely for those in that state, but has also illuminated others with the light of divine knowledge.

An Invitation to Praise God's Goodness

58. If, then, those men have come through their trials with distinction, if they have become celebrated and illustrious and have left a salutary example to posterity, if they were a source of salvation to their fellow captives, if they were a service to the barbarians in the manner in which they kept their virtue unsullied, and in the marvels they performed because of their piety, why do you find fault with providence which sees to these things? Why do you not rather praise the Keeper of souls, the Guide of creation who directs everything with such wisdom and goodness?

59. I have demonstrated, then, from the Sacred Scriptures that a slave to an evil master can avoid evil, practice virtue, and provide masters with many helps to salvation. And if you examine the slaves round about you, you will see that, although many of them have immoral masters, they themselves spurn depravity, hold restraint in honor, and contract no vice from their masters, but imitate the example of those men of whom we have just spoken. And from what we have said and brought to your notice, you will have learned that our will is free and that God is all-wise in His providence. Consequently, sing a hymn of praise, in that way changing the blasphemy you have just been guilty of into a canticle, letting your tongue which lately was raised against God resound on His behalf, chanting the praises of the providence of the Creator, Christ, our God, to whom be glory forever and ever. Amen.

DISCOURSE 9

That the Pursuit of Justice Is Not Fruitless Even if This Is Not Apparent in the Present Life; and on the Resurrection, Based on Rational Arguments

1. The providence of God in regard to the universe could be established in a few words if all men were willing to heed that salutary exhortation of the sacred writer which clearly proclaims: *Seek not the things that are too strong for you and search not into things that are too deep for you, but the things that are commanded you think on them always.*[1]

2. For if only inquisitive minds abandoned their superfluous and useless questioning, it would be a comparatively simple and easy matter to see providence taking hold of the rudders of the universe and wisely guiding all things. Many men, however, deliberately refuse to see; they close their eyes, block their ears, and refuse to hear the testimony borne from every quarter. They make fun of all the wise, beneficent actions of God, blaspheming, slandering, and weaving countless falsehoods into a web of deceit. So it is right, I think, for us to have undertaken to refute their misrepresentations, slanderous though they were, and to show that they lack foundation.

A Resumé of the Eight Previous Discourses

3. Having invoked the providence they repudiate as our ally and outlining the tenor of our argument we have already spent eight discourses in refuting their ungracious calumnies. And we have summoned as witnesses on our side the very things they rail against:

the sky, the earth, the sea, the air, and all the bodies that inhabit them—animate and inanimate, rational and irrational, winged and footed, sea creatures and amphibian. Besides this, we have shown the wisdom and providence of God manifested in every part of the composition of the human body. Next we considered the God-given gift of reason by which man has discovered agriculture, navigation, medicine, letters, and all the other crafts and sciences which contribute to human happiness.

4. We have shown with God's assistance the place of animals, tame and wild, in the scheme of things, the utility of wealth and poverty, and the need for rulers and ruled. We have also proved that slaves are not corrupted by the wicked life of their masters so long as they wish to persevere in virtue. And we produced arguments from Scripture in support of these assertions.[2]

To the bitter critics of providence we have left the examination of those in slavery at this present time. For it is even now possible to see countless numbers in slavery to wicked masters, and far from imitating the wickedness of their masters they loath it utterly, embrace a life of virtue, and go to the other extreme from their masters.

A New Objection: Cultivating Virtue Is a Useless Pursuit

5. Perhaps critics will take their cue from this for another attack on divine providence, and will assert that those who cultivate virtue labor in vain, sowing on stones, as the proverb has it, and carrying water in a sieve[3] and performing similar tasks, futile since they derive no fruit from them. For there are men, they argue, who live in poverty and whose lot is cast in utter wretchedness. Others trail the harsh yoke of slavery, are oppressed with perpetual toils, and, what is easily the worst feature of all, many who repudiate vice in their own lives are compelled to minister to vicious masters. What reward have these men, they ask? What return does virtue make them? What are the wages of toil? What is the fruit of perspiration? What are the prizes for the contests?

Such Questioning Arises from Confusing Prosperity and Happiness

6. Admittedly we do not see all slaves gaining their freedom, nor all who are poor but upright joining the ranks of the wealthy; no, we see the majority of them remaining in their lowly state. But you, you worldly wretch, measure happiness in terms of what you eat, and taste, and see; your idea of well-being is a lofty carriage, a string of slaves, an elaborate wardrobe, horses well-groomed and decked from head to tail, a hall porter, a stately mansion, banquet halls adorned with Euboean and Thessalian stone and painted, comfortable couches, goblets, furniture, beakers, wines with a fine bouquet, banquets in the style of Sicily or Sybaris, and all the other trappings of a life of softness, license, and luxury.[4]

Men of Virtue Know How to Use Riches

7. Those who practise virtue, on the other hand, usually label these things not as happiness but as the greatest unhappiness and misfortune. The Guardian of the universe has not given men wealth to squander on luxury, or to use for immoral purposes, but rather to administer it wisely and well so as to provide the necessities of life for themselves and to give what is over and above to those in need.

8. This is not merely the divine arrangement about wealth and the framework in which holy men, following the Master, order their affairs. Even you yourselves, who are the victims of the basest ingratitude, are in the habit of rebuking those who misuse riches in this way. Or rather you regard such people as worthy of pardon, but revile divine providence for giving wealth in abundance to wicked men. You also admit that luxury of this sort should not be regarded as well-being, but that a life of justice and temperance deserves the greatest praise and the highest honor and that such a life, whether it is led by a poor man or a rich man, is equally worthy of a crown. In my opinion, even you would doubly crown poor people who strive to be virtuous since they show greater perseverance.

True Happiness Resides in the Possession of God

9. Those who are zealous in the service of God, however, do not get such a reward, nor indeed do those who are concerned about the laws of God look for this return. For praise is often known to injure many, since it makes them less attuned and slows their pace. If a man thinks he has reached the goal of his endeavor—and praise gives him to understand that he has—he stops his race and victory eludes him. This was revealed by the God of the universe, speaking through the prophet: *My people, they that call you blessed, the same deceive you and destroy the way of your steps.*[5] For praise slackens the intensity of their zeal and prevents them from reaching the goal.

10. St. Paul in his race did not listen to those who praised or slandered him, *but forgetting what was behind, and intent on what lay before, pressing on towards the mark of the prize of the heavenly summons.*[6] Those, then, who keep the laws of God do not reckon as reward for their efforts the praise they get from men. They live in expectation of the divine promises. They wait on the presiding Officer of the games. They are on the lookout for lasting crowns. They eagerly await the prizes distributed by God. They wait on the sentence of the just Judge, the resurrection of the body, the ascent into heaven, the choir of angels, and, above all, the uninterrupted vision of the Beloved for whom they traversed the sea of life and surmounted the waves of evil.

11. Their crossing was attended with great difficulties, but they refused to be submerged. Desire of the harbor supported them in their weakness and sustained them in their difficulties. Those who have attained the summit of perfection have as their harbor, not life, nor the resurrection, nor any of these admirable things, but the desired One Himself, for whose sake they counted misfortune a delight, and weary toil the sweetest repose, and time spent in the desert more desirable than city life, and poverty fairer than wealth, and irksome slavery sweeter than any position of authority. This is the reward awaited by the doers of virtue. *It is an inheritance for those that serve God,*[7] as the prophet Isaias exclaims.

12. The blessed David bears testimony to the same thing, composing a hymn of thanksgiving to the Giver of blessings, and saying: *You have given an inheritance to them that fear your name.*[8] Christ, the

Lord, has described the nature of the inheritance in the holy Gospels: *Blessed are the poor in spirit for theirs is the kingdom of heaven. Blessed are the meek for they shall inherit the land.*[9] And so on. You can easily find the relevant text in the Holy Bible. You will find the same thing in the distribution of the talents, the parable of the ten virgins, the metaphorical separation of the lambs and kids, the seed that was oversown with cockle, the net which was let down into the sea in which every kind of fish was taken and afterwards duly picked.[10] Numerous similar examples can be found in the teaching of the apostles.

Virtue Is Admitted To Be a Good Thing Even by Those Who Deny Providence

13. Leaving the investigation of these to scholars—for it would unduly lengthen the discourse—I will proceed to my next point. For it would be both superfluous and tedious to demonstrate the rewards of virtue from Sacred Scripture. Those who believe in a divine providence over men are in no need of our words, but are satisfied with the eyes of faith and the teaching of the divinely inspired Scriptures. Infidels, however, who are engulfed in the darkness of disbelief and afflicted with ingratitude towards God, turn a deaf ear on the Word of God. Passing over, therefore, scriptural proofs for the moment, let us refute them by reason.[11]

Rational Arguments to Prove that Virtue Is Rewarded

14. Let us ask them whether they regard temperance, justice, and the other kinds of virtue as good things and the cause of blessings, or do they regard them as evil? Not even the father of evil himself would ever dare to say that. How could he, seeing that he is at war daily with those who practice such virtues and ever tries to replace temperance by self-indulgence and justice by injustice. Obviously our opponents would have to agree with their master and not attempt to outdo their father in malice. *For the disciple is not above his master,*[12] as the Lord says. Let us ask them another question. If those virtues are noble, nay, passing noble, and good, exceedingly good—a thing that no one short of a raving lunatic would deny—is it not fitting to

call those who love virtue honorable and good, and fitting, too, that they should reap a reward not only equal to their toils but far surpassing them?

15. If the farmer who sows his seeds reaps a more abundant harvest, and the gardener who plants trees has the consolation of seeing the fruits bud, would it not be absurd if those who cultivate virtue and tend this spiritual garden with much toil and perspiration were the only ones whose work is fruitless and whose perspiration goes for nothing? Those who exercise their bodies or their voices get garlands and prizes, and are applauded by spectators. Are those who strive to be good to be held in less esteem than athletes and boxers? Is this contest, which is the major one, to have no spectators, no ring master, no honors, no prize, no crown?

16. Tragic and comic actors have an objective in their art, and endure its hazards in the hope of the rewards. Charioteers take risks in the expectation of victory and a good reputation with the spectators. They get their pay too from the owners. The pilot, looking to port, defies the waves, and, animated by the desire of gain, endures the impact of the breakers. The worker in leather or bronze and artisans in general look to the result of their labors, and the hope of profit joined to their toil produces an admixture of pleasure in the perspiration.[13] Has the pursuit of virtue (whether you wish to call it an art, or a science of combats and contests, or a culture, or a cultivation) no result which can usefully be recalled as a spur in time of desolation? Is it all in vain that temperate men live soberly, fighting against the many subtle passions and trying to quench their ardor?

17. Is it in vain that just men spar with injustice, do not touch what does not belong to them, and give away what does? Is the possession of virtue useless to those who have it? Are those who bear grievous misfortunes with dignity to have no arbitration? It cannot be, it cannot be. For virtue is an admirable and desirable possession, as you would concede if you were directed by the force of conscience. Knowledge of this fact is innate in man, and no one who possesses virtue needs external proofs of it from God or man. Internal proof is ample for such a person.

Wrongdoers by Sinning in Secret Tacitly Admit that Virtue Is a Good Thing

18. Evildoers, too, admit this inasmuch as they sin in secret, and if they are detected they frame excuses for themselves. Burglars, body snatchers, footpads, paramours, murderers, and those who dare to perform similar crimes try to do them under cover of night. Anyone attempting any of these things in daylight would find himself without support. In trying to conceal their methods, then, they reveal their mental attitudes, for they would not conceal them if they thought they were acting properly. In trying to escape notice and in fearing detection, they admit the malice of their conduct. You know, then, most ungrateful creatures, that the possession of virtue is good and that very many toils attend it.

Virtue Is Not Always Rewarded in This Life

19. It is only fitting then that it should be praised by its friends and adversaries alike and that what is attained with such difficulties should get the return that is its due. In this life, however, we see many seeking after virtue and enduring numerous hardships in its cause, but not all enjoy praise and honor as a result. We see some talked about by all as lovers of virtue: these are well known, and when they die they leave an indelible reputation. Others are completely unknown and inconspicuous, and resemble a pearl buried in the deep or an ostrich in the sand.

20. In view of this, let us think to ourselves why it is that of those who hold religion in esteem some achieve great fame and others make no impression at all. Let us also take into consideration the fact that since the Creator and Judge of the universe is just, He will give a just decision on those who have been on his side and will not allow the balance of justice to be upset.

A Future Life Will See Justice Done to All

21. When we see both types of people ending their days—those in high standing and those who are quite worthless, members of the

common herd—let us consider once more that He has prepared another life in which to reward, according to their deserts, those who
have lived the good life. Indeed He has already unmistakably honored some of them by making their crowns of virtue manifest. But
the fact that not all men appear illustrious and distinguished in the
present life reveals the reality of a future life.

22. The honor given to some is a sign of God's justice. The fact
that not all virtuous people get equal returns is a proof of a future life,
and strengthens the expectation of the things to come. For this reason
the Ruler of the universe does not broadcast in this life the names of
all the virtuous, nor does He reprove all who live in sin. He singles
out some for vengeance, revealing the justice of the verdict, hoping
thereby to alarm the others, and He rouses them to repentance. In
not destroying all who do evil He gives us another proof of a future
life.

23. If there is no life after our departure from here below, those
who are reproved in this life are done great injustice and those who
are not escape due punishment. Quite clearly, too, those who devote
themselves to philosophy are done a great injury for they reap no utility or recognition from their study, while others who lead a similar
upright life enjoy great renown. But to call the Fount of Justice unjust
is the last word in blasphemy and transcends the extremes of folly.
Now if the Ruler of the universe is just, as indeed He is, if He sees
everything that is done, if He judges fairly and maintains in equilib-
rium the balance of justice even when it wishes to be upset, it is a
manifestation of His loving mercy and not of any injustice.

For there does exist another life in which those who here escape
punishment will pay the due penalty, and those who enjoyed no return for their efforts at virtue in the present life will obtain the reward
of their strivings. Perhaps you find yourself in agreement with me.

The Pagan Greeks Believed in a Future Life

24. Now the Greeks, though they did not receive a prophet, an
apostle, or an evangelist, were directed by nature alone and were
convinced of the truth of these things, although they were in error

on many points and mingled fable with true doctrines. Their poets[14] and philosophers[15] alike believed and taught that the wicked would be punished and the just rewarded in a future life, and they left a record of their teaching in their writings. Perhaps you, too, persuaded by natural reason, instructed by these truths, and convinced by what has just been said, will join your voice to theirs and agree that these things are so.

What the Soul Might Say to the Judge if It Alone Were Punished

25. It may be urged, however, that only souls will be liable to reward or punishment, and that the body will be cast aside, abandoned to putrefaction as being quite useless and bereft of reason. How could this be? How could the soul only be crowned when it fought and won in company with the body? Or how could it be separated from the body for punishment?

For the punished soul might well speak like this to its Judge: I was not alone, Master, in transgressing your laws. The body was with me in running adrift on the rocks of wickedness. Or rather, if I must speak the truth, it swept me into the abyss of sin. Ensnared by the eyes of the body I plundered other men's couches, soliciting what belonged to another. I desired possessions and riches at which they forced me to look. I fell into the depth of injustice. Its passions enslaved me and took away the freedom you gave me. For I was compelled to serve, a slave like the other passions, and wait on the needs of the body. Appetite forced me to self-indulgence, self-indulgence to gluttony, and gluttony gave rise to unlawful desires.

26. I often yielded reluctantly to the constraints of the flesh and, distressed and greatly pained, I was forced to minister to its desires. Often, too, I resisted and gallantly repelled its attacks. The continual struggle, however, often got the better of me and in wretched thrall I obeyed my sister, the body, and became worn out and exhausted. The pain attacked me again and as it increased I was ensnared. Thenceforth I again suffered its unruly ways and did not know what to do, for the wretched state caused me great annoyance, and yielding to it only intensified the battle and broke down my defenses. Do not,

then, hand me over to punishment on my own, Master, but either deliver both the body and me from evils, or commit it with me to punishment.

What the Body Might Say if It Were Isolated for Punishment

27. The body which has attended on the soul's every wish might likewise say to the just Judge if it had any use of speech: When you fashioned me, Lord, you breathed a soul into me or, if we must establish every step in nature by principles, it was I who enjoyed creation first and then you gave me the vital power of the soul. I was its counterpart during its time in paradise. We passed the same period of conception in the maternal womb. We both came into this life at birth after the pains of travail and enjoyed together the light of day and inhaled the beneficial air.[16]

28. We went through life together. The soul never did anything of any good on its own; with my help it amassed its store of virtue. It was I who kept the sleepless fasts. It was I who lay on the ground and endured all the other mortifications while I built up resources with it here on earth. I lined its prayer with tears. I provided it with a heart when it felt constrained to grieve in the service of the Spirit. It was with my tongue that it continued to chant Your praises. It was through my lips that its petitions reached You. It reaped the fruits of Your loving mercy by raising my hands to heaven. It was on my feet that it ran to Your sacred shrines.

29. I provided the ears for it to receive Your oracles. It used my eyes to look at the sun and moon, the galaxy of stars, the heavens, the earth, the sea, and the whole visible creation and thus it reached a concept of You, concluding from the magnitude and beauty of visible objects that You were the Creator. With my eyes it made captive the spoils of wealth hidden in the Scriptures. With my fingers it committed Your divine teachings to writing, leaving an immortal record of these things. With my hands it erected the houses of prayer throughout the world. With my cooperation it fulfilled the precepts of charity. With my hands it washed the feet of the saints, and helped those in affliction by rendering assistance to their bodily ills.[17]

30. Do not, then, separate me, Master, from my mate who was

joined to me from above. Do not break the union which did not simply come about by chance but was decreed from the beginning by Your heavenly design. Render, instead, the one crown to those who have run the same race. For this is characteristic of Your equity; this befits Your just judgment. In such terms would the body that had served the soul in well-doing speak if it enjoyed the use of speech.

The Just Judge Needs No Such Reminders. Examples of How Men Reward Valor

31. The body and soul that have cooperated in evil will say none of these things, for the Judge needs no such supplication. Just as He directs wisely, so He judges justly. And just as He assigns bodies to souls, so He renders to everyone according to his deserts. If a brave soldier is victorious in battle, his comrades honor him by a likeness of him together with the equipment he used in routing the enemy, either painted, or sculptured, or engraved in stone, or bronze, or wood. If he used a bow in his victory, then he is depicted with a bow; if a sword, then with a sword; and similarly with a helmet or a shield or any other piece of equipment. Now would it not be absurd for the soul that had campaigned with the body and had overcome invisible enemies and was made in the likeness of the Creator of the Universe, to stand bare and deprived of its panoply?

32. The soldier is not the only one seen honored in this way. The athlete is similarly honored, as also the boxer, the runner, the tragic actor, the charioteer. Each of these is represented with the instrument with which he made his conquest. The actor is depicted with his buskins and his general's cloak, with the mask of Oenomaus or Creon[18] all but proclaiming to the world that it was with these he acted and made his conquest. The runner is stripped and in a running position, thus revealing the nature of his contest. The wrestler stands in typical pose or holding the crown and showing the uninformed what kind of competition he contested. The boxer spars with an opponent. The rider shows by his appearance and whip what art he followed to reach victory.

33. Do not you, then, pretend that human nature is less honorable than any of these pursuits which are only its manifestations.

Do not imagine that God is less just than men, for He is the fount of justice. Do not doubt that He will honor those who succeed for Him, just as men do. For if men frequently, with no regard for justice, or rather holding it in very slender esteem, are in the habit of honoring those who engage in worthless, unprofitable contests, how much more will the Judge and Prescriber of virtue honor and crown its great and illustrious exponents, and surpass justice in the size of His gifts?

The Resurrection of the Body Seems Impossible to You, But Is Easy for God

34. I know why you ran adrift into this blasphemy. You judge divine things by the standards of your own weakness, making that the boundary of the divine power, and thinking that what is impossible to you is also impossible with God. But that is not so. By no means. Clay has not the same power as the potter though both have the same nature, seeing that both came from the earth. And the man speaking to Job testifies to this: *Of the same clay you and I were formed.*[19] Yet though the potter and the clay are of the same nature one does not find the same function in each. The one moves, the other is moved; one fashions, the other is fashioned; one mixes, the other is mixed; one shapes, the other takes shape, and the potter changes its shape whatever way he wishes. If, when the nature is the same, the function is different, there will be a greater difference still in function when the natures are different. For it is impossible to compare things that are incomparable. How then could you compare what is created from nothing with what existed from all eternity? Or the temporal with the eternal? Or what is made of clay with the Creator of heaven and earth?

35. Do not think, then, that what is absolutely impossible with you is impossible also with God, for all things are possible and quite easy to the divine nature. He is therefore able to reassemble the body even after it has become decomposed, turned into dust, and scattered in all directions, in rivers, in seas, among birds of prey, or wild beasts, in fire, in water (I am bringing forward all your grounds of

disbelief),[20] and can restore you to your former stature and gracefulness.

Creation Was More Difficult Than the Resurrection of the Body

36. At His merest wish the heavens were made, arched according to His wishes. He wished it and the earth was made underneath, and it was suspended with its foundation as God had determined. *He said the word and light was made.*[21] He gave the order and the waters were assembled. At His next command they were separated from the earth. At His nod the earth was adorned with meadows and groves and all kinds of crop land. He spoke the word and countless species of living creatures were made on land and in the water and in the air. If He did this with a word, surely He can with even greater ease resurrect a body, for it is easier by far to renovate something that already existed than to create the nonexistent without matter.[22]

Nature Teaches and Proclaims a Resurrection

37. If you do not believe this, Paul, the world-famed teacher, will tell you: *Senseless man, that which you sow is not quickened, except it die first. And that which you sow you sow not the body that shall be: but bare grain as of wheat or of some of the rest. But God gives it a body as He will.*[23] If you think that His doctrine is silly and fictitious, examine nature which teaches and proclaims a resurrection.[24] The farmer first plows the furrows, digs, as it were, graves, then scatters the seeds, burying them just as bodies are interred in the tomb. He can do nothing more than this, except that if water is plentiful he can merely apply it.

God's Creative Activity in Nature

38. But God either sends rain from the heavens or waters the seeds from fountains and rivers. Watering and irrigating them in this way and allowing them to decay much like human bodies, He leaves

the seeds of no further use for human consumption but extremely useful to the crops that spring from them. When they receive the moisture and become dilated and decayed, they shoot forth the roots. These get a hold in the surrounding earth, draw in through the roots as through tubes, and give birth to a plant which raises itself aloft. Bit by bit it is nourished in the way I have explained, and sends up the shoot and produces the awn that keeps the fruit concealed, surrounded as it were by its satellites, the ears.

39. Do not disbelieve, then, in the resurrection of the body, since you are constantly seeing reproductions of it and constantly hearing proclamations of it. To strengthen your belief in it let us return to the study of plants. Look at the twigs of the vines and of the other trees or the so-called grafts or the offshoots of the roots. These are apparently dead when cut; placing them in a hole is like placing them in a tomb. Then they are covered with earth, decay, and, when God wishes they strike root, send up shoots, ripen, grow up, and become weighed down with fruit, and the plants surpass in beauty the slips that were buried.[25]

The Creation of the Human Body

40. Why speak of branches, trees, and seeds? Examine with me the formation of your own body. Look at the materials you were formed from, useless, insignificant, and no better than a downward flow. Nevertheless, this useless, insignificant, inanimate matter that lacks a spirit and is altogether devoid of sensibility becomes man at the will of God, and, despite its uniformity, assumes many forms, some tough and durable, others soft and supple, others loose and porous, others compact and dense, others stout and smooth, others slender, reticular, and fibrous, others tubular and porous, others solid and without any pores.[26]

41. And one can see originating from this slender material blood vessels, air passages, and solid joints, soft flesh and solid bones, shining eyes and clear pupils, smooth cheeks, fine hair, and all the other constituents of the human body. Many learned men in this field have tried to describe their use and operation, but words fail them at the wisdom of the Creator and they have ended their discourse with a

song of praise. And these were not of our fold but belonged to the sheep wandering outside it.[27] Nevertheless, enjoying the good pastures, with no one to guide and instruct them but nature alone, they praised with all their might the Pastor, Protector, and Maker of the universe. You, however, besides nature, have the law to teach you, and the prophets who treat of religious matters, and the company of apostles teaching you about the present and foretelling what is to come. Recognize, then, the benefit of salvation which is conferred on you from every side.

The Last Day Will See Justice Done to All

42. The nature of embryos and the initial formation of human beings are sufficient proof for you of the resurrection of the body. Imagine the maternal womb as the earth, the matrix as the tomb, the semen as the most insignificant portion of nature resembling the dust that remains of the body, which is altogether imperceptible to man, but is visible to God, for no one escapes that eye. *In His hand are the ends of the earth, and He Himself has measured the water in His hand, and the heavens with His span, and the whole earth with the flat of His hand.*[28] It is easy for Him to see the contents of His hand. Indeed it would be quite easy for you yourself. For if you wish to mingle millet, lentil, wheat, and barley, you can easily distinguish them again if you wish. If, then, the ends of the earth are in the hands of God, it is quite easy for Him to separate even elements that are completely intermingled.

43. Imagine, then, the matrix as the tomb, the semen, the mortal remains, the birth as the Creator, the birth pangs as the last day of life and the fearful voice of the archangel. *For the trumpet shall sound and the dead shall rise again incorruptible.*[29] Then shall we render the accounts of our deeds in life. Then shall we give an explanation of what good we have done or what evil. Then the hidden thoughts of our mind will be revealed to all. Then all men will stand at the judgment seat of Christ, so that each may reap what his mortal life has earned, good or ill, according to his deeds.[30]

44. Fear these things, brethren. Lay aside hatred of providence. Avoid this wretched ill-will. Enough of this blasphemy; it is inexcusable. Make a pact of friendship with the Creator that He may di-

rect us as friends and not throw us out of the ship like enemies. Sing the praises of the rudders of providence, so that by their guidance you may escape the breakers of the present life and may enjoy these tranquil harbors in Christ Jesus Our Lord, because to Him is due all glory forever and ever. Amen.

DISCOURSE 10

THAT GOD FROM THE OUTSET HAS EXTENDED HIS CARE TO ALL MEN AND NOT ONLY TO THE JEWS; AND CONCERNING THE INCARNATION OF THE SAVIOR

Mysteries Are Inscrutable

1. I am well and truly aware that the sea of divine wisdom and providence is unfathomable. And I am mindful too of the most holy prophet exclaiming: *Your judgments are deep as the abyss.*[1] I am also mindful of the great herald of truth, the inspired Paul, who also said: *O the depth of the riches, of the wisdom, and of the knowledge of God. How incomprehensible are His judgments and how unsearchable His ways.*[2] We do not then recklessly dare the impossible but marvel with all our might at the words of God and praise Him to the best of our ability.

Curiosity Leads to Confusion

2. For we know that those who try to look at the sun longer than necessary[3] do not enjoy what they desire but weaken their sight, and instead of deriving light from it behold darkness. The human spirit is obviously confused in the very same way. For often, misled by curiosity, it tries to discover what support the earth has, what is its foundation, on what is it upheld, or again of what nature are the highest heavens, and what exists outside the universe,[4] but far from reaching a successful conclusion to such investigations man is filled in the end with great confusion and doubt.

The Limitations of Knowledge

3. The blessed Paul, knowing this weakness of the human intellect, addresses us in the following terms: *If any man think that he knows anything, he has not yet known as he ought to know.*[5] And again: *We know in part: and we prophesy in part. But when that which is perfect is come, that which is in part shall be done away.*[6] And in another place: *I see now through a glass in a dark manner; but then face to face. Now I know in part; but then I shall know even as I am known.*[7] And again: *When I was a child I spoke as a child, I understood as a child, I thought as a child. But when I became a man, I put away the things of a child.*[8]

4. This holy man provides all these examples in his desire to convince all men to check the mind's insatiable curiosity lest it should attempt the impossible, and also to await a complete knowledge of these things in the life to come. This is why he calls the mind given to us in the present time *that of a child*. Comparing it to the teaching of the law he calls it *perfect*, but comparing it to the life without suffering or without end, he calls it *childish*. Now this is a clear proof of divine providence. For God, wisely directing all things and knowing how puffed up we become with arrogance, has not given a clear knowledge of divine mysteries even to the saints. For *knowledge puffs up*,[9] as St. Paul knew, and how right he was.

The Virtuous Praise God Even in Adversity

5. But God has set up this prize of virtue so that, having nobly contended in this life, after divesting ourselves of the passions and investing our body with freedom from corruption and concupiscence, we might then receive perfect knowledge, liable to no further injury in that we have been delivered from the passions and placed outside the dangers of combat. Let us, then, not essay the impossible, but rather let us be satisfied with what we possess, sing hymns to our good Master as we go, and praise His beneficence for what we have.

Justice Will Prevail Ultimately

6. Do we see some virtuous men living in glory, honor, and respect? Let us do reverence to the One who established virtue as a prize or goal, and proclaimed it as right and just. Do we see others espousing the good life with equal eagerness but not attaining to the same good name among men? Let us not be perturbed, my friend, but rather trust that they who strive earnestly for the prize of endurance will be proclaimed for so doing in the world to come, as we have said in the preceding discourse. And let us not hurl blasphemous words against providence.

7. For it is absurd, the height of stupidity, nay, of extreme insanity, for those only to sing the praises of the Pilot who ride the rough waves and are borne on the breakers, and who pass their lives in great misfortune, while those who are situated outside the range of fire, as the proverb has it, being spectators rather than contestants, hurl their blasphemous taunts at the ringmaster when they cannot pelt him literally. That those who cultivate virtue praise the God of the universe not merely when they are borne on favorable winds, but even when they are struggling with billow and storm, can be perceived from the exclamation of the blessed David, a man who spent a lifetime in warfare and struggle with countless misfortunes: *What shall I render to the Lord for all the things that He has rendered to me?*[10]

8. You can likewise hear the saintly Daniel[11] and those holy young men, when they were undergoing those terrible perils, praising God, calling publicly to mind faults which they had not committed, confessing that they were paying the penalty for their offenses, yet never claiming the crowns that were their due, nor finding fault with the yoke of judgment. Oppressed with hunger, the mighty patriarch Abraham,[12] who had received the promises from God, nobly endured its pangs. Twice[13] deprived of his wife, and seeing her in the midst of the barbarians, he gave continuous thanks to Him who had called him, and joyfully sailed the rough seas of life awaiting the fulfillment of the promises.

9. What words, pray, could match his magnanimity? Who can marvel sufficiently at his lofty philosophy? Leaving it, then, to zealous readers to study the narrative and to learn in more detail about

his bravery, his endurance, his temperance, his justice, his constancy, his love of God, in a word his exalted virtue, I shall proceed in my discourse to the characters of the New Testament.

New Testament Endurance in the Pursuit of Virtue

10. Behold Peter and John, those towers of sanctity, pillars of truth, supports of the Church. When scourged by the Jews they are glad and rejoice, *that they were accounted worthy to suffer reproach for the name of Christ*.[14] The writer of these events, when he says that they were scourged, does not say that they bore the lash patiently and with dignity, but that they departed rejoicing and happy. Enduring is one thing, but rejoicing is quite a different matter. For a person often endures the assault of trials but does so in pain and distress. The one who rejoices, on the other hand, proclaims aloud his gladness of soul. Thus the blessed Paul, the greatest exponent of sacred eloquence, exclaims, *I please myself in infirmities, in reproaches, in necessities, in persecutions, in distresses for Christ*.[15] Now he does not say: *I bear* or *I endure*, but *I please myself*, which indicates the intensity of his pleasure. And in another place he says: *Now I rejoice in my sufferings*[16] for Christ. And again: *the sufferings of this time are not worthy to be compared with the glory to come that shall be revealed to us*.[17] And again: *Who shall separate us from the love of Christ? Shall tribulation, or distress, or persecution, or famine, or nakedness, or danger, or the sword?*[18] And a little further on: *For I am sure that neither death, nor life, nor things present, nor things to come, nor height, nor depth, nor any other creature shall be able to separate us from the love of God which is in Christ Jesus, Our Lord*.[19]

11. But the day would not be long enough for me to collect all such statements of this great master of those who strive after perfection. If, then, those who have attained every kind of virtue and reached the summit of perfection, far from being annoyed at the storms in the sea of life, continue to rejoice as if they were borne on a favorable wind, and try not to inquire too closely into these happenings, but to sing the praises of the Pilot even when breakers surge up, gales and squalls lash them, and the sea is in a turbulent swirl, why should you, who are out of the reach of the sea and on dry land, not out on the deep, jibe at what happens, why should you praise the

contestants and criticize at the same time the One who is conducting the contest? For it is only proper, I take it, that those who marvel at the virtue of these contestants should also cherish their judgment. Now they regarded any misfortune endured in preaching the Gospel as the greatest blessing—slaughter, stoning, burning, affront, reviling, imprisonment, hazards on land and on sea, in cities and in the country, at the hands of friends and of strangers.

The Incarnation Is the Supreme Example of God's Loving Care

12. But we have digressed in our discourse. Come, let us say a few words about the Incarnation of Our Savior, which is the summit[20] of God's providence toward men. For nothing shows His immeasurable goodness so well, neither sky, nor earth, nor sea, nor air, nor sun, nor moon, nor stars, nor the whole visible and invisible creation which has been created by a single word, or rather which a word has produced as soon as it was willed, nothing shows His providence so well as the only begotten Son of God, who was *in the form of God,*[21] *the brightness of His glory and the figure of His substance,*[22] who was *in the beginning and was with God and was God, by whom all things were made*[23] taking *the form of a servant to be made in the likeness of man and in habit found as a man,* and He was seen on the earth, and He conversed with man, and He *took our weaknesses and bore our infirmities.*[24] Now the blessed Paul recognized this as the greatest proof of the love of God for men and exclaimed: *But God commends His charity towards us because when as yet we were sinners Christ died for us.*[25] And again: *He that spared not even His own Son, but delivered Him up for us all, how has He not also, with Him, given us all things?*[26]

Christ Became Man to Make Men His Adopted Sons

13. Saint John agrees that this is so: *For God so loved the world as to give His only begotten Son for it so that whosoever believe in Him may not perish but may have life everlasting.*[27] God, then, has not simply a care for men, He has a loving care for them. Such is the excess of His love that He gave us His only begotten Son, consubstantial with Him,

born *before the rising of the daystar*,[28] whom He used as His collaborator in creation, to be our Physician and Savior and to confer through Him the gift of adoptive sonship on us.

14. For when the Creator perceived that mankind had gone over to the standard of the hated tyrant and had fallen into the very abyss of evil, trampling recklessly on the laws of nature when He saw too that the visible creation, though it manifests and proclaims that it is the work of a Creator, is unable to convince of this fact those who have fallen into the depths of insensibility, He contrived our salvation with wisdom and justice. For He did not wish to liberate us merely in virtue of His omnipotence, nor did He want mercy to be His sole weapon against the enemy who had enslaved our nature—the enemy might misrepresent such mercy as unjust—but instead He contrived a way that was full of kindness and adorned with justice. Uniting conquered nature to His own, He enters the contests, prepares to reverse[29] the defeat, and to retrieve by conquest[30] the one who had been badly vanquished of old and to undo the tyranny of the one who had bitterly enslaved us, and restore us to our former freedom.

15. For this reason, Christ the Lord is born like us from a woman. His birth in addition was a virginal one.[31] For it was a virgin who conceived and gave birth to Christ the Lord. Accordingly when you hear the word Christ, know that He is the only begotten Son, the Logos born from the Father before the ages, who has put on human nature, and do not think that this incarnation is something sordid, for nothing can pollute this unblemished nature.[32]

16. If the sun, being corporeal, for it is visible and admits of dissolution, cannot be polluted when it passes through corpses, putrid mud, and many other evil-smelling substances,[33] much more impervious to such pollution is the maker of the sun, the Creator of the universe, the incorporeal one, the invisible, the unchangeable, the one who always remains the same.

17. And that those things are so, the following reflection will bear out. We both assert and believe that his nature is infinite, for we have heard him exclaim: *Do I not fill the heavens and the earth, says the Lord.*[34] And, *Heaven is my throne, the earth is the footstool for my feet.* And, *who has measured the waters with his hand, the heavens with his palm, and the whole earth with the span of his hand?*[35] and many questions of a similar nature. And the blessed David exclaims: *In his hand are the ends of*

the earth. And the divine Paul: *For in him we live, and move, and are.*[36] If, therefore, we live and move, and are in him, as the saying of the apostle goes, there is no part of the world devoid of God. But among created things, some things are sacred and some are profane; some goods are fragrant, some fetid, while among human beings some are adorned with piety, others wallow in wickedness. He, however, who fills all things delights in those who fear him, but hates *all the workers of iniquity and will destroy all who speak falsehood and the bloody and deceitful man the Lord will abhor and with Him the base man will not dwell.*[37] Nothing then injures Him who cannot be defiled.

18. If those who practice medicine do not themselves contract the wounds they are engaged in attending, but restore health to the ailing without incurring any injury themselves in the process, the supreme Artist, God, who has an impassible nature that is superior to change and does not admit of mutation, will certainly derive no defilement whatever from healing us.[38] Let us marvel, then, at Him for not entrusting our salvation to angels, but for undertaking in person the healing of mankind.

Christ's Earthly Life

19. Christ, Our Lord, then, born in this manner, is fed by His mother as we are: He reclines in a manger, the feeding place of animals, both to rebuke men for their unreasonableness and to reveal His own benevolence in that, as God, being the One who nourished us, He became as man the nourishment of men who had become as senseless as the animals. Now, however, human nature, having shed its ignorance and recovered the use of reason, the nourishment received at the mystical table, typified by the manger, and men are taught that *man when he was in honor did not understand, but was compared to senseless beasts and was like them.*[39] A manger received that divine, spiritual food. When nature returned to itself and recognized clearly that the divine likeness was in it,[40] this nourishment next passed to the spiritual table.

20. Christ next received circumcision and offered sacrifices, for He was man and human nature should submit to the observance of law. As man He flees to Egypt, although He is present everywhere

as God and assists all men, as Sacred Scripture says.[41] Although free from the stain of sin He comes to John the Baptist and submits to baptism to fulfil all justice. He is proclaimed from on high by the Father and is manifested by the Spirit. For the Father exclaimed from heaven: *This is My beloved Son in whom I am well pleased.*[42] And the Holy Spirit, appearing in the form of a dove, drew the voice to Himself and explained to the bystanders who He was who had received testimony from the Father.

21. Next He proceeds to the struggles with the devil.[43] The desert becomes the scene of the struggles, the spectators are the crowds of angels, the enemy is the enemy of truth. The devil, when he heard His voice, mindful of the forebodings of the prophet, feared the contest. He could not bear the flash of His virtue, yet he was compelled to struggle; when he recognized the voice, he dreaded the fight. He, however, who created our nature and champions our cause, who crowns our efforts and presides over our conflicts, does not fear the antagonist.

22. He does not scare away the beast, but encourages him, provokes him to combat, so that He may wipe out the earlier victory. He allows His own body to feel hungry after its forty days' fast. He does not allow it to fast longer than those who had fasted previously so that its true humanity might be believed in. The enemy saw hunger and hoped for victory; he attacked with confidence, and thought he saw the old Adam when he saw the passion of hunger. He went up to Him as to Adam, but found the Creator of Adam in Adam's nature and said to Him: *If you are the Son of God, command that these stones be made bread,*[44] producing the word of heaven for confirmation and wishing to have it ratified by a miracle of loaves.

23. From this you can clearly see how our adversary utilizes us in his vicious attacks. If he sees that we are hungry, he makes his attack on that front. But our Savior, although He is hungry and in need of food, does not proceed to work a miracle. He repels the tyrant with a text from Scripture, saying: *Not on bread alone will man live but on every word that proceeds from the mouth of God.*[45] He answered as man, concealing His divinity for the moment, and gained a human victory. Bread, He says, is not the only support in life for man, but every word spoken by God is calculated to give life to hungry men.

24. We believe that, if God willed it, human life could be sus-

tained without bread. When he had loosened the toils of the enemy in this manner and had shown that his second and third attacks were unavailing, making His answers as man that He might regain the supremacy lost by man, He routs the enemy, puts an end to the tyranny exercised by this common scourge of humanity, and is ministered to by the onlooking angels: *Angels came*, we are told, *and ministered to Him*.[46]

25. Next He performed countless miracles. He made wine from water without shoots or earth; from five loaves He fed many thousands; with a word He made the lame walk, cleansed the lepers, gave life to withered hands, gave the gift of sound vision to sightless eyes. He opened tombs and instructed the imprisoned and fetid corpses to run and flee from the hands of death, to listen to the call of the Creator, and not to be held captive by the gates or chains of death.[47] After doing these things and very much else besides, He is maligned by the Jews and freely submits to their plots, for He foresees the salvation of men that would result therefrom.

26. These things, indeed, He had foretold from the beginning through the prophet: *I do not resist:* he said, *I do not shrink, I have given my back to the strikers and my cheeks to them that slapped them. I have not turned away my face from them that reviled me and spat on me.*[48] He foretold these things and suffered them; He was nailed to the cross, paying the penalty not for personal sins (*for he did not sin, neither was guilt found in his mouth*),[49] but paying the debt of our nature. For our nature was in debt after transgressing the laws of its Maker. And since it was in debt and unable to pay, the Creator Himself in His wisdom devised a way of paying the debt; taking human limbs as capital He invested it wisely and justly in paying the debt and freeing human nature.

27. Our evidence for this is in Isaias and Paul, one of whom foretold the passion and the other interpreted the prophecy after it was fulfilled. The same Spirit spoke through both of them: *A man in distress, and used to enduring suffering,*[50] naming him from what he saw, for He suffered in his vision. *This man*, he says, *bears our sufferings and endures pains for us. We have reckoned him to be in pain, smitten by God, and in distress.*[51]

28. Those who saw Him nailed to the cross presumed that He was being punished for countless misdeeds and was paying the pen-

alty for personal faults. It was for this reason that the Jews nailed Him between two malefactors, wishing thereby to gain for Him an evil reputation. But the Holy Spirit teaches through the prophet that He was wounded for our iniquities and weakened for our sins. He makes this clearer in what follows: *Chastisement for our peace was inflicted on Him and by His bruises we were healed.*[52] We were enemies of God, in that we had offended Him, so chastisement and retribution were due from us.

29. We did not, however, settle the debt. Our Savior settled it Himself. And by so suffering He bequeathed peace with God to us. What follows makes this clearer: *All we like sheep have gone astray; man has lost his way. And so He has been led as a sheep to the slaughter and dumb as a lamb before his shearer.*[53] It was fitting for Him to heal like by like, and to recall the other wandering sheep by a sheep. He became a sheep, without being changed into one, or without being altered, or without quitting His own essence. He plainly assumed the nature of a sheep and, just as the ram is the leader of the sheepfold, so He became the leader of His fold and made all the sheep follow Him.

30. As a sheep, then, He became a victim and was offered a sacrifice on behalf of the entire race. Not without reason did the prophet mention slaughter and shearing in the same breath. Since He was God and man, the divine nature remained intact after the body had been slaughtered. Of necessity, then, the inspired Isaias depicted for us the slaughter of a sheep and the shearing of a lamb. For, according to him, he was sheared as well as slaughtered. For He endured death in His humanity. But as God He remained alive and impassible, and gave the fleece of His body to the shearers.[54] Thus the blessed Isaias described for us the sufferings of our Savior and taught us their cause.

31. And the God-like Paul expressly said: *Christ has redeemed us from the curse of the law, being made a curse for us. For it is written: "Cursed is everyone that hangs on a tree."*[55] In saying *for us*, He showed that though He was Himself innocent and free of all blame He paid our debt and deemed us worthy of freedom, although we lay under countless penalties and were compelled to live in slavery as a result. He redeemed us at the price of His own blood.

32. Thus Paul says in another place: *We were ransomed at a great price.*[56] And again: *In your knowledge a weak brother is lost for whom Christ died:*[57] Because of this He undertook death on a cross since this kind

of death in the eyes of the law was cursed. Cursed too was our nature in transgressing the law. For it is written: *Cursed be he that does not abide by the things laid down in the book of the law.*[58] And so He takes on Himself the common curse and resolves it by being unjustly put to death. For although He lay outside the curse (*for He did no sin, neither was guilt found in his mouth*),[59] He endured the death of sinners and took action against the common enemy, nature's avenging spirit.

The Crucified Christ Addresses the Devil

33. He became the ally and advocate of our nature and addressed our deadly enemy in these apt terms:[60] You are caught, you utter wretch; you are laid low in your own snares; your sword has entered your own heart; your bows are broken; you have dug a trench and have fallen into it yourself. The nets you set have ensnared your hands. Tell me, why have you nailed My body to the cross and committed it to death? What kind of evil did you see in Me? Or what transgression of the law? Examine me more closely now, naked on the cross; look at My tongue free of defilement, My ears free of maliciousness, My eyes that do not admit anything impure from without, My hands that kept away from any wrongdoing, being adorned rather with all justice, My feet that, to quote the prophet, did not run in the way of wickedness but traversed the course of virtue. Submit every part of My body to minute examination. Examine the movements of My soul. If even the slightest fault is discovered, then it is right and fair that I should be detained. For those who sin are deserving of death.

34. If, however, you discover nothing forbidden by the divine law and everything that it commands, I shall not allow you to detain what it is not lawful to detain. Nay, rather, I shall open the prison of death for all others and will detain you alone for transgressing the divine limit. The divine law condemned evil-doers to die, but you have committed a blameless person to the bonds of death. And this extreme harshness was caused by your insatiable selfishness. In taking one man unjustly, you are justly deprived of all those in your bondage. In eating forbidden fruit, you vomit all that you have eaten already, and you will be a lesson to all men to

be satisfied with what they have and abstain from what does not belong to them.

35. Remember why Adam, the father of the human race, was delivered to death. He owned all the trees in paradise but was dissatisfied with what he was given; the enjoyment of all the trees in their abundance was not enough for him. He dared to touch the tree of knowledge which his Maker had forbidden him to touch. Through his insatiable disease and unlawful desire he was deprived of paradise. I will subject you to these very penalties. For it would be unjust if the one who was seduced should suffer such a loss and the seducer did not incur a like penalty. Since then, after getting power over sinners, you touched One who did no wrong, surrender your power, quit your tyrannous position. I will liberate all from death, not merely as an exercise of mercy, but in justice and mercy, and not in virtue of any arbitrary power, but as a legitimate exercise of power.

36. I have paid the debt for human nature. Though not liable to death, I have endured it; though not subject to it, I underwent it; though not required to render an account, I was enlisted with those so required; though free of debt, I was ranked with the debtors. I have then paid nature's debt, and in enduring an unjust death I have freed those for whom death is deserved. By being unjustly detained, I release from prison those who are justly kept there. Oh! harsh avenger of sin, look at the bill of nature effaced, look at it nailed to the cross and the decree of sin abolished.[61] See how no trace of sin is entered.

37. The eyes of this body have paid for eyes that looked on evil things; those ears have paid for ears that were exposed to filth; this tongue for tongues that moved in transgression of the law; those hands for hands that performed wicked deeds; those other limbs for limbs which perpetrated evil of whatever kind. Now that the debt is paid, it is fitting that those who were detained in prison on its account should be released, and should recover their former freedom, and should enter into their patrimony.

Christ by His Resurrection Bequeathed the Hope of a General
Resurrection

38. With these words the Lord resurrected His own body and
engendered the hope of a resurrection in mankind, giving His own
resurrection as a pledge to all.⁶² Let no one think that we prattle idly
in this matter; the holy Gospels and the apostolic instructions are our
sources for the truth of these things. For we heard the words of the
Lord Himself: *The prince of this world comes and in Me he does not find*
*anything.*⁶³ I have not, He means, any marks of sin; I have a body free
of all transgression. Yet, although he finds nothing in Me, he will
deliver Me up to death as if I were liable to countless penalties. I endure it, however, for I wish to eject him from his tyranny in a spirit
of strict justice. Wherefore He says, too, in another place: *Now is the*
*judgment of this world, now shall the prince of this world be cast out.*⁶⁴

39. When the judgment and trial take place, he will be condemned and sentenced. He will be ejected from his tyranny for giving an unjust sentence against Me. And to show that, as well as
freeing His own body from the power of death, He will free all mankind as well, He goes on to add: *And I, if I be lifted up from the earth,*
*will draw all men to Myself.*⁶⁵ I will not allow the body which I have
assumed to rise by itself; I will see that all men will rise as well. It
was for that reason I came and took the form of a servant. That is
why I was led to the slaughter and was *dumb like a lamb before his*
shearer.

40. St. Paul says the same, writing to the Colossians, and
through them to all men: *And to you, when you were dead in your sins and*
the uncircumcision of your flesh, he has given life together with Him, forgiv-
ing us all offenses, blotting out the handwriting of the decree that was ordained
against us. And he has swept it out of the way, fastening it to the cross. And
despoiling the principalities and powers He has exposed them in open show,
*triumphing over them in himself.*⁶⁶ We learn from this that He has paid
the debt for us, blotted out the handwriting against us, nailed it to
the cross, and exposed the principalities and powers, that is the opposing forces, triumphing over them in Himself.

41. That is to say, He who is blameless has shown His body
and soul to them, and convicted those who have given an unjust sentence against Him, and in doing this all human nature is quickened

together with Him. It is possible to find countless other testimonies in Sacred Scripture demonstrating the truth of this. If we wished to collect them all, however, and to interpret them all suitably, the task would assume boundless proportions. Leaving the collection of them to the scholars, I will continue with my discourse.

42. Christ the Lord, then, after He had destroyed death and ensured our salvation in this manner, returned to heaven, leaving behind Him the hope of a similar ascent to those who cultivate sanctity. *And I, if only I am lifted up*, He says, *will draw all men to Myself.*[67]

43. Such is the loving care of the God of the universe for men. Such providence has the Creator exercised for His thankless creation. Such is the attention of the prototype for His own image. He fashioned it from the beginning and honored it with His own likeness. But it was ungrateful to its Maker, destroyed the divine image, received the characteristics of wild beasts, and changed from divine into animal form. The Creator did not look askance at what had assumed animal form, but renewed it, restored it to its pristine splendor, gave it back its old gracefulness, and made those His sons who were unworthy to be His servants.

God Ordained the Incarnation from All Eternity

44. Now there are some who work not at all,[68] as St. Paul says, but are meddlesome and curious about unlawful things, and strive to measure the abyss of wisdom with their own reasonings, and ask: Why did God not arrange this economy from the beginning, instead of after a lapse of many thousands of years?[69] Since such curiosity is very daring and bold, going beyond the extremes of madness, those who raise such questions should answer them themselves.

Providence in Old Testament Times

45. To show that God did not set up this economy through any change of purpose but had arranged things in that way from the very beginning, come, let us produce the Sacred Scripture and listen first to the words of Christ Our Lord in the Gospels: *Come, you blessed of My Father, possess you the kingdom prepared for you from the foundation of*

the world.[70] If He prepared from the foundation of the world the kingdom for the apostles and for those who received the faith from them,
it is plain that God's will was the same from the beginning and that
He did not have one plan now and a different one later. For His economy is opportune at each moment of time and His teachings adapted
to human capacities. Thus it was that He gave the command about
the tree to Adam[71] as if he were a newly born child. It would have
been superfluous to give him the whole law about adultery, murder,
false testimony, and injustice. With whom would he commit adultery, seeing that there was only one woman? Whom would he murder, with no one to provoke him? Against whom would he weave
false testimony or perpetrate an injustice? Therefore, the only precept he got was the one concerning the tree, suited to an infant or to
newly born children.

46. Then, after a long number of years the human race multiplied, and He gave Noah laws about foods. He bade him eat freely
of all meats, that is to say, clean ones (for He was Himself the author
of the distinction), only forbidding him to touch blood.[72] Then again,
after a long space of time, He called Abraham,[73] ordered him to quit
his native country, led him into what was formerly known as Canaan
but is now called Palestine, and gave him the precept about circumcision, so that his descendants might regard the removal of the pre-
puce as a sign of their religion.

47. Then under stress of famine[74] he led around the herald of
religion everywhere, displaying his own form of worship to the
Egyptians and Palestinians. He allowed his wife to be stolen by the
barbarians,[75] but defended her when she was taken away; he
scourged her captives and did not allow the woman-hunters to hold
their quarry: they had her in their toils, but were not allowed to make
off with her. They were themselves taken in invisible toils and
learned by experience the love God has for the stranger. The rulers
of those races summoned the stranger, the foreigner, the alien, and
became his suppliants. Seizing the opportunity, he instructed the ignorant in the elements of religion. Injustice opened up the road to
sanctity and unlawful desire heralded their knowledge of God.

48. It was the same in the disposition of providence towards
Isaac and Jacob. The former was a benefactor to Abimelech,[76] the
latter revealed the true God to Laban,[77] and exposed the weakness of

gods which had only an apparent, but no real, existence. He showed the same regard towards Joseph.[78] He permitted him first to be enslaved, but after slavery, calumny, and imprisonment, he handed over the control of Egypt to him. He preached monotheism first to the cupbearer, and then to the Pharaoh. When he took control he showed wisdom in his guidance of the whole ship. Thus when the Israelites multiplied, God wished to free them from Egyptian bondage[79] and He accomplished this with many great wonders, thereby making them famous.

49. For He selected this one nation to teach the knowledge of God to all the others. Just as He had selected one man—at one time Moses, at another Joshua, at another Samuel, at another some other of the prophets—to look after the welfare of this race, one man who benefited his fellows by practicing true wisdom, so through the one race, Israel, He called all the races of the earth that shared the same nature to share the same religion. Rahab, the harlot, testifies that this is so.[80] Though she belonged to a different race and was a harlot, she relied solely on their reputation, accepted their religion, abandoned her own beliefs, and entrusted herself to strangers. *We have heard*, she said, *what things the Lord your God has done to the Egyptians and fear of you fell on us*.[81] Accordingly, she made a pact with the spies and sealed it with an oath.

50. The Philistines also testify to this. They feared the presence of the ark and said to one another: *This is the God who struck Egypt. Woe to us Philistines*.[82] Then God gave the ark to the Philistines to convict His people of transgressing the law. For He could not make those who flagrantly broke the law its upholders. But in giving the ark He safeguarded His majesty, teaching the Philistines that it was sinful men they had conquered and not God. So Dagon[83] who was adored as God by them (although he was a dumb, senseless idol) was made to fall before the ark and God prepared to stage a spectacle for the spectators, so that the Philistines might perceive the difference between false god and true God.

51. In their folly, they raised him up again only to see him fallen a second time and brought to his knees, so to speak. Behaving thus with singular stupidity, and reluctant to recognize the difference, they were taught by experience not to run to excess. Having learned their lesson they returned to their senses, shook off their drunken igno-

rance, returned the ark, as was fitting, to its proper admirers, having honored it with votive offerings.[84] They confessed their chastisements and instructed those who received it about the manner of its return.

52. God did the same to Baltassar.[85] For when the people had lapsed into the depths of impiety loot was sent to Babylon and the sacred vessels became the spoils of the enemy. Now Nabuchodonosor, since they were sacred, removed them from profane use and brought them to the temples of those whom they cultivated as gods.[86] His son, Baltassar, however, had not learned his lesson sufficiently from his father's disasters and did not calculate the penalty he should pay for such arrogance; having honored, as he thought, these sacred vessels, he brought out the vessels once consecrated to God, drank from them—the wretch—and handed round the vessels that should not be touched to his fellow drinkers. While this was going on, the decision against the accursed wretch was produced and a hand of somebody invisible wrote on the wall the sentence of God. Baltassar was held in doubt, unable to read or understand the import of what was written.

53. Then his mother brought into the court Daniel, who often solved such problems for his father.[87] Daniel read and interpreted it, and told him the cause of the punishment, saying:[88] We have been made captives to pay the penalty for our sins. And God has given those vessels consecrated by us to our vanquisher to teach us that He suffered us to offer sacrifices which He did not need and accepted our offerings as long as we remained holy, because He wished to be of help to us. But when we drifted into impiety He rejected the gifts we offered. Your father then, accepting the rebuke, worshipped as he thought best, withdrawing objects from profane use and offering them to his supposed gods. You have no use for such worship, you have fallen into the abyss of arrogance and have drunk from the sacred vessels. The reason the Lord gives you such a lesson to end your arrogance is not His care for inanimate objects, but His loving care for men, and He proposes your punishment as a lesson in discipline for many. So much he said, and that night Baltassar paid the penalty.

54. Behold, then, how the Maker of the universe has always shown a loving care for mankind, not merely for the race of the descendants of Abraham, but for all the descendants of Adam; through one tribe He has led all tribes to a knowledge of Himself. He used them for this purpose both when they were religious and when they

were paying the penalty for their sins. For instance, Nabuchodono-sor, the arrogant tyrant, who raised up the golden image and called on all to adore it, saying: *I will exalt my throne above the stars. I will ascend above the height of the clouds. I will be like the most High. I will gather in my hand the whole earth as a nest, as eggs that lie abandoned will I gather it.*[89]

55. Not through angels has the God of the universe preached moderation, but through those taken captive by Him. For when Na-buchodonosor saw the three youths who had refused to do the royal command, despise the dreaded fire as if it were merely a joke and tread on those coals as if they were a bed of roses, and praise God from the midst of such flames, he marvels at the wonder, is struck with terror at the Author of the wonder, bids everybody worship the God of such marvels, calls Him the Highest, the God of all, the Sovereign.

56. Likewise that Assyrian,[90] raving against him and using these frenzied words: *The Lord God shall not deliver you from my hand*, and, *Where are the gods of the nations?*[91] To show him his weakness He compels him to fly alone, the countless multitude in whom he greatly prided being stricken dead in a moment of time by a single angel. Likewise, He sent Jonas to preach penance to the Ninivites. Reluctant to obey, he foolishly attempts to fly but is constrained by the waves, and is taken into custody by a whale.[92] The animal returns the man to where he was instructed to preach.

57. When the great mystery of the divine economy was about to be accomplished and the proclamation of the divine Incarnation had to be spread throughout the world, then that people, which had been selected from other nations for special favor from the beginning of time, was dispersed throughout the world, so that all those who wrongly believed in polytheism might be made to believe that there is but one God, Maker of heaven and earth, and in this way the preaching of the divine apostles was facilitated.

Jewish Opposition Helped the Christian Faith

58. Now some one may say perhaps: The Jews, far from advancing the teaching of Christ, were greatly opposed to it, and were

an obstacle to the Gentiles who wished to believe. If one is willing to examine this matter thoroughly, he will find that Jewish opposition was a help to Gentile faith. Discussion with the Jews, and proof from the law and the prophets, clearly condemned their folly and showed the Gentiles that the Christian religion was divinely revealed. The testimony of enemies rendered the preaching worthy of credence.

59. For the preachers spoke of Abraham, the patriarch, who received the promises, and of Isaac, the fruit of the promise, of Jacob, who received his father's blessing, and of Juda, who inherited the same paternal blessing, of Moses, who foretold those events, of King David, who predicted them, of Isaias and Jeremiah, who prophesied them, of Ezechiel and Daniel, who proclaimed them through the inspiration of the Spirit, and of the whole chorus of prophets who told us clearly of our doings in advance. When they that heard these things saw that the Jews accepted these utterances as divine, when they saw too the miracles performed in the name of Christ, taking these signs as guarantees of the preaching, they accepted the doctrine without any difficulty, believed in the God that was preached to them, and repudiated the wretched conduct of the Jews. Thus the incredulity of the Jews[93] was no impediment to the divine message, but rather their very resistance to it made it worthy of credence.

60. For the opposition of the Jews caused witnesses of the Master to be brought to light and these refuted falsehood and revealed the light of truth. Thus has the God of the universe brought about the salvation of mankind from on high, giving due care to every period of time.

St. Paul, teaching this, says: *As long as the heir is a child he differs nothing from a servant though he be lord of all. But he is under tutors and governors until the time appointed by the father. So we also, when we were children, were slaving at the elements of worldly knowledge. But when the fullness of time arrived God sent out His Son born from a woman, born under the law, that He might ransom those under the law, that we might receive adoptive sonship.*[94]

61. That God did not come to this decision as an afterthought but had so decreed from the beginning of time, let the same witness testify in his Epistle to the Corinthians: *We speak wisdom among the perfect: yet not the wisdom of this world, neither of the princes of this world whose power is to be abrogated. But we speak the wisdom of God in a mystery,*

a wisdom which is hidden, which God ordained before the world unto our glory: which none of the princes of this world knew. For if they had known it they would never have crucified the Lord of glory.[95] For it was not through envy of their happiness that they afforded men this occasion for great good fortune, but through ignorance of the end of the mystery they raved against the Savior of our souls and unwittingly donated to us the loftiest blessings. The mystery was hidden but ordained before the world.

62. Knowing this, and aware of the all-pervading providence of God, and seeing His unlimited love for men and His immeasurable mercy, stop raving against the Creator, learn to praise His goodness, repay His great blessings with words of gratitude. Offer the incense of your praise to God. Defile not your tongue with blasphemy, but make it an instrument of praise, fulfilling the purpose for which it was made. Reverence what can be seen of the divine plan and do not trouble yourself about what is hidden. Await a full knowledge of these things in the life to come. When we are divested of the passions we will attain to perfect knowledge. Do not imitate Adam who dared to pick forbidden fruit. Do not touch what is hidden, but wait patiently on a full knowledge of these things in God's good time. Attend to wisdom, saying: *Do not say: What is this, or what is that? For all things were made to supply a need.*[96] From every source, then, collect occasions for praise and, combining these in one hymn, offer it in union with us to the Creator, the Giver of blessings, the Savior Christ, our true God, to whom be glory, adoration, and lofty praise for endless ages. Amen.

NOTES

LIST OF ABBREVIATIONS

ACW	Ancient Christian Writers
AJP	American Journal of Philology (Baltimore 1880–)
Azéma	Y. Azéma, ed., *Théodoret de Cyr. Discours sur la Providence* (Paris 1954)
CAH	Cambridge Ancient History (London-New York 1923–1939; rev. ed. Cambridge, England 1961–)
Canivet, *Entre.*	P. Canivet, *Histoire d'une entreprise apologétique au Ve siècle* (Paris 1957)
CP	Classical Philology (Chicago 1906–)
CQ	Classical Quarterly (London 1907–)
CSEL	Corpus scriptorum ecclesiasticorum latinorum (Vienna 1866–)
ClW	Classical World
DACL	Dictionnaire d'archaéologie chrétienne et de liturgie (Paris 1903–1953)
DCB	Dictionary of Christian Biography, Literature, Sects and Doctrines (London 1877–1887)
DHGE	Dictionnaire d'histoire et de géographie ecclésiastiques (Paris 1912–)
Diels, *Dox.*	H. Diels, *Doxographi Graeci* (Berlin 1929)
Diels-Kranz	H. Diels—W. Kranz, *Die Fragmente der Vorsokratiker* (3 vols., Berlin 1951–1952)
DOP	Dumbarton Oaks Papers
DPAC	Dizionario patristico e di antichita cristiane
DSp	Dictionnaire de spiritualité

DTC	Dictionnaire de théologie catholique (Paris 1903–1950)
ERE	Encyclopedia of Religion and Ethics
EThL	Ephemerides theologicae lovaniensis
GCS	Die griechischen christlichen Schriftsteller der ersten drei Jahrhunderte (Leipzig 1897–)
Guthrie, *History*	W. K. C. Guthrie, *A History of Greek Philosophy* (Cambridge 1962–1981).
HSCP	Harvard Studies in Classical Philology (Cambridge, Mass. 1890–)
HThR	Harvard Theological Review (Cambridge, Mass. 1908–)
JAC	Jahrbuch für Antike und Christentum (Münster 1958–)
JTS	Journal of Theological Studies (London 1899–1949; n.s. 1950–)
LCC	Library of Christian Classics
LCL	Loeb Classical Library
LTK	Lexikon für Antike und Christentum
Mansi	J. D. Mansi, *Sacrorum conciliorum nova et amplissima collectio* (Florence 1759–1798; reprint and continuation, Paris and Leipzig 1901–1927)
MG	*Patrologia graeca*, ed. J. P. Migne (Paris 1857–1866)
ML	*Patrologia latina*, ed. J. P. Migne (Paris 1844–1855)
Montalverne	J. Montalverne, *Theodoreti Cyrensis doctrina antiquior de Verbo 'inhumanato'* (Studia Antoniana 1; Rome 1948)
MSR	Mélanges de science religieuse
NCE	New Catholic Encyclopedia
NPNF	Library of Nicene and Post-Nicene Fathers
OCD^2	Oxford Classical Dictionary, 2nd ed.

ODCC²	Oxford Dictionary of the Christian Church, 2nd ed.
OECT	Oxford Early Christian Texts
Perrin, *L'Homme*	M. Perrin, *L'homme antique et Chrétien: L'anthropologie de Lactance, 250–325* (Théol. historique 59, Paris 1981)
PW	A. Pauly-G. Wissowa-W. Kroll, *Realencyclopädie der klassischen Altertumswissenschaft* (Stuttgart 1893–)
RAC	Reallexikon für Antike und Christentum (Stuttgart 1941 [1950]–)
REG	Revue des études grecs
RHE	Revue d'histoire ecclésiastique
RSPhTh	Revue des sciences philosophiques et théologiques
RTL	Revue théologique de Louvain
SC	Sources chrétiennes (Paris 1940–)
SVF	J. von Arnim, *Stoicorum veterum fragmenta* (4 vols., 1921–1924; repr. Stuttgart 1964)
TRE	Theologische Realenzklopädie
TU	Texte und Untersuchungen zur Geschichte der altchristlichen Literatur (Berlin 1882–)
ZKG	Zeitschrift für Kirchengeschichte
ZTK	Zeitschrift für Theologie und Kirche

INTRODUCTION

1. See J. L. Schulze and J. A. Noesselt, edd., *Theodoretus, Opera omnia* (Halle 1769–1774) 5 volumes; reprinted in J. P. Migne, ed., *Patrologia graeca* 80–84. For details see J. Quasten, *Patrology* 3 (Westminster, Md. 1960) 536–554. See also M. Geerard, CPG 111, no. 6211, which announces a new edition of *De providentia* in preparation by Y. Azéma. For a preliminary list of mss., see Azéma 9 n. 2. See also nos. 6200–6288 for details on Theodoret's other works.

G. Koch, *Struckturen und Geschichte des Heils in der Theologie des Theodoret von Kyros* (Frankfurt am Main 1974) 19–56, contains an excellent bibliography. See also G. Ettlinger, *Theodoret of Cyrus, Eranistes* (Oxford 1975) xi–xiii. For Theodoret as church historian, cf. G. F. Chesnut, *The First Christian Histories: Eusebius, Socrates, Sozomen, Theodoret and Evagrius* (Théologie historique 46, Paris 1977; 2nd ed., revised and enlarged, Macon, Ga. 1986); L. Parmentier, *Theodoret, Kirchengeschichte* (GCS 44, Berlin 1954).

2. Cf. Garnerii, "Dissertatio 1: Historia Theodoreti" in MG 84.89–198.

3. Cf. R. Ceillier, *Histoire générale des auteurs sacrés et ecclésiastiques* 10 (Paris 1891) 19–142.

4. A. Bertram, *Theodoreti episcopi Cyrensis doctrina christologica* (Hildesheim 1883).

5. L. S. N. Tilloment, *Mémoires pour servir a l'histoire ecclésiastique* 15 (Paris 1711) 207–340.

6. Cf. J. Montalverne, *Theodoreti Cyrensis doctrina antiquior de Verbo inhumato* (Rome 1948) 2 f.

7. Cf. B. Altaner and A. Stuiber, *Patrologie* (9th ed., Freiburg 1978) 341. See also Quasten, *Patrology* 3.536; P. Canivet, *Théodoret de Cyr, Thérapeutique des maladies helléniques* (SC 57, Paris 1958) 7.

8. See P. Canivet, "Théodoret et le monachisme syrien avant le

concile de Chalcedoine" in *Théologie de la vie monastique* (Paris 1961) 241–282.

For Theodoret as exegete see G. Ashby, *Theodoret of Cyrus as Exegete of the Old Testament* (Grahamstown 1972) and "The hermeneutic approach of Theodoret of Cyrrhus to the Old Testament," Studia Patristica 15 (= TU 128, Berlin 1984) 131–135; M. Simonetti, "La tecnica esegetica di Teodoreto nel Commento ai Salmi," in *Vetera Christianorum* 23 (1986) 81–116; I. Sanna, "Spirito e grazia nel commento alla Lettera ai Romani di Teodoreto di Ciro e sua dependenza in quest' opera da Giovanni Crisostomo e Teodoro di Mopsustia" in *Lateranum* 48 (1982) 238–260; P. M. Parvis, *Theodoret's Commentary on the Epistles of St. Paul: Historical Setting and Exegetical Practice* (diss. Oxford University 1975).

For his secular knowledge, see Canivet, *Entre*. passim, esp. 35 f., 131 f., 290, 298. On the sources of Theodoret's secular knowledge, see especially Canivet, *Entre*. 255–275, where they are effectively reduced to five main sources: 1. Clement of Alexandria; 2. Eusebius of Caesarea; 3. The *Placita* of Aëtius, a Peripatetic philosopher of the 2nd century A.D.; 4. The *Epitome* of Plutarch, now lost but apparently preserved in its entirety in Eusebius, *Praep. evang.* 14; and 5. What Canivet calls "La source X." By this he understands some collection or florilegium in which Theodoret could have found citations from, for example, Plato's *Republic*, not already in Eusebius, but without having to resort to the Platonic corpus directly. Theodoret himself acknowledges his debt to Aëtius (*Affect.* 4.31).

The manner in which Theodoret compiled the many quotations in the *Eranistes* has already been studied in L. Saltet, "Les sources de l'Ερανιστής de Théodoret" in RHE 6 (1905) 289–303, 513–536, 741–754. See also G. Ettlinger, *Theodoret of Cyrus, Eranistes* 9–35; Y. Azéma, "Citations d'auteurs et allusions profanes dans la correspondance de Théodoret" in *Uberlieferungsgeschichtliche Untersuchungen* (TU 125, Berlin 1981) 5–13; G. J. M. Bartelink, "Homère dans des oeuvres de Théodoret de Cyr" in *Orpheus* 11 (1981) 2–28. See further A. Leroy-Molinghen, "Théodoret de Cyr et Grégoire de Nazianze" in J. Mossay, ed., *II. Symposium Nazianzenum* (Paderborn 1983) 181–186 for a test case of Theodoret's fidelity in quotation in his *Eranistes*.

Nemesius, *De natura hominis*, may also have helped for *De prov-*

identia though this is rightly doubted by R. W. Sharples, "Nemesius of Emesa and Some Theories of Divine Providence" in VigC 37 (1983) 141–156.

9. On Cyrus, see E. Frezouls, "Recherches sur le ville de Cyrrhus" in *Annales archaeologiques de Syrie* 4.5 (1954–55) 90–128; "Cyrrhus" in DHGE 13.1186 f. On Nicerte, see P. Canivet-A. Leroy-Molinghen, edd., *Théodoret de Cyr: Histoire des moines de Syrie* SC 234, 252, n. 2; P. Canivet, *Le monachisme syrien*, 137–139.

10. Theodoret, *Ep.* 113 (SC 111.62).

11. On the Robber Synod, see W. H. C. Frend, *The Rise of Christianity* (Philadelphia 1984) 766–770; J. Flemming, *Akten der ephesinischen Synode 449* (German tr. J. Hoffmann, AAWG Phil.-hist. Kl., N.F. 15,1) 104 f.

12. On Theodoret at Chalcedon, see Frend, *op. cit.* 771–772; A. J. Festugière, *Ephèse et Chalcedoine. Actes des Conciles;* P. T. R. Gray, *The Defence of Chalcedon in the East (451–553)* (Leiden 1979) 82–88. For dating his death to 460, not 457, see Y. Azéma, "La date de la mort de Theodoret de Cyr," *Pallas* 31 (1984) 137–155, 192–193.

13. See J. H. Newman, *Historical Sketches* (London 1876) 2.303–367, esp. 323.

14. *Op. cit.* 208. For excellent recent portraits of Theodoret, see Jean-Noel Guinot, "Un évèque exégète: Théodoret de Cyr," in C. Mondesert, ed., *Le monde grec ancien et la Bible* (Paris 1984) 335–360; and M. Smolak, "Theodoret von Cyrus," in M. Greschat, ed., *Gestalten der Kirchengeschichte, Alte Kirche* II (Stuttgart 1984) 2.239–250.

15. *Ep.* 113 (SC 111.64).

16. MG 84.345–346.

17. On dating the *Interp. in Ps.* to a little later than 435, see B. Croke, "Dating Theodoret's Church History and Commentary on the Psalms," *Byzantion* 54 (1984) 59–74.

18. J. Schulte, *Theodoret von Cyrus als Apologet* (Vienna 1904) 24.

19. Bardenhewer, 4.232; Altaner-Stuiber, *Patrologie;* P. C. da Mazzarino, *La dottrina di Teodoreto di Ciro sull' unione ipostatica delle due nature in Cristo* (Rome 1941).

20. DTC 15.1, 299–325.

21. Quasten, *Patrology*, 3.545.

22. E. Peterson, "I sermoni sulla Provvidenza sono conferenze

(non omelie) per il publico colto di Antiochia," in *Enciclopedie Cattolica* 11.1927.

23. Galen is mentioned in *Affect.* 5.82 as one of the ancients who wrote on the nature of the soul, but without explicit citation.

24. Garnerius writes in MG 84.346: *Dicti sunt igitur Antiochiae, in urbe Orientis primaria, quae quia litteris Graecis erat excultissima, imo litterarum fons uberrimus, tantarum deliciarum sensum habere potuit, quas Cyrensium ruditas ac pene barbaries non capiebat. De his ergo praesertim sermonibus, propter admirabilem eloquentiam, interpretor Theodoreti verba, de Ioanne Antiocheno sibi, cum diceret, plaudente: 'Disserentibus nobis sic afficiebatur, ut ambas saepe manus non teneret, et de sede sua consurgeret,'.* . . .

25. On providence, see "Vorsehung" in LTK 10.885–889; "Providence" in DB 5.802–803; "Providentia" in RE Supplbd. 14.562–565; "Vorsehung" in *Biblisches Reallexicon* 2.961–962; "Provvidenza" in DPAC 2942–2945. For the Greek Fathers, see esp. DTC 13,1.941–960. For a conspectus of theological literature on the subject, see L. Korinek, "Bulletin de théologie naturelle des années 1957–1960" in *Gregorianum* 41.3 (1960) 486–517. J. Walsh and P. G. Walsh, *Divine Providence and Human Suffering* (Message of the Fathers 17, Wilmington 1985) contains many apposite texts. See also R. Frangiotti, *La politique de Dieu selon la doctrine traditionnelle de la Providence divine* (Strasbourg 1983); Leo Scheffczyk, "Schopfung und Vorsehung" in M. Schmaus and A. Grillmeier, edd., *Handbuch der Dogmengeschichte* (Band II, Faszikel 2d, Freiburg 1963) 1–70.

26. Cicero, *De natura Deorum*, book 2.

27. For providence in Stoicism see J. von Arnim, ed., *Stoicorum Veterum Fragmenta* (Leipzig 1921–24), esp. vol. 4 s.v. πρόνοια. See also M. Dragona-Monachou, "Providence and Fate in Stoicism in Preneoplatonism: Chalcidius as an Authority on Cleanthes' theodicy (SVF 2.933)" in *Philosophia* (Athens) 3 (1973) 262–306; H. Dörrie, "Der Begriff 'Pronoia' in Stoa und Platonismus," *FZPhTh* 24 (1977) 60–87; J. Den Boeft, *Calcidius on Fate* (Leiden 1970).

The word "pronoia" is not found in the extant works of Epicurus, but later it became a "catchword" according to N. De Witt, *Epicurus and His Philosophy* (Minnesota University Press 1954) 179. For Epicurus' denial of providence, see C. J. de Vogel, *Greek Philosophy* 3,845, 852, and also RAC 5.681–800, esp. 781 ff.

28. For providence in Judaism, cf. H.-F. Weiss, *Untersuchungen zur Kosmologie des hellenistischen und palastinischen Judentums* (= TU 97, Berlin 1966). For Philo, see C. J. de Vogel, *Greek Philosophy* 3.1290b.

29. Cf. Job 36.27; Isa. 10.5–10. See E. F. Sutcliffe, *Providence and Suffering in the Old and New Testaments* (London 1955); P. Imschoot, *Théologie de l'ancien Testament* 1 (Paris 1954) 107–113; L. Scheffczyk, *op. cit.* 1–12 (O.T.), 13–29 (N.T.); H. Holsstein, "Gouvernement spirituel l. Le gouvernement divin dans l'Écriture," DSp 6.644–648.

30. Wisd. 14.3, 17.2, on which see P. Heinisch, *Das Buch der Weisheit* (Munster 1912) *ad loc.*

31. See S. Schulz, "Gottes Vorsehung bei Lukas," in *Zeitschrift fur die neutestamentliche Wissenschaft* 54 (1963) 104–116.

32. See Diels, *Dox.*; A. P. Bos, *Providentia Divina: The Theme of Divine Pronoia in Plato and Aristotle* (Assen/Amsterdam 1976). On Theodoret's attitude to Plato, see D. S. Wallace-Hadrill, *Christian Antioch* 101–103.

33. E. R. Dodds, ed., *Proclus, The Elements of Theology* (Oxford 1933). G. W. Clarke, in his introduction to *The Octavius of Marcus Minucius Felix* (ACW 39) notes (p. 28): "As is well known, in the rhetorical curriculum current at this time figured the *controversia* designed to train a student in deliberative and forensic oratory. . . . Quintilian tells us specifically that one such *thesis* was *an providentia mundus regatur* ('whether the world is governed by providence'). Later, Greek rhetoricians of the second century, Aelius Theon and Hermogenes, in their rhetorical handbooks mention the same topic, and Aelius Theon actually gives elaborate and detailed instructions for dealing with this particular thesis." On Proclus, see *Procle. Trois études sur la Providence:* texte établi et traduit par Daniel Isaac (Paris 1977); W. Beierwaltes, "Pronoia und Freiheit in der Philosophie des Proklos," *FZPhTh* 24 (1977) 88–111.

34. See *Affect.* 6 (SC 57.275) and Canivet, *Entre.* 312. For providence in Plotinus, see V. Schubert, *Pronoia und Logos. Die Rechtfertigung der Weltordnung bei Plotin* (Munchen-Salzburg 1968).

35. See A. M. Malingrey, ed., *Saint Jean Chrysostome, Sur la Providence* (SC 79, Paris 1961).

36. Garnerii Dissertatio II in MG 84.345.

37. Azéma 22–24.

38. For instance, Quasten, *Patrology*. 3.544: "one of the best specimens of Theodoret's eloquence and style."
39. In DTC 15.1.307.
40. DTC 13.1.956.
41. Azéma 90.
42. The entry is in The National Union Catalog, Pre-1956 Imprints, v. 589 (Mansell 1978) p. 323: "Theodoretus, Bp. of Cyrrhus. The mirror of diuine prouidence. Containing a collection of Theodoret his arguments: declaring the prouidence of God to appeare notably both in the heauens and in the earth, and in all things therein contained: taken out of his workes De providentia. London, Printed by T.C. [reed] for I. Smithick, 1602. 'Extracted and digested into method by a learned divine now deceased.'—Editor's pref. signed: I.C."

For other translations in French or German, see Azéma 7 n.1.

DISCOURSE 1

1. The proemium is a very good example of *captatio benevolentiae*, including an example of *prokataleipsis* ("let no one contradict me at the outset"). It should be compared with the start of Eusebius, *Praeparatio evangelica* 8.14, a chapter also dealing with divine providence, excerpted from Philo, *De providentia*. There God is seen as no tyrant but a king deserving the name of father. Likewise Eusebius, *Praep. evang.* 7.11.4, tells us that the theology of the Hebrews teaches us that the entire world is not left to itself by the one who constituted it, as an orphan abandoned by its father, but that for eternity it is administered by the providence of God so well that God is not just the demiurge and creator of the universe, but also its savior and administrator, its king and leader.

The wall of Theodosius II (408–450) was built around 430/431 and would be fresh in his hearers' memories; cf. G. Downey, "The Wall of Theodosius at Antioch," AJP 62 (1941) 207–213, and his *A History of Antioch*, 452.

2. A patristic commonplace. Cf. Tatian, *Oratio ad Graecos* 4.3: "Nor is the ineffable God to be bribed, for he is entirely free of needs

and must not be misrepresented by us as in need of anything"; Athanasius, *Contra gentes* 28: "For it is accepted that God is in need of no one but is self-sufficient and complete in himself."

3. On truth simple, falsehood complex, cf. Euripides, *Phoenissae* 469–72, quoted in Clement, *Stromata* 1.8.40, an important source for Clement's views on the essentially fraudulent aspect of dialectic. Clement, in the same context, quotes a fragment of Euripides, *Antiope* frag. 206:

My son, well-spoken discourses could be false and could vanquish truth by elegance of words.

Whoever vanquishes by glibness of speech may be wise, but I prefer deeds to words.

There is a similar sentiment in the beginning of Theodoret's Discourse 7. For the same sentiment, cf. Theodoret, *Graecarum affectionum curatio* 2.8. On the allegorical interpretation of poetic fables, cf. Cicero, *ND* 111.63. On Greek poets as purveyors of polytheism, cf. *Affect.* 3.4, naming Homer and Hesiod. Theophilus of Antioch, *Ad Autolycum* 2.5–7, makes the same charge against Homer and Hesiod, as had Plato, *Euthyphro* 6b and *Republica* 2.

4. On the flowing beard and long hair, cf. "Haar," RAC Lief. 98 (1984) 176–203, esp. 190, 195–97; Arnobius, *Adversus nationes* 6.21 (= ACW 8.474; and also see 8.599, note 150). Chrysostom, *Ep. ad 1 Cor. hom.* 26 (PG 61.213), has the same expression. On the Cynics, see ERE 4.378–383, 9.298–300. For the use of the *tribon* by philosophers, cf. Justin Martyr, *Dialogus cum Tryphone Judaeo* 1, a chapter which makes providence a prime concern of the philosopher. On the beard, cf. Clement, *Paidagogos* 3.11.60: "A man's head should be bald unless he has crisp, curly hair, but his chin should be covered with a beard."

5. On the poets, cf. Athanasius, *Gent.* 15. Origen, *Commentary in Rom.* 3 (MG 14.926), accused the Epicureans of cloaking their base language about the gods in ornate language: *Erat in hominibus dogma quod summum bonum pronuntiaret esse voluptatem: in quo et illud consequenter asseritur, non esse Providentiam, quippe si non ex legibus sed ex voluptate vivendum: et haec lauti satis ornatoque sermone, et argumentis validissimis per innumera volumina digeruntur.*

6. In *Affect.* 3.49, Theodoret has the same, with some additions: "They call carnal desire Aphrodite and Eros; anger, Ares; drunken-

ness, Dionysus; theft, Hermes; reason, Athena; the arts, since they use fire as helpers, Hephaistos." (= Clement, *Strom.* 4.9.52): "For as the Greeks call iron by the name of Ares and wine by that of Dionysus. . . . "

In the creation of Pandora, described in Hesiod, *Opera et dies* 50–105, Hermes instructed her in every kind of guile and deceit, Athena taught her handiwork and to weave the embroidered web, and Aphrodite shed grace about her head and grievous desire and wasting passion.

On Aphrodite, Theodoret, *Affect.* 3.53, quotes Antisthenes, *frag.* 35 (= Clement, *Strom.* 11.20.107): "I would pierce Aphrodite with my arrows if I got her, because she has corrupted so many of our good, noble women."

For the etymology of Ares, see Eusebius, *Praep. evang.* 3.1.9. On his anger, cf. Athenagoras, *Legatio* 21.3 (in the first sentence he quotes Homer, *Il.* 15.568, and in the concluding sentence he quotes Homer, *Il.* 5.31): "He raged as when Ares with his spear. . . . Be silent, Homer, a god does not rage; yet you can tell me of a god who is bloodthirsty and a bane of men. Ares, Ares, bane of men, bloodthirsty one."

On Dionysus, cf. Athanasius, *Gent.* 24: "The Indians worship Dionysus, calling him symbolically wine." For Dionysus, see Cicero, *ND* 2.62.

Hermes is the god of thieves in Aristophanes (*Plutus,* 1155; *Pax,* 1141); Euripides (*Rhesus,* 217); Plutarch (*Quaestiones Graecae,* 55). For the association of Hermes and theft, cf. "Hermes," *RE* 8,1 738–792, esp. 780–781. For his theft of the cattle of Apollo, see *Homeric Hymn to Hermes* 175, and T. W. Allen, W. R. Halliday, and E. E. Sikes, *The Homeric Hymns* (Oxford 1936) 270–274, 291f. Eusebius, *Praep. evang.* 11.1.8, attributes to Hermes the invention of writing, control of sacrifices to the gods, invention of the lyre, hermeneutics, and discovery of the olive. All four deities are listed in a passage in Theagenes; cf. Diels-Kranz 1.52.8–12.

7. Cf. Theodoret, *Affect.* 2.27, quoting Plato, *Cratylus* 397cd (= Eusebius, *Praep. evang.* 1.9.12): "I suspect that the sun, moon, earth, stars, and heaven, which are still the gods of many barbarians, were the only gods known to the aboriginal Hellenes. Seeing that they were always moving and running, from their running nature they

were called runners. . . . " Theodoret repeats the *Cratylus* quotation in *Affect.* 3.7. Eusebius, *Praep. evang.* 14.20: οὐδὲν ὑπὲρ τὰ ὁρωμένα νοῆσαι δυνηθέντες.

8. He is thinking especially of Empedocles; cf. *Affect.* 2.10: (ἀρχὴν) ὁ δὲ ᾿Ακραγαντίνος ᾿Εμπεδοκλῆς τὰ στοιχεῖος ᾿έφη τὰ τεσσάρα. Lactantius, *Institutiones divinae* 2.12: "Empedocles, whom you would not know whether to place among philosophers or poets because he wrote on the nature of things in verse, as did Lucretius and Varro among the Romans, set down four elements: fire, air, water, and earth." Eusebius, *Praep, evang.* 3.10.10, asks: "What kind of a god could he be whose constituent parts are the earth and the earth's mountains? What logic would call god the brother and parent of fire, of water, of air, products of irrational and corruptible matter?" Lucretius, *De rerum natura* 2.9.11: *Et qui quattuor ex rebus posse omnia rentur ex igni, terra, atque anima procrescere et imbri. Quorum Acragantinus cum primis Empedocles est.*

9. Clement, *Protrepticus* 5.64, gives a typical doxographic account of these pre-Socratic views: The elements were the first principles sung about by them—Thales, the Milesian, water; Anaximenes, a Milesian also, air; his successor a little later was Diogenes of Apollonia. Parmenides of Elea proposed fire and earth as gods; only one of those elements, fire, was deified by Hippasos of Metapontos and Heraclitus of Ephesus; Empedocles added to the four elements strife and friendship. See also Minucius Felix, *Octavius* 19.4 (= ACW 39.83). Theodoret is more specific in *Affect.* 2.9 and 2.10.

On Thales, see Guthrie, *History* 1.45–72, and Nemesius, *Nat. hom.* 5.

10. Theodoret quotes Plotinus, *Enneads* 3.2.2, in *Affect.* 6.59: "To attribute to chance and to fortune the cause and organization of all this universe is foolish and characteristic of a man possessed of neither intelligence nor sense." See especially D. Amand, *Fatalisme et liberté dans l'antiquité grecque* (Louvain 1945); and for a recent good survey, G. Verbeke, "Fatalism and Freedom" in *The Presence of Stoicism in Medieval Thought* (Washington 1983) 71–96.

11. Theodoret, in *Affect.* 4.15, names as champions of a single world Thales, Pythagoras, Anaxagoras, Parmenides, Melissus, Heraclitus, Plato, Aristotle, and Zeno, "but, on the other hand, Anaxi-

mander, Anaximenes, Archelaos, Xenophanes, Diogenes, Leucippus, Democritus, and Epicurus affirm that there are many and infinite worlds." See Aëtius, *Placita* 11.1.2–3, and M. Ninci, *Aporia ed entusiasmo* 28–29, 115. Eusebius, *Praep. evang.* 1.8, names Diogenes of Apollonia as a believer in a plurality of worlds.

12. In *Affect.* 2.112 Theodoret names three atheists—Diagoras of Melos (not Miletos, as he wrongly says), Theodore of Cyrene, and Euhemeros of Tegea. Here he gives Plutarch as his source (cf. *De placitis philosophorum* 1.7), though he is only using Eusebius, *Praep. evang.* 14.16.1. See "Atheismus," RAC 1.866–870.

In *Affect.* 3.4 Theodoret tells us that "the atheists are not only Diagoras of Miletos, Theodore of Cyrene and Euhemeros of Tegea and their followers who completely denied that the gods existed as we know from Plutarch," but also Homer, Hesiod, and groups of philosophers, fabulous inventors of innumerable bands of gods. See also Clement, *Protrep.* 2.24 (GCS 1.18); *Stromata* 6.8.67 (GCS 2.465).

M. Winiarczyk, "Wer Galt im Altertum als Atheist," *Philologus* 128 (1984) 157–183, provides a prosopography of 68 such "atheists." See also W. Fahr, *Theous Nomizein. Zum Problem der Anfänge des Atheismus bei den Griechen* (Hildesheim 1969).

13. Theodoret, in *Affect.* 6.6, reports that Epicurus, son of Neocles, and his following say that God exists but that he is turned toward himself and is unwilling to care for others (= *Sent.* 1, frag. 359). Epicurus is the favorite butt of the Fathers. Among useless topics for research, Gregory Nazianzus lists *Or.* 27: "Then there is Epicurus' atheism, or his atoms, or his ideal of pleasure, unworthy of a philosopher, or Aristotle's low conception of providence, the artful character of his logic, his mortal view of the soul, and the human-centered nature of his teaching."

Clement, *Strom.* 1.11.50, says that Paul criticised the philosophy of Epicurus in Acts (cf. Acts 17.18) for denying providence and divinizing pleasure. In Theophilus *Ad Autol.* 2.4, the Stoic Chrysippus is lumped with Epicurus as believing that God did not exercise providence (cf. Plutarch, *De Stoicorum repugnantiis* 38.1052c).

Lactantius, *De ira dei* 4, says: "He who takes away all force, therefore, all substance from God, what else does he say except that there is no God at all. Marcus Tullius, in fact, relates that it was said by Posidonius that Epicurus believed this, that there were no gods, but that the things which he spoke about the gods he had said for the sake of driving away ill will, and so, in his words he left the gods but in very fact he removed them, to whom he assigned no motion, no function" (FOTC 54.66). For Marcus Tullius cf. Cicero, *ND* 1.44.123. Origen suspects that Celsus is an Epicurean; cf. *Contra Celsum* 4.75. The Epicurean tradition continued in other philosophers; cf. Lactantius, *De opificio dei* 2: "I often marvel at the folly of those philosophers in the wake of Epicurus who condemn the works of nature that they may show that the world is formed and governed by no providence" (FOTC 54.10). See "Epikur," RAC 5.681 ff.; "Epikur," RE Supplementband XI.

14. Theodoret explicitly names Aristotle for this; see *Affect.* 5.47 ("leaving the rest under fate"), 6.7; also *Haereticarum fabularum compendium* 5.10. This view was falsely attributed to Aristotle by many of the Fathers: Tatian, *Or.* 2; Athenagoras, *Leg.* 25; Clement, *Strom.* 5.14.90; Eusebius, *Praep. evang.* 15.5.1. See A. P. Bos, *Providentia Divina: The Theme of Divine Pronoia in Plato and Aristotle* (Assen/Amsterdam 1976) 5 and 29 n. 1; also A. J. Festugière, *L'Idéal religieux des grecs et l'evangile* (Gabalda 1932): Excursus C: Aristôte dans la littérature grecque chrétienne, jusqu'à Théodoret, 221–263.

For Aristotle see Canivet, *Entre.* 214. Theodoret never speaks well of him, probably because his dialectic was employed by the Arians and the Anomeans; cf. *Affect.* 5.72.

15. Clement, *Strom.* 5.14.128, with a Philemon fragment, which is reproduced in Theodoret, *Affect.* 6.16 (Also in Eusebius, *Praep. evang.* 13.13.55.)

> Fortune is no divinity to us.
> There's no such god.
> But what befalls by chance
> and of itself,
> to each is Fortune called.

(Philemon, frag. 137, CAF 11.520)

Cf. Origen, *Cels.* 4.75: "(Celsus), like a true Epicurean, maintaining that these things are the product of chance, and not of the work of providence."

16. From *Affect.* 6.13 it is clear at whom this is aimed: "Not only those around Democritus and Chrysippus and Epicurus say that

everything occurs according to necessity, calling fate necessity, but also the much touted Pythagoras said that necessity encompassed the cosmos."

Many of the Fathers composed works on fate; cf. Canivet, *Entre.* 96–98. See Justin Martyr, *Apologiae* 7: "But the Stoics claimed that everything took place by the necessity of fate."

See the definition of *heimarmene* in Aulus Gellius, *Noct. Att.* 7.2.1 (**RAC** fasc.) from the 4th book of Chrysippus, *Peri pronoias.* See "Fatum (Heimarmene)," **RAC** 7.524–636; "Heimarmene," RE 7.2622–2645; and an extended treatment in Festugière, *op. cit.* 101–115. See also the section *De Fato* in **SVF** 2.264–298; also Canivet, *Entre.* 85 f., 214 f., 312 f.

17. He means Marcion; cf. *Haer.* 1.24 and 5.16. See "Marcion," DS 10.311–321; R. J. Hoffmann, *Marcion: On the Restitution of Christianity* (Chico, CA 1984).

In *Ep.* 81, Theodoret speaks of "8 villages of Marcionites, 1 village of Eunomians, 1 village of Arians." According to DCB 4.906, "Cyrrhus was not more fertile in ascetics than in heretics. . . . Eunomians, Arians, Marcionites, and the adherents of other still wilder distortions of the pure religion of Christ abounded."

18. For Manicheism, cf. Theodoret, *Haer.* 1.26. For other texts, see A. Adam, *Texte zum Manichaismus* (Berlin 1969); H. C. Puech, *Le Manichéisme* (Paris 1949); also "Mani et Manichéisme," DSp 10.198–215; F. Decret, *Aspects du manichéisme dans l'Afrique romaine* (Paris 1970).

19. He has Arianism in mind; cf. *Haer.* 4.1 and 4.3.

20. On Macedonius, cf. *Haer.* 5.3. Theodoret wrote three books, *Adversus Macedonianos*, now lost.

21. The "economy" for Theodoret means the Incarnation; cf. *Affect.* 6.74 and 6.92, on which see Canivet, *Entre.* 340. For Docetism, cf. DSp 3.1463–1468; DPAC 1.1001.

22. He is clearly thinking of Apollinarius; cf. *Ep.* 104 (MG 83.1300). See also *Haer.* 4.8. Theodoret devoted almost the whole of his *De incarnatione* to the Apollinarist heresy (MG 75.1189B), wrongly ascribed to Cyril. See Bertram, *op. cit.*, 48 f.; D. S. Wallace-Hadrill, *Christian Antioch* 134–136. On Apollinarism, cf. **RAC** 1.520–522; **TRE** 3.362–371; DHGE 3.962–982; DPAC 1.281–285.

23. Theodoret deals in a very orderly way with "all the other

arrays of heretics" in his *Haer.* For the military vocabulary here, cf.
2 Cor. 10.5.

24. The language is a close paraphrase of Eph. 6.11–17.

25. For similar cumulative listing of descriptive nouns and adjectives, cf. Chrysostom, *Ad eos qui scandalizati sunt* 1.7 (MG 52.491). For Stoic overtones, cf. Cicero, *ND* 2.78–80. Stylistically, the passage affords a good example of asyndeton.

26. Ps. 102(101).27–28. Chrysostom, *Ad populum Antiochenum de statuis* 9 (MG 49.114), has the same thought about the agelessness of the heavens.

27. Cf. Gregory Nazianzus, *Or.* 28.29: "What makes the sun a beacon for the whole world to look at, a chorus-leader, so to speak, who puts the other stars in the shade, outdoing them. . . . Its mild temperature and ordered movement give warmth without burning." See W. K. C. Guthrie, "Anaximenes and ΤΟ ΚΡΥΣΤΑΛΛΟΕΙΔΕΣ," *CQ* 49 (1956) 40–44; ibid., *History* 1.135 f.

28. Cf. Isa. 40.22, quoted in a similar context in Theophilus, *Ad Autol.* 2.13. On "like an arch", cf. A. B. Cook, *Zeus* 1.60.422. On "like a tent", cf. Cook, *Zeus*, 1.58 ff. Cf. Chrysostom, *Stat.* 10 (MG 49.114): φύσει πολέμια ἀλλήλοις ὄντα καὶ ἐχθρά.

29. On God, not fortune, holding the rudder, cf. Cicero *De officiis* 2.6; Lactantius, *Div. inst.*3.29. Cf. Chrysostom, *loc. cit.*: εἰ κατέλιπε αὐτὸν ἐρημὸν τῆσ οἰκείας προνοίας, with an elaborate development of the ship-metaphor.

30. For the beginning-to-walk image, cf. Chrysostom, *In cap. 1 Gen.* hom. 2 (MG 53.205).

31. Cf. Basil, *Homiliae in hexaëmeron* 1: "As for the saying, 'He has founded it upon the seas' (Ps. 24(23).2), what else does it signify than that the water is spread around the earth on all sides? Now, how does water, which exists as a fluid and naturally tends to flow downward, remain hanging without support and never flow away?"

32. For fire going normally upwards, cf. SVF 2.434; Seneca, *Quaestiones Naturales* 71.102; Chrysostom, *Stat.* 10 (MG 49.112). The opposing view is held in Lucretius, *De rerum nat.* 1.184–293.

33. On the Demiurgos, cf. Xenophon, *Memorabilia* 1.4.9; Plato, *Timaeus* 40C and *Repub.* 530A; Festugière, "Proclus le Demiurge de Platon," *Hermes Trismegisthus* 4.275–292; "Demiourgos," RAC 3.694–

711. See also Eusebius, *Praep. evang.* 7.12–16, with its quotations from Philo, Plato, Aristoboulos, Numenius, Plotinus, and Amelius.

34. On water suspended aloft merely by God's word, cf. Ambrose, *Hexaëmeron* 4.2.8.

35. Cf. Basil, *Hexaëm.* 6: "Come, then; for just as those unaccustomed to cities are taken by the hand and led around, so also I myself shall guide you, as strangers, to the hidden wonders of this great city" (FOTC 46.84).

36. Cf. Gen. 1.15; Plato, *Repub.* 7.530A; Theophilus, *Ad Autol.* 2.13.

37. For the image of sisterly days and nights, cf. *Affect.* 4.59. See also Chrysostom, *Stat.* 9: "For just as certain sisters dividing their father's inheritance among themselves with much affection . . . even so too the day and night distribute the year with such an equity of parts, with the utmost accuracy" (NPNF 9.402).

38. Cf. Chrysostom, *De compunctione ad Stelechium* 2 (MG 47.418). For the medico-cosmological origin of this notion, cf. G. Vlastos, "Equality and Justice in Early Greek Cosmologies," **CP** 42 (1947) 156–178.

39. On frost, rain, mud, and mire, cf. Downey, *op. cit.* 18, which tells of rains in Antioch, sometimes of torrential proportions (often cloudbursts) during the winter rainy season, lasting from November to March or April. Frequently the rain is so heavy that streams and ravines cannot carry it all off, and the "result is a heavy wash of loose stones, soil and debris carried down and deposited on the level part of the site between the mountain and river."

40. Cf. Cyril of Jerusalem, *Cat.* 9.7: "A servant would receive no rest from his masters did not the darkness bring a necessary respite . . . he who was yesterday toilworn comes forth vigorous in the morning because of the night's rest." See also Chrysostom, *Scand.* (MG 52.494).

41. Ps. 104(103).19–23.

42. Cf. Chrysostom, *Compunct.* 2 2.5 (MG 47.418).

43. Theodoret asks the same question in *Quaestiones in Genesim* 1 (MG 80.97) and devotes most of Discourse 5 in the present series to the answer. See Chrysostom, *Scand.* 4.2–3.

44. On the measures of time, cf. Plato, *Timaeus* 47; Theodoret, *Quaest. in Gen.* 1 (MG 80.89); Clement, *Protrep.* 4.63.

45. Cf. Apoc. 21.25 and 22.5; Augustine, *De civ. Dei* 22.30: "Heaven, too, will be the fulfillment of the Sabbath rest foretold in the command, 'Be still and see that I am God' (Ps. 46[45].10). This indeed will be the ultimate Sabbath that has no evening and which the Lord foreshadowed in the account of His creation: 'And God rested on the seventh day. . . . ' " See C. Parma, *Pronoia und Providentia. Der Vorsehungsbegriff Plotins und Augustins* (Leiden 1971).

46. Theodoret talks of the moon being *dichotomos* in a Manichean context in *Haer.* 1.26 (MG 83.380). See also Aëtius, *Placita* 2.27.1; ps.-Aristotle, *De mundo* 399ab; and Lorimer, *Some Notes on the Text of Ps.-Aristotle* (Oxford 1925) 96.

47. See Arnim, SVF 2.201.26; Diogenes Laertius 7.151. Basil, *Hex.* 6.8, is very similar: "Then comes Spring, which causes all plants to bud, . . . and now the sun, moving thence toward the summer solstice in a northerly direction, offers us the longest days . . . it dries up all the land, aiding in this way the seeds to mature and hurrying the fruits of the trees to ripeness" (FOTC 46.95).

48. Cf. Arnim, SVF 2.202.2, quoting Stobaeus; Philo, *De aetern. mundi* 109. See P. Duhem, "La procession des Equinoxes," in his *Le système du monde* 2.190–204. On the succession of the seasons, cf. A. Lebedev, "The Cosmos as a Stadium: Agonistic Metaphors in Heraclitus' Cosmology," *Phronesis* 30 (1985) 131 ff.

49. Theodoret, *Haer.* 5.10; Athanasius, *Gent.* 19; Lactantius, *Div. instit.* 7.3: "But, since, as we see, a marvellous plan does govern the world and all its parts; since there is order in the heavens and an even course of stars and heavenly lights in their very variety; since the marking of seasons is constant and wondrous; since the varied fecundity of the earth, the evenness of the fields, the foundations and ramparts of the mountains, the green richness of forests, the very bountiful overflow of waters, the timely flooding of rivers, the opulent and rich content of the sea, the various and useful blowing of the winds, and all things else are according to the highest plan, who is so blind as to think that these things were done without cause, in which the wonderful arrangement of a most provident reason gleams forth?"

50. On spring, cf. Theodoret, *Quaest. in Gen.* 1 (MG 80.96); SVF 2.693 (Diog. Laert. 7.151); Chrysostom, *Stat.* 9: "Who can describe the perfect order of the seasons and how these, like some virgins dancing in a circle, succeed one another with the happiest

harmony, and how those who are in the middle cease not to pass over to the opposite ones with a gradual and noiseless transition?" (LNPF 9.402).

51. Cf. SVF 2.693. Azéma, *Disc.* 113, sees the filiation of this argument coming from Xenophon, *Memorabilia* 4.3.9, with Chrysostom, *Stat.* 9.3, as the immediate source.

52. Cf. Downey, *op. cit.* 493–560.

53. Cf. Downey, *op. cit.* 21.

54. For similar appeals to the stars, cf. Diels, *Dox.* 293.9; Eusebius, *Praep. evang.* 15.46; Chrysostom, *Scand.* 7.11 (SC 79.114); *In c. 1 Gen.* hom. 6 (MG 53.59).

55. See E. S. McCartney, "The Classical Astral Weather Chart for Rustics and for Seamen," CW 20 (1926) 43–49, 51–54.

56. Ps. 139(138).6.

57. Ps. 104(103).24, also quoted in *Affect.* 4.65. Chrysostom also rests his hearers lest they tire in learning to walk; *In cap. 1 Genesis,* hom. 2, (MG 53.26)

58. "The practice of concluding a literary composition with a short prayer of praise or petition, accompanied by an optative of wish expressed or implied, is traceable to the short but formal manner in which Saint Paul was wont to end his epistles." D. C. Fives, *The use of the optative mood in the works of Theodoret of Cyrus* (Patristic Studies 50; Washington, D.C. 1937) 3.

DISCOURSE 2

1. The elaborate pilot-of-the-ship metaphor is also utilized by Theodoret in *Affect.* 6.2. For earlier patristic usages, cf. Theophilus, *Ad Autol.* 1.5; Chrysostom, *Hom. 19 in Eph.* (MG 62,131), *Stat.* 10.5: "For if a ship does not hold together without a pilot but soon founders, how could the world have held together so long a time if there was no one governing its course? And that I may not enlarge, suppose the world to be a ship, the earth . . . a keel, the sky . . . the sail, men . . . the passengers. . . . How is it, then, that during so long a time there was no shipwreck?" (LNPF 9.408).

For κυβερνᾶν in the pre-Socratics, see Guthrie, *op. cit.* 88. For the Stoic origins of the metaphor, cf. Salvian, *De gubernatione Dei* 1.1: "The Stoics bear witness that He remains, taking the place of the helmsman, within that which He directs" (FOTC 3.27). Plutarch, *De defectu oraculorum* 12, speaks of "the archons of the great city, the general of the invincible host, the pilot who always manages the universe with saving care." Such metaphors were prominent in the language of Orphism and Pythagoreanism; cf. A. E. Taylor, *A Commentary on Plato's Timaeus* (Oxford 1928) 264–266.

2. This may be an indication that the discourses were actually delivered and at close intervals; cf. 1.13 and 4.13. But Azéma 119 n. 24 is sceptical: "A moins de supposer une fiction bien improbable, les sermons sur la Providence ont donc été réellement prononcés."

3. See Disc. 1 n. 14. Cyril of Jerusalem, *Catech.* 8.2, says "that some . . . pervert the text, 'And your faithfulness to the skies' (Ps. 108[107].5), and have dared to circumscribe the providence of God by skies and heaven, and to alienate from God the things of earth, forgetting the Psalm which says, 'If I go up to the heavens, you are there; if I sink to the nether world, you are present there' (Ps. 139[138].8)" (FOTC 61.180).

4. Cicero, *ND* 2.101, speaks of *aer . . . tum fusus et extenuatus sublime fertur, tum autem concretus in nubes cogitur umoremque colligens terram auget imbribus, tum effluens huc et illuc ventos effecit*. See also Gregory of Nyssa, *Apologia in Hexaëmeron* (MG 44.96); ps.-Justin, *Cohortatio ad Graecos* 3; Gregory of Nazianzus, *Or.* 28.2; John Damascene, *De fid. orthod.* 2.8.

5. Philo, *De providentia* 67 (SVF 2.33.1146): *animantium imprimis esca est et ciborum omnium potuumque frequentissima*.

6. Cf. Basil, *Hex. 3:* "And yet, we see the great wisdom of the universal Ruler, which changes the sun from one side to the other, in order that it may not ruin the orderly arrangement with its excessive heat by remaining always in the same place. Now he leads it to the southern part about the time of the winter solstice, now transfers it to the sign of the equinox, and from there brings it back to the northern parts during the summer solstice, so that by its gradual shifting a good temperature is preserved in the regions around the earth" (FOTC 46.49).

7. See Deut. 33:13–15 (LXX). For a similar description of rain

and frost, see Basil, *Hex. 6:* "It is winter when the sun tarries in the southern parts and produces much night shadow in the region about us, so that the air above the earth is chilled and all the damp exhalations, gathering around us, provide a source for rains and frost and indescribably great snows" (FOTC 46.95). See also *Hex. 3.*

8. Clement, *Protrep.* 4.63.5, warns: "Let none of you worship the sun, but direct your desires toward the maker of the sun; do not deify the cosmos, but search for the demiurge of the cosmos." On the "apparent" troubles, cf. Chrysostom, *Stat.* 10.7: "He made the world not only wonderful and vast, but also corruptible and perishable: and placed therein many evidences of its weakness: and what He did with respect to the apostles He did with respect to the whole world. . . . Since they used to perform many great and astonishing signs and wonders, he suffered them constantly to be scourged, to be expelled, to inhabit the dungeons, to encounter bodily infirmities, to be in continual tribulations, lest the greatness of their miracles should make them to be accounted gods amongst mankind" (LNPF 9.409).

9. On air being shared equally by all, cf. Clement, *Paid.* 2.12.119. On the sun helping to distinguish colors, cf. Clement, *Strom.* 6.10.83.

10. On the cool breezes of Antioch, cf. Downey, *op. cit.* 20. On the providential nature of cool breezes, cf. Cicero, *ND* 2.131; Chrysostom, *Expos. in Ps. 134* and *Scand.* 7.22.

11. On the conceit, earth as nurse, mother, and grave, cf. Gregory Nazianzus, *Or.* 33.9; John Chrysostom, *Hom. 9 in Gen.* (MG 53.77b).

12. Dan. 7.25

13. For an idyllic portrait of a wooded mountain, cf. Basil, *Ep.* 14, addressed to Gregory Nazianzus; cf. Wallace-Hadrill, *op. cit.* 87–91, where Gregory of Nyssa, *Ep.* 15, is also quoted: "Above, a densely wooded mountain stretches with its long ridge covered at all points by the foliage of oaks."

14. Cf. Downey, *op. cit.* 19, n.17, on the thickly wooded hills and mountain sides of Antioch, quoting Libanius, *Oratio* 11.19.

15. Cf. Chrysostom, *Stat.* 10.3: "The world, though subsisting five thousand years, has not suffered shipwreck" (PG 49.114, NPNF 9.408). Cf. also Wallace-Hadrill, *op. cit.* 17: "On the age of the earth,

Origen taunts Celsus with allowing himself to be forced into a position in which he argues that the world is comparatively recent in origin, not yet ten thousand years old."

16. On fountains, cf. Lactantius, *Div. instit.* 7.3: *fontium saluberrima eruptio, fluminum opportuna inundatio;* Basil, *Hex. 3.6;* Clement, *Recognitions* 8.24: "What shall we say of fountains and rivers, which flow with perpetual motion into the sea? And, by the divine providence, neither does their abundant supply fail, nor does the sea . . . experience any increase." On water going upwards, cf. Discourse 1.22.

17. Insistence on God's providence in the creation of hot springs may have been occasioned by the necessity to reject the cult of Artemis Thermia; cf. J. H. Creon, "Artemis Thermia and Apollo Thermios," *Mnemosyne* 9 (1956) 193–220; and also his "Hot springs and healing," *Mnemosyne* 14 (1961) 140–141. For Lucretius' explanation of hot springs, see *De rerum natura* 6.848–905 and Bailey's note, 3.1684. See Diogenes Laertius 7.123: "The ever-flowing springs, made for enjoyment and for health, unfailingly offer their breasts to sustain the life of man"; Clement of Rome, *1 Epistle to the Corinthians* 20; Gregory of Nazianzus, *Or.* 28: "Under caverns these flow until forced out by the pressure of the wind, their temperature raised in the vehemence of the struggle, they erupt at the least opportunity. This way they provide us all over the world with hot springs, and through the force of the contrast with a free natural corrective"; Gregory of Nyssa, *De pauperibus amandis* (MG 46.464A). See also Cicero, *ND* 2.8.

18. See *Haer.* 2.26: "They (the Manichees) consider all things possessed of spirit—fire, water, air, plants, seeds—for which reason those whom they call the perfect do not break bread or cut vegetables, but they openly regard those who do such things as killers. But they nonetheless eat what is broken or cut by others" (MG 83.280D). Clement, *Strom.* 3.3.12, says that the Marcionites refuse to marry, use the food made by the Creator and breathe His air. Cf. H.-Ch. Puech, *Le Manichéisme* (Paris 1949) 89–90; "Manicheism," **ERE** 8.394 f.; "Manichéisme," **DTC** 9.1841–95; "Mani-Manicheisms," **DPAC** 2076–2081; "Manichaeism," *NCE* 9.153; "Mani et Manichéisme," **DSp** 10.198–215; P. Brown, "The diffusion of Manichaeism in the Roman Empire," **JRS** 59 (1969) 92–103. See also Origen, *Cels.* 8.31.

19. For the same argument, cf. *Affect.* 4.52. Cf. *Haer.* 5.10 (PG
83.484c), where Theodoret connects Aristotle's limitation of providence at the moon with this dilemma. For a similar dilemma posed
as an Epicurean objection, cf. Lactantius, *De ira Dei* 13.19, on which
see E. P. Meijering, *God, Being, History* (Amsterdam 1975) 30–31. See
also Irenaeus, *Adv. haer.* 5.4.1. Clement of Alexandria poses the same
dilemmas, *Strom.* 7.2, ed. Butterfield (= GCS 3.6.20, ed. Stählin).

20. Acts 17.25. Irenaeus, *Adv. haer.* 4.14.1: *Igitur initio non quasi
indigens Deus hominis, plasmavit Adam, sed ut haberet in quem collocaret
sua beneficia.* Clement, *Protrep.* 4.63; Chrysostom, *Compunct.* 2 (MG
47.418); John Damascene, *Contra Manichaeos* 33 ff. (MG 94.1540 f.).

21. Cf. Plato, *Timaeus* 29; Philo, *De mundi opificio* ch. 5 and the
other citations in "Création" in DTC 3.2165. See also Plotinus, *Enneads* 2.9.17, 16–17, and Pindar, *Olymp.* 8.71–72 (as noted in V. Cil-
ento, "Mito e poesia nelle Enneadi di Plotino," in *Les sources de Plotin*
[Geneva 1960] 243–323).

Cyril of Alexandria, *Contra Julianum* (MG 76.604), assigns to
Plato the view that God is envious. See W. J. Malley, *Hellenism and
Christianity* (Rome 1978) 85, 105–106, 323–327. For pagan views on
divine envy, cf. J. C. Opstelten, *Sophocles and Greek Pessimism* (Amsterdam 1952) appendix 232–239.

22. Ps. 95(94).4, on which see Theodoret, *In Ps. 94* (MG
80.1641).

23. Isa. 40.12, on which see Theodoret, *In Isa.* ch. 40 (MG
81.405).

24. Cf. Cicero *ND* 2.100: *At vero quanta maris est pulchritudo, quae
species universi, quae multitudo et varietas insularum, quae amoenitates or-
arum ac litorum, quot genera beluarum.*

25. On the variety of fish see Basil, *Hex.7:* " . . . every sort of
fish, those which have a skin and those which have not . . . to review
them all would be to undertake to count the waves of the ocean or
measure its waters in the hollow of the hand." Ambrose, *Hex.* 5.1:
Numera, si potes, omnium piscium genera vel minutorum; Chrysostom,
Stat. 10 (MG 49.113).

26. Cf. Chrysostom, *Stat.* 9: "Each thing remains held, as it
were, by a kind of bridle and band; preserved by the will of the Creator within its own boundaries, and their strife becomes a source of

peace to the whole" (LNPF 9.404). Gregory of Nazianzus, *Or.* 28.27: "What binding force brought the sea together? What causes it to swell yet stay in position as if in awe of the land, its neighbor?"

27. Cf. Job 38.11; Jer. 5.22. Basil, quoting Jer. 5.22, adds: "With the weakest of all things, sand, the sea, irresistible in its violence, is bridled. And yet, what would have hindered the Red Sea from invading the whole of Egypt, which was lower than it, and joining with the other sea adjacent to Egypt, had it not been fettered by the command of the Creator?" (FOTC 46.58). Clement of Alexandria, *Protrep.* 1.5: "It (The divine song) let loose the fluid ocean and yet has prevented it encroaching the land. The earth, again, which has been in a state of commotion, has established and fixed the sea as its boundary." See also *Affect.* 4.61.

28. See Origen, *Cels.* 4.76: "The want of necessaries caused the products of other places also to be conveyed by means of the arts of sailing and pilotage . . . so that even on that account we might admire Providence. . . . " Cf. Basil, *Hex.* 4: "The sea is good in the eyes of God. . . . By this means it gives us the boon of general information, supplies the merchant with his wealth, and easily provides for the necessities of life, allowing the rich to export their superfluities, and blessing the poor with the supply of what they lack."

On the restraining divine law, cf. Chrysostom, *Stat.* 9, *Homily 13 in Philippians*. Already in Clement of Rome, *Letter to the Corinthians* 20.6 (= ACW 1.22), we read: "The basin of the boundless sea, firmly built by His creative act for the collecting of the waters, does not burst the barriers set up all around it . . ." Ambrose, *Hex.* 3.5: *bonum mare, tamquam hospitium fluviorum, fons imbrium, dirivatio adluvionum, invectio conmeatum, quo sibi distantes populi copulantur, . . . subsidium in necessitatibus, refugium in periculis, gratia in voluptatibus, salubritas valetudinis, separatorum conjunctio, itineris conpendium, transfugium laborantum, subsidium vectigalium, sterilitatis alimentum.* Chrysostom, *Compunct.* 2, in a lengthy treatment of the same theme, says that, lest distance militate against friendship, the sea is spread throughout the earth to make our dwelling on earth seem as if we all inhabited the same one house.

29. Isa. 23.4

30. Cf. "Sidon," **DB** 5.1704–1706; **LTK** 9.534–535. Tyre and Sidon are envied, says Clement, *Paid.* 2.10.115 (SC 108.216), be-

cause of the purple dye extracted from their shellfish. On polytheism in Sidon, cf. *Affect.* 8.15 which mentions Tyre and other cities where the malady of error was propagated.

31. See Wallace-Hadrill, *op. cit.* 9–12. Cf. Basil, *Hex. 6.4:* "And, as to the significance of these things, who does not know how useful they are for our livelihood? It is possible for the sailor to keep his ship inside the harbors if he has foreseen dangers from the winds. It is possible for the traveller from afar to avoid injuries by awaiting a change in the sullen sky. And farmers, busy with seeds and the care of plants, find from the indications in the sky all the opportune times for their labors" (FOTC 46.90). For stars as navigational aids, see also Clement of Alexandria, *Strom.* 6.16.143; Origen, *De principiis* 111.1.18.

Discourse 3

1. Discourse 1 of *Affect.* also begins with the reflection that soul and body alike need medical therapy. In dealing with anthropology in *Affect.* 5.16, Theodoret tells us that his sources for his treatment of man's soul are the commentaries of Plutarch, Porphyry, and Aëtius; and for the body (5.82), the works of Hippocrates, Galen, Plato, Xenophon, Aristotle, and Theophrastus. See further Canivet, *Entre.* 116–121, 209–215, and Arnim, *SVF* 3.457. Chrysippus had written a work entitled *Peri psyches.*

For medical knowledge in the Fathers, cf. J. F. Frings, *Medizin und Artzt bei den Griechischen Kirchenvätern bis Chrysostomos* (Bonn 1959); J. Janini Cuesta, *La Antropologia y la Medicina pastoral de san Gregorio de Nisa* (Madrid 1946). For Theodoret's medical knowledge, see Canivet, *Entre.* 307–308; Azéma, 71; A. Harrent, *Les écoles d'Antioche* (Paris 1898) 151–161. For general orientation, cf. D. S. Wallace-Hadrill, *The Greek Patristic View of Nature* (New York 1968) 40–65; J. Kollesch und D. Nickel, *Antike Heilskunst. Ausgewählte Texte aus dem medizinischen Schrifttum der Griechen und Römer* (Leipzig 1979).

Theodoret, *Haer.* 5.9 (MG 83.477) specifies the Manichees as those in need of therapy. Chrysostom, *Scand.* 1.1, starts out similarly.

2. For the medical vocabulary, cf. Hierocles, *De providentia* (*apud* Photius, *Bibliotheca* cod. 251).

3. In *Haer.* 1.26 we are told that the Manichees believed that man was fashioned not by God but by Sacla, the principle of matter.

4. Note that the summary of the previous discourses utilizes the rhetorical device of arsis and thesis; cf. J. M. Campbell, *The Influence of the Second Sophistic on the Style of the Sermons of St. Basil the Great* (Patristic Studies; Washington, DC 1922) 29. It was the errors of the Epicureans in regard to the creation of the human body (e.g., Lucretius, *De rerum natura* 5.834) that led Christian writers to an examination of the body; cf. Eusebius, *Praep. evang.* 14.26; Lactantius, *De opificio Dei* 6: "At this point I cannot refrain from exposing again the foolishness of Epicurus—for all of Lucretius' ravings are his. . . . Of course to make place for those atoms of his, he had to rule out Divine providence. But when he saw that there is a marvelous system of providence existing within all things that breathe, what emptiness for that scoundrel to say that there had existed strange animals in which the system had ceased" (FOTC 54.20).

5. The Manichees are labelled blasphemers in *Haer.* 1.26.

6. For the Epicurean attack on this teleological view, cf. Lucretius, *De rerum natura* 4.823–42. Aëtius, *Placita* 4.19 (= Diels, *Dox.* 407–410), summarises the teachings of Plato, Epicurus, Democritus, the Stoics, Anaxagoras, and Pythagoras on the voice. For Aristotle, see C. Tanus, ed., *Musici scriptores Graeci* (Teubner 1895) 3–14.

7. For the mouth resembling a bronze-reeded organ with bellows, cf. Aristotle, *De iuventute et senectute* 474a; Cicero, *ND* 2.149; also Basil, *In illud, attende tibi ipsi* (MG 31.217); Gregory of Nyssa, *De hominis opificio* 9; Nemesius, *De natura hominis* 14; Meletius, *De natura hominis* 11; Lactantius, *De opificio Dei* 15.

8. The idea that man's nature is but an imitation of universal nature and that the arts of man are but a replica of the natural arts of the bodily functions is adumbrated in the *De diaeta* of the Hippocratic collection, which is strongly under the influence of Heraclitus; cf. C. J. Singer, *Greek Biology and Greek Medicine* (Oxford 1922) 11–12; Festugière, *La révelation d'Hermes Trismegiste* 1.127; F. Solmsen, *Aristotle's Systems of the Physical World* (Ithaca 1960) 103 n. 41.

9. Cf. Aristotle, *Historia animalium* 492b, 495a, and *Partibus animalium* 664b; Galen, *De usu partium* 7.3.3; Cicero, *ND* 2.136; Ne-

NOTES TO TEXT 183

mesius, *De natura hominis* (MG 40.712ab). For the bellows simile, cf. Gregory of Nyssa, *De hominis opificio* 30. See also Wallace-Hadrill, *op. cit.* 45: "Gregory of Nyssa expands this: the heart . . . is situated at the back of the lungs, and by expansion and contraction draws to itself a supply of air much as bellows draw air to a furnace. The action is spontaneous. The lungs also force air up the windpipe, and as the air strikes against the membraneous protuberances which divide this flute-like passage 'in a circular arrangement', it utters a sound in the manner of a flute". See also Plutarch, *Epitome* (*apud* Aëtius, *Placita*, 4.22); Diels, *Dox.* 413.9.

10. In *Haer.* 5.9, the teeth are likened to strings and the tongue to a plectrum, a Stoic notion; cf. Cicero, *ND* 2.149, and Pease's note with citations. Nemesius was probably Theodoret's immediate source. Gregory of Nyssa, in *Answers to Eunomius, Second Book* (NPNF 5².270) describes the voice production similarly: "For our speech is uttered by the organs of speech, the windpipe, the tongue, the teeth, and the mouth, the inhalation of air from without, and the breath from within, working together to produce the utterance. For the windpipe, fitting into the throat like a flute, emits a sound from below; and the roof of the mouth, by reason of the void space above extending to the nostrils, like some musical instrument gives volume from above to the voice. And the cheeks, too, are aids to speech, contracting and expanding in accordance with their structural arrangement, or propelling the voice through a narrow passage by various movements of the tongue, which it effects now with one part of itself, now another, giving hardness or softness to the sound which passes over it by contact with the teeth or with the palate. Again, the service of the lips contributes not a little to the result, affecting the voice by the variety of their distinctive movements, and helping to shape the words as they are uttered." For the Greek text, see W. Jaeger, ed. *Gregorii Nysseni opera* 1 (1960) 283, where the similarity of the passage to Gregory's *De hominis opificio* is noted.

11. See Arnim, **SVF** 2.227.36, Diels, *Dox* 516.8; Origen, *Cels.* 2.72 (quoted in **SVF** 2.43.138); Basil, *Homily in Ps. 28* (MG 30.73d).

12. The "smoky substance" apparently is supposed to come from the heat of the heart. See Nemesius, *op. cit.* (MG 40.693, 699); Gregory of Nyssa, *Hex.* (MG 44.97b); Meletius, *De natura hominis* (MG 64.1092d, 1109); Diels, *Dox.* 388.

13. On the heart, see Aristotle, *PA* 3.3.665a, *HA* 496a, 3.51a. That the pneuma was hot was a Stoic notion; cf. Diels, *Dox.* 388; Janini Cuesta, *op. cit.* 112.

14. Cf. Wallace-Hadrill, *op. cit.* 41: "The patristic view of human physiology is dominated by the Stoic physiology elaborated in the second century by Galen. There is almost unquestioned agreement that the physiological function of veins is to transmit blood, which is produced by the liver, and the function of arteries to transmit *pneuma*, or spirit, which is inhaled by the lungs and warmed by the heart." See Aristotle, *PA* 3.6.668b; *HA* 589a; *De Resp.* 10.475b. See also *Clem. Recog.* 8.30 (MG 1.1386). For a similar description, see Basil, *Hex.* 7.1: "We have lungs, internal organs of loose texture and many passages, which receive air by the dilation of the chest, fan away our inner heat, and refresh us" (FOTC 46.107). Gregory of Nyssa, *De hominis opificio* 30, 19, speaks of other organs, to subserve the continuance of life, importing by their own means the proper supplies, as the stomach and the lungs, the latter fanning by respiration the heat at the heart, the former introducing the nourishment for the internal organs. See also Lactantius, *De opificio Dei* 11, and Perrin 144–147.

15. He may have Galen in mind; but his proximate source may well have been Nemesius, *loc. cit.* 712, or Gregory of Nyssa, *De hominis opificio* 12.2. Wallace-Hadrill, *op. cit.* 42, deserves quotation at length: "There is little attempt to define *pneuma;* it is assumed to be the vital principle of life. Heat, writes Gregory of Nyssa, has its origin in the heart, since loss of heat and death are seen to go together. 'From the heart, pipe-like passages which grow from one another in many ramifications diffuse through the whole body the warm and fiery *pneuma.* . . . ' Gregory envisages the heart as simply the source of warm air or *pneuma.* Theodoret agrees that the heart is the source of warmth, and adds that it needs cooling by the pure air inhaled through the trachea and the 'smooth passages' to the left ventricle of the heart. The air is warmed and transmitted to the lung to be expelled through the 'rough artery', presumably the trachea. Theodoret differs from Gregory in associating the heart with blood as well as with air and *pneuma.*"

For a full treatment of *pneuma*, see G. Verbeke, *Évolution de la doctrine du pneuma du stoïcisme a saint Augustin* (Louvain 1945). See also

Pease's note on *ventriculum cordis* in Cicero, *ND* 2.910. On the lungs, cf. Plato, *Timaeus* 70cd, and Aristotle, *HA* 1.17.1. Aristotle does not know that the lungs are two-fold; *PA* 3, 6–7 and esp. 3.7.699b (noted by Perrin, 141, n. 482). Cicero, *ND* 2.136: *In pulmonibus autem inest raritas quaedam et adsimilis spongiis mollitudo ad hauriendum spiritum aptissima.* Pliny, *Nat. hist.* 11.88, speaks of *pulmo . . . spongiosus ac fistulis inanibus cavis.*

16. Rom. 11.33. Chrysostom, *Scand.* 2.6 (SC 79.62), uses this text in an elaborate passage on providence; so also *De incomp. nat.* (SC 28.96).

17. Ps. 106(105).2.

18. Ps. 104(103).24.

19. Cf. Gregory of Nyssa, *De hominis opificio* 9, and Janini Cuesta, *op. cit.* 64–65.

20. Cf. *Haer.* 5.9 and n. 10 above.

21. On the statue lacking perception, reasoning, and voluntary movement, see Athenagoras, *Legatio* 16; cf. Clement of Alexandria, *Protrep.* 10.98.

22. On man the image of God, cf. Quasten, *Patrol.* 3.292–293, 539 and bibliographies. See especially J. Gross, *La divinisation du chrétien d'après les Péres grecs* (Paris 1938) 273 ff.; H. Merki, *Homoiosis Theo. Von den platonischen Angleichung an Gott zur Gottähnlichkeit bei Gregor von Nyssa* (Freiburg 1952); H. Crouzel, *Théologie de l'image de Dieu chez Origène* (Paris 1956); Perrin, 424, n. 206; E. Montmasson, "L'homme crée a l'image de Dieu d'après Théodoret de Cyr et Procope de Gaza," *Echos d'Orient* 14 (1911) 334–339; 15 (1912) 154–162.

23. Cf. Plato, *Repub.* 7.520c.

24. On the heart cf. C. R. S. Harris, *The Heart and the Vascular System in Ancient Greek Medicine, from Alcmaeon to Galen* (Oxford 1973). Cf. Gregory of Nyssa, *De hominis opificio* 30 (MG 44.248b); Chrysostom, *Stat.* 11.9 (MG 49.124). See Lactantius, *De opificio hominis* 14.3.

25. Cf. Aristotle, *PA* 3.7.69a; Gregory of Nyssa, *loc. cit.*; Chrysostom, *Stat.* 11.9.

26. This is a vague reference to the pulse; cf. Gregory of Nyssa, *loc. cit.*; Meletius, *De natura hominis*, (MG 64.1108d) is more explicit. Janini Cuesta, *op. cit.* 139, sees the influence here of Gregory of Nyssa. The connection between pulse and fever is dealt with in Discourse 4.

27. On the lungs, see Aristotle, *PA* 2.3; Gregory of Nyssa, *De hominis opificio* 30; Lactantius, *De opificio Dei* 11 and Perrin, 140–141, 144. The simile of the soft blanket is found also in Chrysostom, *Stat.* 11 (MG 49.124), and is already in Plato, *Timaeus* 70d. See also Meletius (MG 64.1132c); Pliny, *NH* 11.188; Basil, *Hex.* 7.1.

28. On the **vena cava,** cf. Cicero, *ND* 2.137.

29. Nemesius, *De natura hominis* 23, is a detailed treatment of mastication. See also Plato, *Timaeus* 71b. In *Eranistes*, Dialog 3 (ed. Ettlinger) 190–191, there is a similar physiological disquisition on mastication with regard to the forbidden fruit.

30. Aristotle, *PA* 3.7.670A. See also Meletius (MG 64.1109a, 1117a), Lactantius, *De opificio Dei* 10, treats of the mouth's two functions, speaking and eating; cf. Perrin, 116.

31. On the "strainers" of the liver, cf. Aristotle, *PA* 3.7.670A; Plato, *Timaeus* 71; Athenagoras, *Res.* 5 (OECT ed. W. R. Schoedel) 101 and notes 3–5. On the spleen, cf. Plato, *Timaeus* 72c; Aristotle *PA* 3.7.670a.

32. On the gall-bladder, cf. Plato, *Timaeus* 91a; Alexander Aphrodisias, *Problemata* 1.40; Cicero, *ND* 2.55.137; Nemesius (MG 40.696); Meletius (MG 64.1101a). See Lactantius, *De opificio Dei* 11, and Perrin 147–150.

33. Cf. Gregory of Nyssa, *De hominis opificio* 30 (MG 44.252D).

34. Praxagoras of Cos (fl. 340–320) was the first to make this clear distinction; cf. G. Sarton, *Introduction to the History of Science* 1 (Washington 1927) 146. See also W. Scott, ed., *Hermetica* **2.255.**

"Arteries, however, transmit blood and pneuma, and are double-walled in order to prevent the highly volatile pneuma from escaping prematurely. Veins are placed in close proximity to arteries, so that the warmth of the pneuma in the latter can ensure a proper flow of blood in the former, since blood congeals if allowed to cool." Wallace-Hadrill, *op. cit.* 43, who notes: "There is no evidence that Clement of Alexandria or Gregory of Nyssa were conversant at first hand with Galen's text. Theodoret, in describing arteries as conveyors of blood as well as pneuma, is closer to Galen's view." See also M.-P. Duminil, *Le sang, les vaisseaux, le coeur dans la collection hippocratique. Anatomie et physiologie* (Paris 1983).

35. Cf. Aristotle, *PA* 2.9.654b; Meletius, *De natura hominis* (MG 64.1129A).

36. Cf. Wallace-Hadrill, *op. cit.* 87: "Theodoret, who leads his reader through almost Eusebian wastes of cosmological speculation, enlivens his account of Providence by comparing the human body to a well-drained and ventilated house, or by a reference to a dog greeting its master with lowered ears and wagging tail." Cf. *DCB* 4.907: "From his own ecclesiastical revenues—which must therefore have been far from small—Theodoret erected public porticoes, built two bridges on the largest scale, provided baths for the people, and finding the city (of Cyrrhus) without any regular water supply, he constructed an aqueduct, so that water was as abundant as it had been scarce before. While at the same time by the formation of a catchwater drain, he guarded it against inundation from the marshes." Cf. Theodoret, *Epp.* 79 (SC 98.186) and 81 (SC 98.196); J. H. Newman, *Historical Essays* 322.

37. On the respiratory system, see Aëtius, *Placita* 4.22 (Diels, *Dox.* 411–414); Meletius, *De natura hominis* (MG 64.1201–1204); Aristotle, *De respiratione* 473a and *PA* 668a. See also D. J. Furley and J. S. Wilke, *Galen on Respiration and the Arteries* (Princeton 1984).

38. Cf. Aristotle, *PA* 3.5.668a; Galen, *De usu partium* 4.1.227.

39. Wallace-Hadrill, *op. cit.* 51, notes that the process of digestion is described in almost identical terms by Athenagoras and Theodoret. Cf. Athenagoras, *Res.* 5; Nemesius, *De natura hominis* (MG 40.696a).

40. Gregory of Nyssa likens the liver to a fountain from which rivers of blood flow; cf. *De opificio hominis* 30 (MG 44.45a). On the liver producing nourishment, cf. Singer, *op. cit.* 66–69.

41. Saturninus, the Gnostic, who taught at Antioch during Hadrian's reign (c. 125 A.D.), held that man was created by the fallen angels but had not the power of speech or of standing erect, being obliged to crawl on the earth until the supreme father took pity on him, sent forth a spark of divine life which enabled him to assume an erect posture and live.

42. The notion of man as the only upright creature is already found in the Old Testament (Eccle. 7.30) and was a commonplace in Greek and Latin literature from Xenophon, *Memorabilia* 1.4.11. It is found in Aristotle, *PA* 2.10.656a; Galen, *De usu partium* 3.1.4.178; Clement of Alexandria, *Strom.* 4.26; Basil, *Hom. in illud: Attende tibi ipsi* (MG 31.216cd) and *Hex.* 9.2. Gregory of Nyssa devoted part of

the eighth chapter of *De hominis opificio* (MG 44.143) to why is man made upright, on which see Janini Cuesta, *op. cit.* 61. The Stoics were interested in the same question: see Cicero, *ND* 2.140. See also Seneca, *Ep.* 94.56 and *Dialog* 8.5.4; Sallust, *Jugurtha* 18.1; Juvenal, *Satire* 15.147; Macrobius, *In somnium Scipionis* 1.14; Lactantius, *De opificio hominis* 8, on which see Perrin 68–77. On the three articulations, cf. Wallace-Hadrill, *op. cit.* 58.

43. On the buttocks, cf. Aristotle, *PA* 4.10.689b; Meletius (MG 64.1260c).

44. Cf. Cicero, *ND* 2.158, and Pease, 956.

45. This elaborate parenthesis on human reason is close to Nemesius, *De natura hominis* 1 (MG 40.533), whose panegyric on human reason owes much to the Posidonian doctrine that man is the crown of the natural order.

46. The spine, here likened to a stout pillar, is likened to the keel of a ship in Nemesius, *De natura hominis* 28 (MG 40.716b), and Meletius, *De natura hominis* (MG 64.1160a). The image derives from Plutarch, *De placitis philosophorum* 5.17 (= Diels, *Dox.* 190 n.2), and is also found in Lactantius, *De opificio hominis* 5 (CSEL 27.19.18), on which cf. Perrin 77–79.

47. On the spine, cf. Aristotle, *PA* 3.7.516a, 655a.; Lactantius, *De opificio Dei* 5.4–5, and Perrin, 77–78. See also Gregory of Nyssa, *De hominis opificio* 30 (MG 44.252A). Cf. R. B. Onians, *The Origins of European Thought About the Body, the Mind, the Soul, the World, Time, and Fate* (Cambridge 1951) 149 ff. Meletius compares the neck to a charioteer (MG 64.1157).

48. On the neck and trachea, cf. Lactantius, *De opificio Dei* 7.11.5, on which cf. Perrin 138–140.

49. Cf. Cicero, *ND* 2.56.140; Macrobius, *De somnio Scipionis* 1.6 (ed. Stahl, 116); Isidore, *De differentiis rerum* 17.49 (ML 83.78); Lactantius, *De opificio Dei* 7 (SC 213.146); Chrysostom, *De fato et providentia* 1 (MG 50.752).

50. Chrysostom has the helmet comparison in *Stat.* 11.8 (MG 49.123); see also Meletius, *De natura hominis* (MG 64.1153D).

51. On the brain's two coverings, cf. Aristotle, *HA* 494b. Theodoret makes the same point in *Haer.* 5.9 (MG 83.381AB) and *Affect.* 5.22 (SC 57.232), where Erasistratus is said to have taught that this

was the seat of τὸ ἡγεμονικόν (= Diels, *Dox.* 291 n.3). Erasistratus was the most illustrious doctor of the 3rd century B.C.

52. Cf. Aristotle, *Gener. anim.* 2.2.22; Chrysostom, *Stat.* 11 (MG 49.123).

53. On eyebrows acting like eaves of a house, eyelashes like palisades, cf. Aristotle, *PA* 658B. See also Cicero, *ND* 2.923, and the numerous parallels adduced by Pease.

54. On the protective role of eyelashes, cf. Plato, *Timaeus* 45e; Xenophon, *Memorabilia* 1.4.6; Basil, *De struct. hominis* 2.16 (SC 160.274–276); Lactantius, *De opificio Dei* 10, on which see SC 214.322–325.

55. Cf. Cicero, *ND* 2.143, and Pease's note on *munitae . . . tamquam vallo*. See also Chrysostom, *Stat.* 11 (MG 49.123).

56. Cf. Cicero, *De senectute* 51; Manilius, *Astronomica* 5.271; Pliny, *NH* 18.52.

57. On the eye, see "Auge", *RAC* 1.957–960 and the sources there listed, esp. Xenophon, *Mem.* 1.4.6; Aristotle, *PA* 2.15; Cicero, *ND* 2.57, 140, 144; Aulus Gellius, *Noctae Atticae* 5.16; Philo, *De opificio mundi* 48; Galen, *De usu partium* 10.1, 2, 7, 9.

58. Cf. Gregory of Nazianzus, *Or.* 28.27 (SC 250.160).

59. On the nose, cf. Aristotle, *De anima* 11.9. The functions and language are Stoic; cf. Diels, *Dox.* 399. Lactantius, *De opificio dei* 10, also assigns the nose three functions, on which see Perrin, *L'Homme* 111–115, 137.

60. See Plato, *Timaeus* 76A; Aristotle, *HA* 491B and *PA* 2.8.653B; Meletius, *De natura hominis* (MG 64.1149), who says that the three sutures signify the Trinity, according to some of the Fathers. Cf. Chrysostom, *Stat.* 11. (MG 49.123); Nemesius, *De natura hominis* (MG 40.649, 651) and *Hom.* 13 (MG 40.664).

61. On the ear, cf. Lactantius, *De opificio Dei* 14.7, on which cf. Perrin 107–110. For the Epicurean view of hearing, cf. Lucretius, *De rerum natura* 4.524.614. On the difference between treble and bass, cf. Cicero, *ND* 2.931, and Pease's note for patristic references. See Clement of Alexandria, *Strom.* 8.9.32.

62. 2 Tim. 4.3.

63. Ps. 16(15).8.

DISCOURSE 4

1. Ps. 19(18).1, on which see A. S. Pease, "Coeli enarrant," **HThR** 34 (1941) 163–200. For Theodoret's own exegesis cf. *In Ps. 19(18)* (MG 80.992), where the argument by analogy is also employed.

2. Cf. Philo, *De monarchia* 33–35; Chrysostom, *Stat.* 9.2 (MG 49.106), and *In Ps.* 146(145).3 (MG 55.522); Gregory of Nyssa, *Hex.* (MG 44.73), *Contra Eunomium* 12 (MG 45.984).

3. Cf. Diogenes Laertius 7.55 (**SVF** 3.212.25). The voice is defined as smitten air in Origen, *Hom. on Genesis* 3.2.

4. For such extended comparison, see J. M. Campbell, *op. cit.* ch. 9. For the analogy of arguing from the well-built house to the architect cf. Cicero, *ND* 2.154: *est enim mundus quasi communis deorum atque hominum domus aut urbs utrorumque*, on which see Pease 2.950 for patristic parallels. Cf. "Gottesbeweis 2. Der kosmologische Weg," **RAC** 11.969.

5. Cf. *Affect.* 3.16–20.

6. Cf. Philo, *De monarchia* 33–35. See also "Bauen," **RAC** 1.1265–78.

7. Ps. 19(18).3, on which see Theodoret, *In Ps. 18* (MG 80.992–993).

8. See Theodoret, *Discourse* 1.24.

9. Ps. 19(18).4.

10. Ps. 139(138).6. The elaborate development of this text which follows is a good example of prosopopoeia; cf. J. M. Campbell, *op. cit.* 58. On the marvel of man's command over the rest of creation, cf. Sophocles, *Antigone* 332–372, a theme which Theodoret further develops in Discourse 5.

11. Cf. Theodoret, *Affect.* 4.64. Chrysostom likewise marvels at this union of opposites, *Stat.* 11.2 (MG 49.122) and Cyril of Jerusalem, *Catechesis* 12.30 (MG 33.761): "The production of bodies from bodies, though strange, is nevertheless possible. For the dust of the earth to become man is still more wonderful. For a mass of clay to take on the vesture and splendor of eyes is surely more wonderful. For simple dust to issue forth at once into firm bones, soft lungs, and various other members is a wonderful thing. For dust to become an-

imated and traverse the earth by its own motion and build houses, is a wonderful thing" (FOTC 61.246).

12. Cf. Theodoret, *In Ps. 138.6* (MG 80.1936b).

13. Cf. Eusebius, *Praep. evang.* 14.26.

14. Cf. Eusebius, *loc. cit.* 5–7.

15. For Plato, *Symposium* 181d, the first growth of beard indicated the first signs of dawning intelligence. See "Barbe," *DS* 1.1242–43; "Haar," **RAC** 13.195–197.

16. Cf. Epictetus, *Discourse* 1.16, on which see "Epiktet," **RAC** 5.599–681, esp. 657; "Epiktete," **DSp** 4.1.822–842.

17. Cf. Gen. 2.25; Aristotle, *HA* 518b; Cyril of Jerusalem, *Catechesis* 9.15 (MG 33.653).

18. Gen. 2.25.

19. Cf. Gen. 3.7.

20. Gen. 1.31.

21. Gen. 2.18.

22. Gen. 1.28.

23. Cf. 1 Cor. 12.22.

24. Cf. Xenophon, *Mem.* 1.4.6, and *De sublimitate* 4.3.5, based on the Xenophon passage (ed. Rhys Roberts, 51): "It was worthy of an Amphicrates and not of a Xenophon to call our eyes 'modest maidens'." Cicero, *ND* 2.56: *ut in aedificiis architecti avertunt ab oculis . . . sic natura res similes procul amandavit a sensibus.*

25. Cf. Gregory of Nyssa, *De hominis opificio* 30.21, where we are told (MG 44.249) that solid matter rejected by the liver passes to the bowels which revolve the matter in their manifold windings and for a time retain it.

26. Cf. Plato, *Timaeus* 73, where we learn that such preoccupation with eating would make the whole race an enemy to philosophy and music, and also rebellious against the divinest element within us. Cf. Gregory of Nyssa, *loc. cit.*

27. On the hands, see Wallace-Hadrill, *op. cit.* 58; Xenophon, *Mem.* 1.4.11; Galen, *De usu partium* 1.4; Cicero, *ND* 2.150; Eusebius, *Praep. evang.* 14.26; Meletius, *De natura hominis* (MG 64.1244–52); Chrysostom, *Stat* 9.4 (MG 49.109); Lactantius, *De opificio hominis* (CSEL 27.1.19, 37), on which see Perrin 80–82. On the general theme, cf. K. Gross, "Lob der Hand im klassischen und christlichen Altertum," *Gymnasium* 83 (1977) 423–440.

28. On the three joints, cf. Galen, *De utilitate partium corporis*, quoted in Azéma, 162, n. 74; Perrin, 80. See also Eusebius, *Praep. evang.* 14.26.

29. On the nails, cf. Chrysostom, *Stat.* 11.3; Lactantius, *De opificio Dei* 10: "The curvature of matching joints is flexible; the form of the nails, rounded and tightly grasping the ends of the fingers with curved protection lest the softness of the flesh falter in the function of holding, furnishes great ornament" (FOTC 54.30), on which see Perrin 81 and n. 198; **RAC** 7.910 f.

30. See Basil, *Hex.* 9.5; Gregory of Nyssa, *De opificio hominis* (MG 44.141a); Chrysostom, *Stat.* 11.4 (MG 49.125a).

31. Cf. Gregory of Nyssa, *op. cit.* (MG 44.140–146).

32. Cf. Chrysostom, *Stat.* 11.4 (MG 49.124).

33. Cf. Clement, *Paidagogos* 2.11,116

34. Cf. Cicero, *ND* 2.151: *iam vero operibus hominum id est manibus*, and note Pease's edition, 941; Lactantius, *De opificio hominis* 10. In praising the hand, Lactantius, *op. cit.* 3, says: "strength and vigor of body are not of such great importance that you would want to be without the function of speech, nor the free passage of the birds through the air such a thing that you would want to be in need of hands" (FOTC 54.13), on which cf. Perrin, 79–80.

35. Cf. Chrysostom, *In illud: Salutate Priscillam* (MG 51.194), and *In Genesim sermo 3.1* (MG 54.592).

36. Clement, *Strom.* 1.16, names Atlas, the Libyan, as the inventor of the ship (SC 30.104); cf. Theodoret, *Affect.* 1.20; Theophrastus, *In plantatione* 5.7.

37. On the origin of ships, cf. Clement, *Strom.* 6.11.94.

38. Eusebius, *Praep. evang.* 1.10, in his *Epitome Phoenicum Theologiae* (SC 206.190) credits Hephaestus with inventing the fisherman's gear.

39. Chrysostom, *In Matthaeum hom.* 52.4 (MG 58.523), has a long section on the mutual interdependence of the crafts of the farmer, the smith, the carpenter, the cobbler, the builder, and the woodman. See also Origen, *Cels.* 4.76; Theodoret, *Affect.* 4.50–51.

40. Cf. Cicero, *ND* 2.151: *Nos e terrae cavernis ferrum elicimus . . . nos aeris, argenti, auri venas penitus abditas invenimus;* Chrysostom, *In cap. 1 Gen.* 2 (MG 53.28).

See Clement, *Protrep.* 4.52, for the mining operations necessary to construct a statue to Serapis; also Clement, *Strom.* 1.16; Pliny, *Nat. hist.* 7.197: *aes conflare et temperare Aristoteles Lydum Scythen monstrasse, Theoophrastus Delam Phrygem putant—ferrum Hesiodus in Creta eos qui vocati sunt Dactyli Idaei.*

41. Cf. Chrysostom, *In cap. 1 Gen. hom.* 2.2 and *In ep. 1 ad Corinth. hom.* 17.

42. Cf. Chrysostom, *loc. cit.*, Theodoret, *Eranistes Dial.* 1, said that sand, "when it is subjected to heat, first becomes fluid, then is changed and congealed into glass."

43. Cf. Clement of Alexandria, *Paidagogos* 2.3.35.

44. Job 38.36 (LXX).

45. Cf. Lucretius, *De rerum natura* 5.1351–56; Origen, *Cels.* 4.76.

46. Cf. Clement, *Paidagogos* 2.10.109: "[These kinds of garments] must all be renounced, together with the art that produces them: gold embroideries, purple-dyed robes, those embroidered with figurines . . . as well as the saffron-hued Bacchic mantle dipped in myrrh, and the expensive multi-colored mantle of costly skins with figures dyed in purple."

47. Ps. 117(116).1.

48. Cf. Lucretius, *De rerum natura* 6.1075; Pliny, *Nat. hist.* 8.48, 9.36.

49. Cf. Pliny, *Nat. hist.* 22–23.

50. Cf. Basil, *Regulae fusius tractae* interrog. 55 (MG 31.1044–52); Athenagoras, *De resurrectione* 6.

51. Cf. Chrysostom, *Stat.* 3 and 10 (MG 49.52 and 113).

52. Cf. Gen. 1.11 and Theodoret, *Quaest. in Gen. 1* (MG 80.93). Theodoret, *Haer.* 10 (MG 83.485), instances opium and cicuta as such drugs. See also Chrysostom, *In Genes.* 3 (MG 54.596). Titus of Bostra, *Adversus Manichaeos* 2.25 (MG 18.1184), has a section: "*Nullae herbae lethiferae,*" and Basil the Great, *Hex.* 5, has an extended treatment of the same theme. This, in turn, is imitated by Ambrose, *Hexaemeron* 3, both mentioning starlings feeding on hemlock without any ill-effects, and quails on hellebore, while, as for humans: "Why need I speak of opium which has come to be used almost daily, inasmuch as severe intestinal pains are allayed by its use?" (FOTC 42.96 f.).

53. Chrysostom also feels "at sea" in examining providence; cf. *De compunct.* 2 (MG 47.419).

54. On grammar as the distinguishing characteristic of man, cf. Pliny, *Nat. Hist.* 7.58; see also *Stobaei Florilegium* 3 (Lipsiae 1838) 110–120.

55. For the beginnings of grammar, cf. Clement, *Strom.* 1.16.79. Theodoret, *Affect* 1.20 (= Clement, *Strom.* 1.16.74), says that the alphabet was an invention of the Phoenicians, as the Greeks themselves testify, and that Cadmus introduced it into Greece. See also ps.-Justin, *Cohortatio* 12; Cicero, *ND* 2.1112–14.

56. Cf. Nemesius, *De natura hominis* 8 (MG 40.653). On letter-writing in antiquity, see M. R. P. McGuire, "Letters and Letter Carriers in Antiquity," **CW** 53 (1960) 148–153, 184 f., 199 f. The invention of letter-writing is ascribed to Atossa, queen of Persia, by Clement, *Strom.* 1.16.76, quoting Hellanikos. For the extent of Theodoret's own letter-writing, see M. Wagner, "A Chapter in Byzantine Epistolography: the Letters of Theodoret of Cyrus," **DOP** 4 (1948) 127 ff. For an edition of Theodoret's letters, see Y. Azéma, *Theodoret de Cyr. Correspondence* (SC 40.98.111, 3 vols., Paris 1955, 1964, 1965).

57. Chrysostom sees the same providential design in the unequal length of the fingers, *Stat.* 11.3 (MG 49.124). See also Lactantius, *De opificio Dei* 10.24, and Perrin, 82–84. See "Finger," **RAC** 7.909–946, esp. 937 f.

58. Ps. 139(138).6.

DISCOURSE 5

1. The quadrivium is here named by Theodoret. In *Affect.* 1.19 he gives credit to the Egyptians for the discovery of geometry and astronomy, while the Tyrennians invented the trumpet and the Phrygians the flute. Cf. Eusebius, *Praep. evang.* 14.11 and 13. Clement, *Strom.* 1.16.74 (SC 30.104), traces the beginnings of geometry to Egypt and has remarks on music similar to the present section. See also *Strom.* 1.19.93 (SC 30.119); ps.-Basil, *De hominis structura* 2 (MG 30.48). See "Enkyklios Paideia," **RAC** 5.365–398.

2. See Clement, *Strom.* 6.11 (GCS 2.477) for a very similar de-

scription of the functions of music. See also Theodoret, *Affect.* 6.53; and Canivet, *Entre.* 305–307.

3. See "Biene," **RAC** 2. 274–284, especially 279 ff.; also **RE** 31.431–450. On their community life, see Aristotle, *HA* 9.40.623b–627b; Virgil, *Georgics* 4.153–178; Pliny, *Nat. hist.* 11.4–23; Origen, *Cels.* 4.80–84 (SC 136.384–394); Basil, *Hex.* 8 (SC 26.446); Chrysostom, *Stat.* 12 (MG 49.129); Gregory Nazianzus, *Or.* 28.25.

4. Cf. Plato, *Protagoras* 320d: "In his allotment he gave to some creatures strength without speed, and equipped the weaker kinds with speed. Some he armed with weapons, while to the unarmed he gave some other faculty and so contrived means for their preservation."

5. Cf. Aelian, *De nat. anim.* 5.11. Origen, *Cels.* 4.76 (SC 136.372), says: "Celsus, desirous of maintaining that providence created the products of the earth not more on our account than for the wildest animals, says though we struggle and persevere we sustain ourselves only with difficulty and toil, whereas for them 'everything grows without sowing and tillage.' "

6. For descriptions of the construction of honeycombs, see Aristotle, *HA* 9.623a–624b; Aelian, *De nat. anim.* 1.59; Pliny, *Nat. hist.* 11.6.

7. Cf. Basil, *Hex.* 8: "Notice how the discoveries of geometry are merely incidental to the very wise bee. The cells of the honeycombs are all hexagonal and equilateral, not resting upon each other in a straight line, lest the supports, coinciding with the empty cells, might meet with disaster; but the corners of the hexagons below form a base and support for those resting upon them, so that they safely sustain the weights above them and hold the liquid separate in each cell" (FOTC 46.124 f.). See Philo, *De animalibus adv. Alexandrum*, ed. Aucher (= SVF 2.731): *Considera utrum apes et araneae, puta quod textrices istae sunt, illae favum mellis creabunt, iuxta artisne industriam ingeniosam (id faciant), aut absque ratione per actionem naturalem.*

8. Cf. Philo, *loc. cit.*: *admirabilis habenda diligentia quae tamen non a disciplina deducta est.*

9. Cf. Philo, *loc. cit.*

10. Cf. Aelian, *De nat. anim.* 5.13 (= SVF 2.731). Cf. Plutarch, *Moralia 2: De fortuna* 99b: κανόσι καὶ σταθμαῖς καὶ μέτροις καὶ

196   THEODORET OF CYRUS ON DIVINE PROVIDENCE

ἀριθμοῖς πανταχοῦ χρῶνται. Basil, *Hex.* 8: "The Book of Proverbs calls it wise and industrious" (cf. Prov. 6.8a [LXX]).

11. Cf. Philo, *De animalibus* (= SVF 2.733): *Dico tamen haec providentiae, non animalium ratione carentium, sed eius qui universam moderatur naturam esse tribuenda.* Pliny, *Nat. hist.* 11.4, says that bees, alone of all insects, have been created for the benefit of humanity.

12. Gregory of Nyssa, *On Canticle of Canticles* (PG 44.960b): ᾿εμπορεύεἰαι, ἧς τοὺς πόνους βασιλεῖς τε καὶ ἰδιῶται πρὸς ὑγείαν προσφέρονται.

13. See Origen, *Cels.* 4.81, where Celsus makes much of the political skills of the bee. Basil, *Hex.* 8: "Some of these unreasoning creatures even have a government, if a feature of government is to make the activity of all the individuals center in one common end. They have a common dwelling place, they fly in the air together, they work at the same work together." Cf. Chrysostom, *Stat.* 12.2: "Take from the bee at once a lesson in neatness, industry and social concord." See also Aristotle, *HA* 626; Aelian, *De nat. anim. 1.59;* Philo, *De animalibus* (SVF 2.733).

14. Cf. Aelian, *De nat. anim.* 5.10.11d; Origen, *Cels.* 4.81. On the expulsion of the drone, cf. Aristotle, *De gen. animal.* 3.10.760b.

15. Prov. 6.6. See also Origen, *Cels.* 4.83 (SC 136.388); Gregory of Nyssa, *Contra Eunomium* 10.1 (MG 45.828).

16. The Septuagint adds the parallel passage on the bee, quoted also in Clement, *Strom.* 1.6.33; Basil, *Hex.* 8.4; Chrysostom, *Scand.* 7.20. See also S. O. Dickerman, "Some Stock Illustrations of Animal Intelligence in Greek Psychology," *TAPA* 42 (1911) 123–130, esp. 125.

17. Jer. 8.7.
18. Isa. 1.3
19. Ps. 49(48).13.
20. The Scriptural references are Ezech. 13.4; 22.27; Ps. 49(48).13; Matt. 24.28; Ps. 58(57).4. See Clement of Alexandria, *Protrep.* 1.4.
21. Cant. 1.9,15; 4.1, on which see Theodoret, *In cant. cant.* (MG 81.28).
22. John 10.27, 14, a conflated text.
23. John 10.11.
24. Matt. 25.33.

25. For the expression "eye of soul", cf. Irenaeus, *Adv. haer.* 4.38–39; Chrysostom, *In Ps. 6* (MG 55.77): "The eye of the soul is the faculty to judge and to reason, which is obscured by the consciousness of our faults."

26. Matt. 24.28.

27. Cf. Aristotle, *HA* 9.39; Cic. *ND* 2.123; Chrysostom, *Stat.* 12 (MG 49.129). Democritus, frag. 154, called men the pupils of the animals, of the spider in weaving and mending, of the swallow in building, and of the songbirds in song. On nets, cf. Gregory of Nyssa, *In verba, Faciamus hominem* (MG 44.268).

28. Cf. Basil, *De hom. struct.* 1 (MG 29.24b); Gregory of Nyssa, *In verba, Faciamus hom. 1* (MG 44.268) and *Ep.* 21 (MG 46.1085c).

29. Cf. Theodoret, *Quaestiones in Octateuchum* (MG 80.108); Clement, *Strom.* 5.14. According to Plutarch (*De fortuna* 98), man alone has been "abandoned by Nature—yet by one gift all this she mitigates, the gift of reason, diligence and forethought." See also Basil, *De hom. struct.* 1.

30. See Origen, *Cels.* 4.78 and 97. Chrysostom, *Stat.* 11, says of the subservience of the ox: "There are many, forsooth, who bring forward the objection: If man be king of the brutes, why have many animals an advantage over him in strength, agility, and fleetness? For the horse is swifter, the ox is more enduring, the eagle is lighter, and the lion stronger than man" (NPNF 9.416). On the ox, cf. Aelian, *De nat. anim.* 2.57, which adds, to the list of the various uses of the ox, the colorful detail that in death his carcass produces bees.

31. Ps. 73(72).22 f.

32. On the breaking in of the horse, cf. Clement, *Paid.* 1.5.15. On the horse in warfare, cf. P. Vigneron, *Le cheval dans l'antiquité greco-romaine* (Paris 1968).

33. On the elephant, cf. "Elefant," RE 5². 2248–2257; **RAC** 4.1001–1026; "Eléfant," **DACL** 4.2.2265 f.; and, more recently, H. H. Scullard, *The Elephant in the Greek and Roman World* (Ithaca, 1974).

34. On the elephant's use of his proboscis for feeding, cf. Lactantius, *De opificio Dei* 5.12. For an amusing account of an elephant's behavior at a banquet, cf. Aelian, *De nat. anim.* 2.11.

On using the proboscis to retrieve coins, cf. Suetonius, *Divus Iulius* 53.2.

35. For archers on an elephant's back, cf. Philostratus, *Life of*

Apollonius 11.13; Procopius, *History of Gothic Wars* VIII.13.4; Polybius, 5.84–85.

36. See Pliny, *NH* 8.61, about a dog's struggle with an elephant in the presence of Alexander the Great. On dog's devotion to master, cf. Aelian, *De nat. anim.* 6.25.

37. Cf. Plotinus, *Enneads* 3.2.9: "It would be feeble indeed to complain of animals biting man"; Cicero, *ND* 2.127; Titus of Bostra, *Adv. Manich.* (MG 18.1181); Lactantius, *De opificio Dei* 2.

38. Plotinus, *loc. cit.* "It is ridiculous to complain that many of them are dangerous—there are dangerous men abroad as well—and if they distrust us, and in their distrust attack us, is that anything to wonder at?"

39. On the folly of men denying that the Creator created wild beasts, see Titus of Bostra, *Adv. Manich.* 2.20.

40. On reptiles, see H. Piesik, *Bildersprache der apostolischen Väter* (Bonn 1961) 110 *s.v.* "Schlange". On their utility cf. Titus of Bostra, *op. cit.* 2.22: *Quid commodi serpentes et scorpiones afferant.*

41. Cf. Philo *De providentia, apud* Eusebius, *Praep. evang.* 8.14.

42. Ps. 104(103).20–23.

43. Ps. 104(103).24.

44. Cf. Philo, *De Providentia* (= Eusebius, *Praep. evang.* 8.14, PG 21.672); Theophilus of Antioch, *Ad Autolycum* 2.17, where we read: "Just so, it turned out that man, the master, sinned and the slaves (= the wild animals, θηρία) sinned with him" (OECT, ed. R. M. Grant, 54).

45. Cf. Gen. 2.19. Cf. Chrysostom, *Hom. 9 in Gen.*: "As evidence, after all, that everything was placed under the human being's control, listen to Scripture saying, 'He brought the wild animals and all the brute beasts to Adam to see what he would call them.' And seeing the animals near him, he didn't shrink back, but like a master giving names to slaves in his service, he gave them all names; the text says, 'They each bore the name Adam gave them,' this being a symbol of his dominion" (FOTC 74.122).

46. Gen. 6.1–8, 22.

47. Dan. 6.18–29.

48. Acts 28.1 ff.

49. Cf. Chrysostom, *In Gen. 3* (MG 54.592): *Timor bestiarum*

utilis homini. For the same pedagogical simile, cf. Chrysostom, *Expos. In Psalm.* 8 (MG 55.119).

50. The disciplinary role of beasts is reinforced by quoting 1 Tim. 1.9. "A discipline (*paideia*) to the wicked, plaything (*paidia*) to the good"—a nice example of paronomasia. Chrysostom, *In Gen. 4* (MG 54.596), says: "Just as a loving father gives over his children to dreaded pedagogues and teachers, so also God has given our nature which belittles his goodness to teachers and pedagogues so that they may drive away its laziness."

51. On God as teacher/doctor, cf. Clement, *Paid.* 1.9.83 (SC 70.258).

52. See J. Wytzes, "Paideia and Pronoia in Clement of Alexandria," **VigC** 9 (1955) 148–158.

DISCOURSE 6

1. Ps. 75(74).5–6. Bossuet makes Psalm 75(74) a focal point in his consideration of divine providence; cf. G. Terstegge, *Providence as Idée-Maitresse in the Works of Bossuet; Theme and Stylistic Motif* (Washington, D.C. 1948). For general orientation, cf. L. W. Countryman, *The Rich Christian in the Church of the Early Empire* (New York 1980); A. Hamman, F. Queré-Jaulmes, *Riches et pauvres dans l'eglise chrétienne* (Paris 1962); A. Solignac, "Pauvreté chrétienne, II. Pères de l'eglise et moines des origines," **DSp** 10.634–647; C. A. Osiek, *Rich and Poor in the Shepherd of Hermas* (Washington, D.C. 1983); C. P. Roth, *St. John Chrysostom, On Wealth and Poverty* (Crestwood, N.Y. 1984). This last is a translation of St. John Chrysostom's homilies 1–4 and 6–7 on Lazarus and the rich man.

2. Ps. 19(18).1.

3. Ps. 19(18).5.

4. In Minucius Felix, *Octavius* 12.2, the pagan Caecilius charges: "Look: some of you, the greater half (the better half, you say), go in need, suffer from cold, from hunger and toil. And yet your god allows it, he connives at it; he will not, or cannot, assist his own followers" (= ACW 39.69). For a reply see *Octavius* 36.3–5 (= ACW

39.119). Philo, *De providentia* 1.37, raises the problem: *probi viri paupertate pressi, impiis ditescentibus et vitam feliciter traducentibus.* On the contrast between wealth and poverty as an objection to providence—a patristic commonplace—see Titus of Bostra, *Adv. Manich.* 2.8 (MG 18.1148); Chrysostom, *Sermones de Anna* 5.3–4 (MG 54.672–674), and *Hom. 66.3 in Matt.* (MG 58.629); A. F. Villemain, *Tableau de l'eloquence chrétienne au IV siècle* (Paris 1851) 144–208; Stobaeus, *Florilegium* 3.173–223.

5. For thin-spun gossamer arguments, cf. Isa. 59.5; Job 8.14; Basil *Hex.* 1 (SC 26^2.94); Chrysostom, *Expos. in Ps. 45* (MG 55.204); Theodoret, *Ep.* 153 (MG 83.1444) and 155 (MG 83.1448, quoting Isa. 59.5).

6. For the favorable wind, cf. Plato, *Laws* 5.742; Theodoret, *Ep.* 15 (SC 40.87).

7. On the four cardinal virtues, see Theodoret, *Affect.* 6.34, (quoting Plato, *Laws* 1.631b–d) and 5.59, where he says that Xenophon praised Cyrus for his prudence, justice, fortitude, and temperance. See C. J. Classen, "Der platonische-stoische Kanon der Kardinaltugenden bei Philon, Clemens Alexandrinus und Origenes" in *Kerygma und Logos. Festschrift C. Andresen* (Göttingen 1979) 68–88. See also Plato, *Republica* 4.427 and *Laws* 12.2.661a–c; Clement, *Strom.* 2.18 (SC 38.96); *Paid.* 2.12.121 (SC 108.230); Philo, *De virtutibus* 15–17.

8. For wine with a fine bouquet (ἀνθοσμία), see Clement, *Protrep.* 2.2.30 (SC 108.66), where this epithet is reserved for Italian wines, in a passage (cf. Athenaeus, *Deipnosophistae* 1.32) denouncing the fad for importing exotic brands like Chian, Thasian, Lesbian, and Cretan. For the variety of drinking glasses, cf. Clement, *Paid.* 2.3.35.

9. Note the cluster of mixed metaphors. For similar clustering, cf. Gregory of Nazianzus, *Or. 14 De pauperum amore* (MG 35.875–879).

10. On the "superfluous burdens" (τῶν περιττῶν φορίων) and "external cares" (τῶν ἔξωθεν θορυβῶν) of the soul, see Theodoret, *Affect.* 5.29–30.

11. Theodoret's psychology is based on Plato, *Republica* 4.440e, where the spirited element (τὸ θυμιστικὸν) of the soul takes up arms on behalf of reason (τὸ λογιστικὸν). See Theodoret, *Affect.* 5.19 and 5.31.

12. Luke 14.33.

13. At *Affect.* 3.53 (SC 57.184) Theodoret identifies Antisthenes as the disciple of Socrates and the teacher of Diogenes, and says that he preferred temperance to pleasure, quoting a fragment about Aphrodite to prove it. Cf. Clement, *Strom.* 2.20.121 (SC 38.125). Theodoret may have Antisthenes in mind here rather than Anaxarchus, although Socrates and Anaxarchus are coupled in Origen, *Cels.* 7.54.56. They were both Cynics. See L. Paguet, *Les cyniques Grecs* (Ottawa 1975). In *Affect.* 8.57 (SC 57.331) Theodoret has a reference to Anaxarchus borrowed also from Clement, *Strom.* 4.8.56 (MG 8.1269). See "Anaxarchus" and "Antisthenes (1)," OCD² 61 and 75. Theodoret has uncomplimentary things to say of Socrates in *Affect.* 12.57–69 (SC 57.436 ff.).

14. On wealth and poverty as indifferent, cf. "Adiaphora," RAC 1.83–87. See also section, "Ethica III, De indifferentibus" in SVF 3.28–39. On wealth and poverty as raw materials or instruments for statuary, cf. Clement, *Quis dives salvetur* 14.

15. On not finding fault with iron or wine, cf. Chrysostom, *Stat.* 15 (MG 49.155–156).

16. On wine as a God-given gift, cf. Ecclus. 31.27, quoted in Clement, *Paid.* 2.2.22–23 (SC 108.52).

17. On tastes, cf. Plato, *Timaeus* 65b–66c; Aëtius, *Placita* 4.18.1,2; *Doxog. Graec.* 407; Nemesius, *De natura hominis* (MG 40.656); and see "Gewürz," RAC 10.1172–1209, esp. 1173–74.

18. 1 Cor. 12.21–23. On the diversity of functions in the bodily parts, cf. Plotinus, *Enneads* 3.5.

19. On the swarm of servants, cf. Clement, *Paid.* 3.4.63 and 3.7.38 (SC 158.60 and 85). On gilded couches, cf. Clement, *Paid.* 2.3.35 and 2.9.77. On the wonders of cookery, cf. *Paid.* 2.1.3.

20. For the one-man/one-trade principle, cf. Plato, *Republica* 2.370; Gregory of Nyssa, *De virginitate* 20.2 (SC 119.494).

21. For the conceit, earth as common hearth, nurse, mother, and tomb, cf. *Disc.* 2.9 and 7.11; *Affect.* 3.15 (SC 79.174).

For the argument that God has been evenhanded in distributing the basic necessities of life, cf. Chrysostom, *Stat.* 2 (MG 49.43) and *In Ep. 2 ad Cor. hom.* 12 (MG 61.488).

22. Clement, *Strom.* 1.1.12 (SC 30.52), says: "For, in a word, exercise produces a healthy condition both in souls and bodies." For

similar quotations, see Chrysostom, *De poenitentia* 5 (MG 49.512); *In Act. Apostolorum hom.* 16 (MG 60.134); *In Joann. hom.* 22 (MG 59.137), which has the further saying that "a frugal board is the mother of health". Both sayings can be traced to Galen (cf. J. Schulte, *Theodoret von Cyrus als Apologet* [Vienna 1904] 45), who insisted in his *On Diet* that "the fundamental condition of health is a correct proportion between work and nutrition." Azéma 214 n. 127 quotes *De sanitate tuenda* (*Galeni opera*, ed. Kuhn, vol. 4). Salvian, *De gubernatione Dei* 1.2: "sickness which, we understand, is the mother of strength".

23. Melito, *Peri Pascha* §§21–29, dramatically describes the destructive progress of death against the first-born in Egypt.

24. For a similar description of the dissolution at death, cf. Chrysostom, *Hom. 23 on 2 Cor.* (MG 61.560).

25. Croesus and Midas are also coupled in Theodoret, *Affect.* 6.53 (SC 57.273). See "Croesus" and "Midas (1)," OCD² 299 and 686.

26. See "Brot," **RAC** 2.611–620, esp. 612 f.

27. Philo had already raised the question and it was also a Stoic preoccupation; cf. Arnim, **SVF** 2.335–341, §6: *Cur mala sint, cum sit providentia*, with citations.

28. Cf. Job 1.10–11.

29. For verandas or porticos in summer, cf. Basil, *In divites* (MG 31.285). For artificially induced airconditioning, cf. Gregory of Nazianzus, *Or. 14, De pauperum amore* (MG 35.875), noted in Azéma 221 n. 133. On fans, cf. "Fächer," **RAC** 7.217–236; Gregory of Nazianzus, *Or. 16* (MG 35.933).

30. For ground as bed, cf. Gen. 28.11, quoted in Clement, *Paid.* 2.9.77. For a similar prosopopoïia on the poor man, cf. Gregory of Nyssa, *De pauperibus amandis* 1 (MG 46.457). See also T. J. Dennis, "The Relationship between Gregory of Nyssa's Attack on Slavery in his fourth homily on Ecclesiastes and his treatise, *De opificio*," in E. A. Livingstone, ed., *Studia Patristica* XVII 3 (1982) 1065–1072.

31. Cf. Dan. 3.24–45.

DISCOURSE 7

1. Cf. Lev. 3.1–5; 6.7–11 (immolated lamb), 12–16 (fine flour); 5.7–10 (two turtledoves), 11–13 (one tenth of an ephah of fine flour).

2. For a lengthy statement on medical guile in outwitting patients, cf. Chrysostom, *De sacerdotio* 1.7 (SC 272.94–95).

3. For similar complaints, cf. Theophrastus, *Characters* (Loeb Classical Library, New York 1929) 82–84.

4. Cf. R. Klein, "Die Sklavenfrage bei Theodoret von Kyrrhos: Die 7. Rede des Bischofs über die Vorsehung," in *Romanitas-Christianitas Festschrift Johannes Straub*, ed. G. Wirth (Berlin 1982) 586–633.

5. The unity of the human race is important for Theodoret's Christology and soteriology; cf. G. Koch, *Strukturen und Geschichte des Heils in der Theologie des Theodoret von Kyros* (Frankfurt am Main 1974).

6. Cf. Theodoret, *Quaest. in Gen.* interrog. 50, 52 (MG 80.152, 156).

7. In Sparta the board of ephors (overseers) consisted of five annually elected members who represented the absent kings in certain of their duties, especially their superintendence of public discipline. Their authority gradually widened until it came to mean a superintendence over the whole commonwealth, including the kings. It included the right of summoning the deliberative and legislative assemblies. Cf. Aristotle, *Politics* 3.1275.

Navarch or *Nauarchos* was the Spartan term for the commander of the fleet, chosen for one year; also a general term for the captain of a ship, regularly so used in the fleets of the Roman Empire. Harmosts: a board of twenty members at Sparta; probably a kind of higher police, whose duty it was to maintain a supervision over the districts inhabited by the *perioechi*, resident aliens.—See articles in *OCD*[2] 388, 488, 722.

8. On larger fish eating smaller ones, cf. Aristotle, *HA* 8.2.591a7; Nemesius, *De nat. hom.* (MG 40.528); Basil, *Hom. 7.3 on Hex.* (SC 26.402); Chrysostom, *In Gen.* 2 (MG 54.596), quoting Habakkuk 1.13–14. See "Fisch 2. Gewalttätigkeit u. Bosheit der Fische," *RAC* 7.1004–1005; W. Parsons, "Lest Men, Like Fishes," *Traditio* 3 (1945) 380–388; Athenagoras, *Legatio* 34.3.

9. Chrysostom, *In laudibus s. Pauli, hom. 4* (SC PG 50.494).

10. For this view of slavery, cf. M. L. W. Laistner, *Christianity and Pagan Culture in the Later Roman Empire* (Ithaca 1951) 115. W. H. C. Frend, *The Rise of Christianity* (Philadelphia 1984) 419 f., 570 f. For a similar justification of slavery, cf. Gregory of Nazianzus, *Or. 14.25 De pauperum amore* (MG 35.889).

11. On the concern about state taxes, cf. Chrysostom, *De sacerdotio* (SC 272.66). See H. G. Liebeschuetz, *Antioch. City and Imperial Administration in the Later Roman Empire* (Oxford 1972); J. B. Bury, *History of the Later Roman Empire* 1 (London 1889; reprint: New York 1958) 45–55. See "Geld (Geldwirtschaft)," **RAC** 9.797–907, esp. 853, 901–907. Salvian, *De gubernatione Dei* 5.7, complains that the poor are taxed disproportionately.

12. Eccles. 5.11.

13. On Noah constructing the ark, cf. Gen. 6.14–22; Origen, *Hom. 2 in Gen.*

14. For Abraham waiting on table, cf. Gen. 18.6 ff.; Origen, *Hom. 4 in Gen.*

15. On Rebecca in menial roles, cf. Gen. 24.15 f.; Origen, *Hom. 10 in Gen.*

16. For Jacob, cf. Gen. 24.29.

17. On Moses' wife, Ziporah, cf. Exod. 2.16. Theodoret, *Quaest. in Ex.* interrog. 4 (MG 80.227), asks: "Why did Moses marry a foreign wife?" He replies: "It was a type of Christ the Lord, who was born in the flesh from the Jews, and called the Church of the gentiles his bride."

18. On archangels, cf. Theodoret, *Affect.* 3.87 (SC 79.196), and Canivet, *Entre.* 101–106; "Démonologie," **DSp** 3.155.

19. On wicked men bringing wicked rulers on themselves as a form of divine chastisement, a stock argument, cf. Eusebius, *Praep. evang.* 8.14.

20. Zach. 11.9 f.

21. A conflated text: Isa. 58.9, 65.24.

DISCOURSE 8

1. Cf. Theophilus, *Ad Autolycum* 1.5.
2. On Abraham cf. Gen. 24.1–67; Theodoret, *In Gen. quaest. 61* (MG 80.166); Chrysostom, *Scand.* 10.1–4 (SC 79.150 ff.).
3. Gen. 24.12–14.
4. Gen. 24.26–27.
5. I.e., Laban, Rebecca's brother; cf. Gen. 24.29.
6. Gen. 24.56.
7. On Joseph, cf. Gen. 37–40; Chrysostom, *Scand.* 10.19–40, 16.2 (SC 79.162–174, 220). For a good comparison of the varied techniques employed by Chrysostom and Theodoret in handling the Joseph episode, cf. Azéma 254 n. 164.
8. Cf. Gen. 37.3.
9. Cf. Gen. 37.5–10. Cf. Philo, *De somniis* 2.1–154.
10. On Potiphar's wife, cf. Gen. 39.1–20; Theodoret, *Quaest. in Gen.* (MG 80.205). See also J. Vergote, *Joseph en Egypt. Genese chap. 37–50* (Louvain 1959) ch. 3; L. Ruppert, *Die Josepherzählung der Genesis* (München 1965) 43–60.
11. Gen. 39.8–9.
12. An extended example of *prosopopoiia*.
13. Gen. 2.15–17; 3.1–24.
14. Cf. Gen. 39.12; Chrysostom, *Scand.* 10.32 (SC 79.170).
15. Cf. Gen. 2.25; 3.7. For an interesting typological development of the theme of Joseph's nakedness in a baptismal garment of innocence, cf. Asterius the Sophist, *Hom. XI in Psalmos;* H. Auf der Maur, *Die Osterhomilien des Asterios Sophistes* (Trier 1967) 49–50.
16. Cf. Gen. 39.14–19.
17. Cf. "Geste u. Gebärde," **RAC** 10.895–902.
18. Cf. Gen. 40.1–7.
19. Gen. 40.7.
20. Gen. 40.8. Cf. Philo, *De somniis* 2.155–214.
21. Gen. 40.14–15.
22. Cf. Gen. 42.1–5.
23. Cf. Gen. 41.1–41.
24. Cf. Gen. 41.53–57.
25. Gen. 42.19, 25–26.

26. I.e., Benjamin; cf. Gen. 35.16, 19.

27. Cf. Gen. 44.6–17.

28. Cf. Gen. 44.18–34.

29. Gen. 45.4.

30. Gen. 45.5.

31. Gen. 45.7–8.

32. On free-will, cf. Theodoret, *Eranistes* Dialogue 1, ed. Ettlinger, 69.

33. On Abdias, cf. 1 Kings 16, 23–32, 40.

34. 1 Kings 18.3–4.

35. Jer. 34–39.

36. Jer. 38.7–9.

37. Jer. 38.10–13.

38. Jer. 39.16–18.

39. 2 Kings 24.18–25, 30.

40. Dan. 1.1.

41. Dan. 1.2.

42. 2 Kings 25.14–15.

43. 2 Kings 25.18–21.

44. Cf. Chrysostom, *Quod nemo laeditur nisi a seipso* (MG 52.477).

45. Cf. Cant. 1.8–15.

46. I.e., Nabopolasser.

47. Dan. 3.1–12.

48. Dan. 3.17–18.

49. Cf. Dan. 3.19–23.

50. Cf. Dan. 3.26–45, 52–90, 93–96.

51. Cf. Dan. 2.24–49; Hippolytus, *Comment. in Dan.* 22–25 (GCS 1/1.82–88).

52. Dan. 2.49, where Daniel, at his own request, remains at the king's court while his three companions are made administrators of the province of Babylon.

53. Notice the elaborate *praeteritio* or paraleipsis.

54. For the pedagogue image, cf. Chrysostom, *In Gen. 4* (MG 54.596).

Discourse 9

1. Ecclus. 3.22. Theodoret, *Affect.* 4.24 (SC 57.210), quotes a similar sentiment from Aeschylus, *Prometheus Vinctus* 44. Such warnings against curiosity are commonplace in Chrysostom; cf. *Scand.* 2.1, 3.10–11 (SC 79.60, 78).

2. This short summary of the previous eight discourses is taken by some as an indication of a chronological break in composition, or delivery, or both, Discourses 1 through 8 being delivered before the Council of Ephesus, and Discourses 9–10 afterwards. For a defence of the interval, cf. Garnerius, *Dissertatio* 2 (MG 84.345 f.), and for its refutation, cf. Schulte, *op. cit.* 23 f.

3. Cf. Theodoret, *Affect.* 4.25 (SC 57.210); Plato, *Republica* 2.363d; *Gorgias* 493b; and Linforth, "Soul and Sieve in Plato's Gorgias," *University of California Publications in Classical Philology* 12 (1944) 295–314. See also Basil, *Ad adulescentes* 9.

4. Sicily, and specifically Syracuse, is also synonymous with luxury and license in Theodoret, *Affect.* 2.25 and 11.3 (SC 57.145, 392); Plato, *Republica* 3.404d and *Letter* 7.326b. On Syracusan tables, Clement, *Paid.* 2.1.18 (SC 108.44), quotes Plato, *Letter* 8: " 'When I arrived,' he said, 'what is here called a life of pleasure, filled with Italian and Syracusan meals, was very repulsive to me.' " Cf. Gregory of Nazianzus, *Or.* 4.72 (MG 35.596). On Sybaris, cf. Chrysostom, *Expositio in Ps.* 110 (109) (MG 55.278); *De resurrectione mortuorum* 1 (MG 50.419); Gregory of Nyssa, *De pauperibus amandis* 1 (MG 46.468). Gregory of Nyssa, *In sanctum Pascha* 3 (MG 46.669d), speaks of elaborate homes adorned with Thessalian and Laconian stone.

5. Isa. 3.12, also quoted by Theodoret, *Ep. 43* (SC 40.107).

6. Phil. 3.13–14. For Christ as presiding officer of the games, cf. *Gregory of Nyssa. The Life of Moses* tr. A. J. Malherbe and E. Ferguson (New York 1978) 29. See also Gregory of Nazianzus, *Or.* 42 *In laudem Basilii.*

7. Isa. 65.9.

8. Ps. 61(60).6, on which see Theodoret, *In Ps. 60* (MG 80.1325).

9. Matt. 5.3–4.

10. Cf. Matt. 25.14–30, 1–13, 31–46; 13.24–30; 25.47–50.

11. This is one of the few places in which Theodoret has recourse to *a priori* reasoning; in common with the Antiochene school he prefers to argue from concrete facts of experience; cf. Schulte, *op. cit.* 108. On the school of Antioch, cf. DTC 1.1435–39; TRE 3.103–113.

12. Matt. 10.24. Theodoret here relaxes in a rare effort at facetiousness.

13. "Syria produced in super-abundance and exported abroad charioteers, athletes, actors, dancers, flute players, harpists, performers on the sambuca, and tumblers and rope-walkers of both sexes," says CAH 11.639. On circus and theater, cf. Lucian, *De saltatione* 76; Libanius, *Oratio* 11.398.5; Julian, *Misopogon* 432b.

14. On the belief of the poets in a future life, cf. Theophilus, *Ad Autolycum* 2.37–38. Cf. T. H.-C. van Eijk, *La résurrection des morts chez les Pères apostoliques* (Théol. hist. 25, Paris 1974).

15. Cf. Plato, *Republica* 615c (quoted in Theodoret, *Affect.* 11.18); *Phaedo* 113a. Theodoret, *Affect.* 5.23, names as believers in the indestructibility of the human soul: Pythagoras, Anaxagoras, Diogenes, Plato, Empedocles, and Xenocrates. In *Affect.* 1.65 (SC 57.121) he quotes Plato, *Gorgias* 524 (= Eusebius, *Praep. evang.* 12.6), to the same effect.

16. This is an elaborate example of *prosopopoiia*. The soul and body, making separate presentations of their case, should be compared to Gregory of Nazianzus, *Sugkrisis Bion* (= MG 37.649–667) ed. H. M. Werhahn (Wiesbaden 1953).

17. See Discourse 4.

18. Creon, king of Thebes, is particularly associated with Sophocles' *Antigone*, *Oedipus Rex*, and *Oedipus at Colonnus*. Oenomaus is the charioteer who competed with the suitors for his daughter, Hippodameia. He was finally beaten by Pelops, thanks to the duplicity of Myrtilus. Cf. Pindar, *Olympian* 1.76, and the famous sculpture on the east pediment of the temple of Zeus at Olympia.

See " 'Maske,' (IV Im Theater)," RE 14².2072–2105; Pollux, *Onamasticon* 4.133–141; T. B. L. Webster, *Greek Theatre Production* (London 1970) 106 (for Pelops) and 111 (for Kreon). Azéma 298 n. 249 cites Demosthenes, *De corona* 180 and 242, where Aeschines is jeered at for playing the role of Oenomaos in a tragedy. Theodoret quotes him from Euripides, *Oenomaos* (frag. 674, Nauck, = Clement, *Strom.* 6.2.18) in *Affect.* 6.90 (SC 57.286).

19. Job 33.6.

20. Many of these grounds for disbelief in bodily resurrection occur in Theophilus, *Ad Autolycum* 1.13; Tertullian, *De carne Christi*, 57; also Origen, *Cels.* 2.5, 7.32, 8.49. See H. Chadwick, "Origen, Celsus and the Resurrection of the Body," HThR 41 (1948) 83–102. Irenaeus, *Adv. haer.* 5.4.1 also deals with God's task in resuscitating bodies. On the need of soul and body to be judged jointly, cf. Athenagoras, *De resurrectione* 20–22.

21. Gen. 1.3.

22. For *creatio ex nihilo*, see G. May, *Schöpfung aus dem Nichts* (Berlin 1978) 22 n. 96; Theodoret, *Affect.* 4.69; Athenagoras, *De resurrectione* 17–18. See A. P. O'Hagan, *Material Re-Creation in the Apostolic Fathers* (TU 100, Berlin 1968), for the beginnings of Christian eschatology.

23. 1 Cor. 15.36–38. See Origen, *De principiis* 2.10.13, for this quotation in a similar context; also Gregory of Nyssa, *In sanctum pascha* 3 (MG 46.669).

24. On nature proclaiming a resurrection, cf. Theophilus, *Ad Autolycum* 1.13 (SC 20.87); Minucius Felix, *Octavius* 34.11 (= ACW 39.116). The common argument is that the wisdom of god effects rebirth of the seasons, nights and days, and the resurrection of seeds and fruits, to show that He can effect the general resurrection of mankind. See R. M. Grant, "The Resurrection of the Body," *Journal of Religion* 28 (1948) 120–130, 188–208, esp. 193 f.

25. For the burial and resurrection of plants, cf. Cicero, *De senectute* 15; Theophilus, *Ad Autolycum* 1.13; Tertullian, *De resurrectione mortuorum* 52 (CCL 2.995).

26. For the terminology, cf. Gregory of Nyssa, *In sanctum pascha* 3 (PG 46.668).

27. He is thinking of Socrates, Hippocrates, Plato, Xenophon, Aristotle, and Galen; cf. *Haer. fab. comp.* 5.9 (PG 83.480a).

28. Ps. 95(94).4 and Isa. 40.2, already quoted in Discourse 2.16.

29. 1 Cor. 15.52. On separating intermingled elements, cf. Cyril of Jerusalem, *Catech.* 18.3.

30. Cf. 2 Cor. 5.10. According to Irenaeus, *Adv. haer.* 4.36.4,

4.40 (SC 100.892, 974), one of the essential acts of divine government is the rewarding of the good and the punishment of the wicked.

DISCOURSE 10

1. Ps. 36(35).7.
2. Rom. 11.33.
3. For Origen, *De Principiis* 1.1.6 (SC 252.98), the manifestation of Divine Providence is like rays of the sun, not the sun itself. Theophilus of Antioch, *Ad Autolycum* 1.2, has the same image, So also Gregory of Nazianzus, *Or.* 28.3 (SC 250.106).
4. In Aristophanes, *Clouds*, Strepsiades encounters such investigations in the *phrontisterion* of Socrates. Theodoret deals with such curiosity on the part of the natural philosophers negatively and at length in *Affect.* 4.5–30.
5. 1 Cor. 8.2.
6. 1 Cor. 13.9–10.
7. 1 Cor. 13.12.
8. 1 Cor. 13.11.
9. 1 Cor. 8.1.
10. Ps. 116(115).12.
11. Dan. 3 and 4.
12. Cf. Gen. 12.10 f.
13. I.e., Sara, once taken by Pharaoh (Gen. 12.15) and a second time by Abimelech (Gen. 20.2).
14. Acts 5.31.
15. 2 Cor. 12.10.
16. Col. 1.24.
17. Rom. 8.18.
18. Rom. 8.35.
19. Rom. 8.38. See I. Sanna, "Spirito e grazia nel *Commento alla Lettera ai Romani* di Teodoreto di Ciro e sua dipendenza in quest' opera, da Giovanni Crisostomo e Teodoro di Mopsuestia," *Lateranum* 48 (1982) 238–260.
20. Cf. Eph. 1.10; God's plan to be carried out in the fullness of time is to bring all things in heaven and earth into one

(ἀνακεφαλαιώσασθαι) under Christ's headship. Cf. Theodoret, *Eranistes*, Florilegium 1, quoting Irenaeus, *Adv. haer.* 3.21 (SC 34.330–332). See also Theodoret, *Affect.* 6.82 (SC 79.284).

21. Cf. Phil. 2.6.

22. Heb. 1.3. See the use of this text in *Eranistes*, Florilegium 2, ed. Ettlinger, 172, where Theophilus of Alexandria is using it in an anti-Origenist context.

23. John. 1.1–3.

24. Phil. 2.7.

25. Rom. 5.8.

26. Rom. 8.32.

27. John. 3.16.

28. Ps. 110(109).3, on which cf. Theodoret, *In Ps. 109* (MG 80.1769).

29. The reading ἀνακαλέσαι in Migne is rejected by Azéma 317, n. 273, in favor of the reading in the Greek edition of 1569, ἀναπαλαίσασθαι.

30. An example of paronomasia.

31. On the virginal birth in Theodoret, see *Eranistes*, ed. Ettlinger, Index of Names, 271 *s.v. Maria, he Parthenos.* See especially Florilegium 1 for the dossier of texts from Ignatius of Antioch, ed. Ettlinger, 95–96, and from Irenaeus, *loc. cit.* 96–98.

32. On Mary as Theotokos, cf. "Gottesgebärerin (θεοτόκος) (*Theotokos*)," RAC 11 (1981) 1071–1103, esp. 1080–87. Cf. Origen, *Cels.* 4.14.

33. Cf. Origen's reply to Celsus, *Cels.*, *loc. cit.* See also Nemesius, *De natura hominis* (MG 40.6018).

34. Jer. 23.24.

35. Isa. 66.1; 40.12.

36. Ps. 95(94).4; Acts 17.28.

37. Ps. 5.5–7.

38. For Christ compared with a doctor who does not contract the wounds which he treats, cf. Origen, *Cels.* 4.15; R. Arbesmann, "The Concept of Christus medicus in St. Augustine," *Traditio* 10 (1954) 1–28.

39. Ps. 49(48).13, 21.

40. On man as image of God, cf. Irenaeus, *Adv. haer.* 5.16.2.

41. Cf. Luke 2.21–24; Matt. 2.14–15.

42. Matt. 3.17.
43. Only the first of the three temptations of Christ is dealt with here; cf. Matt. 4.3–5.
44. Cf. Matt. 4.3.
45. Deut. 8.3; Matt. 4.4.
46. Matt. 4.11.
47. See Azéma 323 n. 285, citing Richard, "Notes," RSPhTh 25 (1936) 459–481.
48. Isa. 50.5–6.
49. Isa. 53.9; 1 Peter 2.22; 1 John 3.5; Heb. 4.15.
50. Isa. 53.3.
51. Isa. 53.4.
52. Isa. 53.5.
53. Isa. 53.6–7.
54. Cf. Irenaeus, *Adv. haer.* 5.14.3, 5.18.1 (SC 153.188, 234).
55. Gal. 3.13.
56. 1 Cor. 6.20.
57. 1 Cor. 8.11.
58. Deut. 27.26.
59. Cf. Gal. 3.10.
60. For similar animadversions of Christ to the devil, cf. R. P. Casey and R. W. Thomson, "A Dialogue between Christ and the Devil," JTS n.s. 6 (1955) 49–65.
61. Cf. Col. 2.14.
62. Cf. John 17.2; Rom. 1.4; Col. 2.12–13.
63. John 14.30.
64. John 12.31.
65. John 12.32.
66. Col. 2.13–15.
67. John 12.32.
68. 2 Thess. 3.11.
69. Celsus had raised objections to the novelty of Christianity; cf. Origen, *Cels.* 1.26, 6.10, and 8.12. Likewise Porphyry; cf. A. Stötzel, "Warum Christus so spät erschien: die apologetische Argumentation des frühen Christentums," ZKG 92 (1981) 147–160.
70. Matt. 25.34.
71. Cf. Gen. 2.16–17.
72. Cf. Gen. 9.3.

73. Cf. Gen. 12.1 f.
74. Cf. Gen. 12.10 f.
75. Cf. Gen. 12.14.
76. Cf. Gen. 26.1 f.
77. Cf. Gen. 30.25 f.
78. Cf. Gen. 37.45.
79. Cf. Exod. 1.
80. Jos. 2.1.
81. Cf. Jos. 2.10.
82. Cf. 1 Sam. 4.8.
83. Cf. 1 Sam. 5.2–4, on which see Theodoret, *Quaest in 1 Sam. (Kings)* 5 (MG 80.540).
84. Cf. 1 Sam. 6.3 f.
85. Cf. Dan. 5.1 f.
86. Cf. Dan. 1.2, on which see Theodoret, *In Dan.* 1 (MG 81.1269).
87. I.e., Nabuchodonoser, Cf. Dan. 2.
88. What follows is a paraphrase of Dan. 5.17–28; cf. Theodoret, *In Dan.* 5 (MG 81.1385–1392).
89. Isa. 14.13–14; 10.14.
90. That is, Sennacherib; cf. Theodoret, *Quaest. in 2(4) Kings* 18, interrog. 102, (MG 81.785). Cf. 2 Kings 18.
91. 2 Kings 18.29, 33.
92. Cf. Jonas 1 and 2, on which see Theodoret, *In Jonae* 2 (MG 81.1729). See also G. Ashby, *Theodoret of Cyrrhus as Exegete of the Old Testament* (Grahamstown, South Africa 1972) 48–50.
93. On Jewish incredulity being an impetus to Gentile belief, cf. Origen, *Cels.* 2.78 (SC 132.470).
94. Gal. 4.1–5.
95. 1 Cor. 2.6–8.
96. Ecclus. 39.21.

INDEXES

1. OLD AND NEW TESTAMENTS

2. GENERAL INDEX

Abdias, 113, 206
Abimelec, 140, 149; Ethiopian
 slave and eunuch, 114
Abraham, 97, 102, 104, 137,
 149, 204, 205; son of, 102;
 servant of, 102
Achab, 113
actors, 129; tragic and comic,
 124
Adam 70, 109, 142; naked and
 unashamed, 109
Adam, A., 171
Adiaphora, 201
Aelian, 195, 196, 197
Aelius Theon, 164
Aeschylus, 206, *P.V.* 207
Aëtius, 161, 182, 201
agriculture, 120
air, 25, 26, 120, 176; shared
 equally by all, 26, 177
Alexander the Great, 198
alimentary system, 37,
allegorical interpretation, 166
alphabet, 57; invented by
 Cadmus, 194
Altaner, B., 1, 3, 160, 162
Amand, G., 168
Ambrose of Milan, *Hex.* 4.2.8:
 173; 5.1: 179
Amelius, 173

Amphicrates, 191
Ananias, 114
Anaxagoras, 182
Anaxarchus, 77, 201
Anaximenes, 165
angels, 96
animals, submissive despite
 size, 66; disciplinary
 function, 71, 199; tame and
 wild, 120
Anthisthenes, 201
Antioch, 1, 2, 3, 163, 164, 177;
 school of, 1, 208
Aphrodite, 11, 166, 167
Appollinarism, 171
Apollinarius, 171
archangels, 98, 204
architect, 47
archons, 98
Ares, 11, 166, 167
Arianism, 1, 2, 171
Aristophanes, 167; *Clouds*, 210
Aristotle, 181, 182, 184, 189,
 197, 203
arithmetic, 59
Arius, 171
ark, Noah's, 70, 71, 90
Arnim, J. von, 159, 163, 174,
 183
arsis and thesis, 182